Suicide Among the Elderly in Long-Term Care Facilities

Recent Titles in
Contributions to the Study of Aging

Suicide Among the Elderly in Long-Term Care Facilities

Nancy J. Osgood,
Barbara A. Brant,
and
Aaron Lipman

HV
6545.2
. O 84
1990
West

CONTRIBUTIONS TO THE STUDY OF AGING, NUMBER 19
Erdman B. Palmore, *Series Adviser*

GREENWOOD PRESS
New York • Westport, Connecticut • London

Library of Congress Cataloging-in-Publication Data

Osgood, Nancy J.
    Suicide among the elderly in long-term care facilities / Nancy J.
Osgood, Barbara A. Brant, and Aaron Lipman.
    p. cm.—(Contributions to the study of aging, ISSN
0732-085X ; no. 19)
    Includes bibliographical references and index.
    ISBN 0-313-26522-4 (lib. bdg. : alk. paper)
    1. Aged—United States—Suicidal behavior. 2. Aged—Long term
care—United States. 3. Suicide—United States—Prevention.
I. Brant, Barbara A. II. Lipman, Aaron, 1925-   III. Title.
IV. Series.
HV6545.2.084   1991
362.2'8'0846—dc20   90–36738

British Library Cataloguing in Publication Data is available.

Library of Congress Catalog Card Number: 90–36738
ISBN: 0–313–26522–4
ISSN: 0732–085X

First published in 1991

Greenwood Press, 88 Post Road West, Westport, Connecticut 06881
An imprint of Greenwood Publishing Group, Inc.

Printed in the United States of America

The paper used in this book complies with the
Permanent Paper Standard issued by the National
Information Standards Organization (Z39.48-1984).

10 9 8 7 6 5 4 3 2 1

Copyright Acknowledgments

The publisher and authors wish to acknowledge the following for permission to extract:

Portions of the Introduction, will appear in "The vulnerable and suicidal elderly" by N. J. Osgood and J. L. McIntosh, in *Understanding and serving vulnerable aged*, edited by Z. Harel P. Erlich, and R. W. Hubbard; New York: Springer Publishing Company, Inc., forthcoming. Used by permission.

Portions of chapter 3, published in N. J. Osgood, BA. Brant, and A. Lipman, "Patterns of suicidal behavior in long-term care facilities," *Omega, Journal of Death and Dying, 19*(1), 69-79; Amityville, NY: Baywood Publishing Co., 1988/89; and in N. J. Osgood and BA. Brant, "Suicidal behavior in long-term care facilities," *Suicide and Life-Threatening Behavior, 20* (2), 113–122; New York: The Guilford Press (Summer 1990).

Shorter versions of some profiles in chapter 5, published in BA. Brant, and N. J. Osgood, "The Suicidal patient in long-term care institutions," *Journal of Gerontological Nursing, 16* (2), 15-18 (1990).

Portions of chapter 7, published in N. J. Osgood and S. B. Thielman, "Geriatrics: Assessment, treatment, and suicidal behavior," in *Suicide over the life cycle*, edited by S. J. Blumenthal and D. J. Kupfer; Washington, DC: American Psychiatric Press, 1990.

THIS BOOK IS WARMLY DEDICATED TO
RESIDENTS AND STAFF OF
LONG-TERM CARE FACILITIES ALL OVER
THE COUNTRY.

CONTENTS

FIGURE AND TABLES

ACKNOWLEDGMENTS

We would like to sincerely thank everyone who made the completion of this book possible. First, our thanks go to all of the administrators, staff, and residents of long-term care facilities surveyed for the valuable information they provided on questionnaires and in interviews. We would especially like to express our gratitude to the staff and residents of the four facilities we visited to complete the in-depth case studies. Their hospitality and cooperation were greatly appreciated by all of us.

We would like to acknowledge the monetary support from Virginia Commonwealth University Faculty Grant-in-Aid program. Without the funds provided for the research, this book would not have been possible.

We would like to thank Nancy Covey for her work on all aspects of the research project. We would especially like to acknowledge her work in completing the case study of New England Health Care Center. Our thanks also go to Ms. Covey for her reading of various chapters of the manuscript. We would also like to thank Dr. Stanley Orchowsky for completing all of the statistical data analysis. Data analysis was a monumental task, and Dr. Orchowsky was always there to complete the next set of statistical manipulations.

Our thanks to all of the faculty members from the School of Nursing at Virginia Commonwealth University/Medical College of Virginia, who took time out of their busy schedules to read and comment on various chapters of the manuscript. In particular, we would like to thank Dr. Lorna Mill Barrell, Dr. Gloria M. Francis, Dr. Mary C. Corley, Dr. Barbara A. Munjas, and Dr. Jean T. Turner. The book is greatly improved, thanks to their careful reading and constructive suggestions.

We would also like to thank Mrs. Alice F. Ritch, Mrs. Mary F. Kehrli,

Ms. Allen Lybrook, and Ms. Cathy Smith, who took the time to read and comment on various chapters of the manuscript. We would also like to thank Cathy Smith for her work in the library completing the numerous references throughout the manuscript.

We especially express our gratitude to Ms. Debra Wood, who patiently typed and edited the manuscript. Our thanks to Ms. Dorothy Silvers for her expert editing.

Finally, we are indebted to our families for their patience and understanding while we busily completed the book. Our special thanks to Cressida and Ray, Alvin and Alice, and Zelda.

INTRODUCTION

A major misconception in our society is that suicide is primarily a phenomenon of adolescence. Until recently, most research and media attention in the United States has focused on the problem of suicide among teens. However, the reality is that suicide is primarily a problem of late life, and the elderly are the most "at risk." In fact, the suicide rate for the elderly is 50 percent higher than that of the young or the nation as a whole. One elderly American takes his or her life every ninety-six minutes (U.S. Bureau of Census, 1986).

The highest rates of suicide for those living in the community are found not among the young, but among those individuals 65 years and older. From 1940 to 1980, the suicide rate for the older population in this country declined markedly due to improvements in the diagnosis and treatment of depression, the increase in numbers of females in the older population, improved economic conditions, and the provision of special services for the elderly. However, from 1980 to 1986, the rates for elderly suicide climbed progressively from 17.1 (per 100,000) to 21.5 (per 100,000) in the population, respectively. In comparison, the rate for the U.S. population was 12.1 (per 100,000), and the rate for 15 to 24 year olds was 13.1 (per 100,000) in 1986 (NCHS, 1988). Not only do older persons kill themselves at a greater rate than their numbers in the population, but they do it with "determination and single-mindedness of purpose" not encountered among younger age groups (Seiden, 1981, p. 265).

The suicide rates recorded and reported for the elderly represent a drastic under-reporting of the problem. Many older adults fail to take life-sustaining medications or follow specified medical regimens; overdose on prescription and over-the-counter medications; mix alcohol and drugs; stop eating or drinking fluids; or have fatal "accidents," which are really suicidal acts. Many of these deaths are certified as "natural or accidental." In addition, many of the suicides in nursing homes and other long-term care facilities result from intentional self-starvation and failure to take medications or follow prescribed medical regimens. These passive suicidal behaviors often result in a debilitated physical condition, increasing the risk of death from pneumonia, cardiac arrest, respiratory failure, and other physical disease conditions. Such deaths are not certified as suicides and do not appear in reported suicide statistics.

Compared to younger individuals, the old openly communicate their suicidal intent less frequently (Jarvis & Boldt, 1980), use more violent and lethal means (McIntosh & Santos, 1985-86), and less often attempt suicide as a means of gaining attention or to cry for help (Pasquali & Bucher, 1981). It is estimated that there are 10 to 20 suicidal attempts for every suicide completion for the population as a whole. Ratios for the young are as high as 200 to 1, while for the elderly the ratio is 4 to 1 (McIntosh, 1985a). Social isolation, lethality of method, greater effort to avoid discovery, delayed medical interventions, and compromised physical conditions with poorer recuperative powers all contribute to successful attempts among the elderly (McIntosh & Santos, 1981).

Some older adults are considerably more vulnerable to suicide than are others. Demographic characteristics associated with vulnerability to suicide in late life include the age of the older adult, gender, race and ethnicity, and marital status. In addition to these characteristics, physical illness and such psychosocial factors as depression, alcoholism, social isolation and loneliness, and bereavement and widowhood, are related to vulnerability to suicide and the increased risk of suicide in this population. Environmental factors also play significant roles in suicide in older adults, particularly for residents of long-term care facilities.

In this chapter, various factors related to suicide in the elderly are examined in detail. The chapter also includes an overview of the scientific study of suicide in long-term care facilities.

DEMOGRAPHIC FACTORS

Age

Not only do suicide rates increase with age and peak past age 65, but within the older population there is also differential vulnerability and higher rates with increasing age. As J. McIntosh (1984) notes, rates are greater among the old-old (75 years of age) compared to the high rates of the young-old (65-74 years of age). If the old-old age group is considered in more detail, suicide rates are usually highest for the 75-84 age group and slightly lower for the oldest-old (85 years of age and older), although in the latter case rates generally remain at levels higher than for any group younger than 65 years old.

Gender

Males kill themselves at all ages at much higher rates and numbers than do women, and gender differences are greatest in old age. Male rates of suicide increase and peak in old age while female rates increase until middle age (mid-40s to mid-50s) and decline thereafter. For 1985, male rates of suicide for all ages combined were 3.9 times those for females while this ratio was 6.1 at age 65 and above and 12.0 for 85 years of age and above (calculated from data in the NCHS annual volume, 1985).

Investigations of both suicide and attempted suicide have shown that relatively more males as a group use violent and lethal methods such as firearms, hanging, and jumping, whereas females usually prefer less-violent techniques such as poisoning and suffocation (McIntosh & Santos, 1982, 1985-1986; Wilson, 1981; Klein-Schwartz, Odera & Booze, 1983). Use of lethal methods increase the likelihood of death from suicidal behavior.

Race and Ethnicity

Suicide rate differences between whites and nonwhites in the United States are great at all ages above 35 and largest above age 65 (McIntosh, in press). Even more pronounced are racial differences in old age by gender. White males are clearly the group most vulnerable to suicide (1985 rate: 43.2 per 100,000) while nonwhite males, white females, and nonwhite females are at considerably lower risk (1985 rates: 14.9, 6.9, and 3.9, respectively). These observations are generally true for blacks, native Americans, and Hispanics (whose rates peak in young adulthood) when specific ethnic rates are calculated. However, Asian-Americans (Chinese-, Japanese-, and Filipino-Americans) display peak rates in old age but at levels lower than for whites (McIntosh, 1985b, 1986, 1987a).

Compared to aging black males and white females, aging white males in American society suffer the most severe losses of social status, power, and money. These losses represent possible explanations for their dramatically higher rates of suicide. R. Maris (1969) and J. McIntosh and J. Santos (1981) have related the high suicide rates of elderly white males to the severe losses of status, power, money, and role relationships formerly provided by participation in work. By comparison, women and minority males, two groups that traditionally have held lower positions in our society, have less to lose on retirement than do white males, and thus tend to display lower rates of suicide than white males.

Maris (1969), McIntosh and Santos (1981), and R. Seiden (1981) all attribute the lower rate of suicide among older blacks as compared to older whites to the greater degree of external constraint imposed on blacks and to their more-intense involvement in family, church, and community.

Marital Status

Recent data (McIntosh, 1987b; Smith, Mercy, & Conn, 1988) indicate that suicide rates are highest for the divorced and widowed with lower rates for single individuals and lowest vulnerability for the married. For the elderly, however, vulnerability to suicide is greatly affected by the gender of the individual. Divorced older adults are the group most vulnerable to suicide; but among elderly males the difference between divorced and widowed is slight, with the single only somewhat lower and the married less than half as vulnerable as are the divorced and widowed. McIntosh (1987b) found that among males 65-74 for 1979-1981 the suicide rates were 66.4, 63.6, 44.0, and 23.4 for the divorced, widowed, single, and married, respectively. Among females of the same ages, however, the rates were much lower in all cases and less disparate (9.9, 8.4, 5.6, and 5.5, respectively).

PSYCHOSOCIAL FACTORS

Depression

Psychological factors play a crucial part in late life suicide. Depression, the major factor in late life suicide, underlies two-thirds of the suicides in the elderly (Gurland & Cross, 1983). Many elderly adults suffer multiple losses, including loss of health, impaired vision and hearing, loss of mobility, financial loss, loss of homes and possessions, loss of independence, cognitive loss and mental impairment, and loss of societal roles in work, family, and the community. These losses may result in stress at a time in life when the individual is least able to resist and cope with stress. These losses and the stress suffered from them often result in feelings of loneliness, depression, and despair (Miller, 1979; Osgood, 1985). Many older individuals experience a deep sense of emptiness and meaninglessness and lose motivation for working, playing, and living. Those who have suffered severe loss and are socially and emotionally isolated often feel rejected and dejected, unwanted, unneeded, and unloved. Their self-esteem suffers, and they view themselves as inadequate and inferior. It is no wonder that many of the elderly, as a whole, confronted as they are with multiple stresses and losses, suffer more from depression than younger individuals. Depression is the most common functional psychiatric disorder of late life.

Depression in the aged has been related to other factors besides loss. Senescent changes in the organism, particularly evolutional changes in the brain and nervous and endocrine systems and accelerated cerebral tissue loss, are factors in the development of depression in late life. Depression may also result from some viral infections and from Parkinson's disease (Birren & Sloane, 1980).

Three major factors have been recognized as contributing to depression and suicide among older persons: haplessness, helplessness, and hopelessness. Lowered self-concept and self-esteem contribute to the haplessness and self-hatred of the aged. M. Seligman (1975) has hypothesized that persons who are unable to control significant life events develop a sense of helplessness. This helplessness, according to Seligman, is the core of depression in elders. Helplessness and hopelessness often go hand in hand and can result in suicidal behavior in the aged. Karl Menninger (1938) characterized the suicides of older adults as a result of the wish to die and identified hopelessness as the major factor in elderly suicide. In notes left by elders contemplating suicide, they often speak of being "tired of life," or "tired of living," a condition referred to by S. H. Cath (1965) as "psychological exhaustion."

Alcoholism

The connection between alcoholism and suicide is well documented (Roy & Linnoila, 1986). More than one-third of all suicides in the United States are related to alcohol. Menninger (1938), in his classic *Man against Himself*, labels alcoholism as a form of "chronic suicide." E. Palola and associates (1982) suggest that alcoholism is a substitute for suicide. Others who have studied alcoholism and suicide claim that both problems are effects of the same causes (i.e., depression, helplessness, and stress). Alcohol and suicide are serious, related problems in the elderly population. Although the association between alcohol and suicide is high in every age group, it is greatly increased in older adults (Blazer, 1982). D. Bienenfeld (1987) reports that the risk of suicide in aging alcoholics is five times greater than in aging nonalcoholic persons.

Many older adults turn to alcohol to relieve depression and loneliness and to escape from the problems and stresses of aging. Ingestion of large quantities of alcohol, however, actually increases depression and anxiety. Alcohol acts as a depressant on the central nervous system and also may alter moods and decrease critical life-evaluating functions of the ego, allowing unconscious self-destructive impulses to gain control. The stimulating effects of alcohol may reduce inhibitions and self-control and contribute to the false courage that may be a factor in suicide. Regular use of alcohol often results in the deterioration of important social relationships, leading to social isolation. The anger, hostility, and belligerence that accompany frequent alcohol use can alienate the depressed person from family members and close friends at a time when those social and emotional supports are needed. Coupled with increased isolation and alienation are intense feelings of shame, guilt, denial, pessimism, and lowered self-concept, all factors in suicidal behavior (Osgood, 1987).

Isolation and Loneliness

Many older adults lose significant others in numerous ways, particularly through death, the loss of contact due to the mobility of family and others, and the tendency on the part of many older adults to remain where they reside. The loss itself may be a motivation to suicide as seen above, but the social isolation leaves fewer social supports and resources in circumstances of suicidal ideation and risk. The old are the group most likely to be socially isolated. Social isolation has been found to have a strong association with increased suicidal vulnerability (Gove & Hughes, 1980; Trout, 1980) and living alone is frequently found among elderly suicides (Cattell, 1988). Loneliness is a common cognitive attribute of suicidal individuals (Shneidman, 1985) and obviously may accompany the social isolation and multiple losses often experienced by older adults (Sainsbury, 1962).

Bereavement and Widowhood

Emile Durkheim (1951) first emphasized the association between widowhood and suicide over one hundred years ago in his seminal work *Suicide*, in which he characterized the vulnerability of the widowed as an indicator of "domestic anomie," that is, a deregulation of behavior associated with the loss of a spouse. Durkheim recognized that participation in the family represented one of the most important ties among society's members. As suggested by Durkheim, the state of marriage and membership in a family integrate societal members by exerting a regulative force on them and by acting as a stimulant to intensive interpersonal relations that draw the members into firm and meaningful union, thereby providing some degree of immunity, the "coefficient of preservation" against suicide. Durkheim viewed the loss of the spouse as weakening the familial integration of the individual. Thus the suicide of widows and widowers may be referred to as both "anomic" and "egoistic." Durkheim's classic explanation for the greater proportion of suicides among widowers as compared to widows, namely that men derive more from marriage than women, reflects an important gender difference among those growing older.

Numerous empirical studies conducted in recent years have confirmed the increased risk of suicide among the widowed, particularly widowed males (MacMahon & Pugh, 1965; Paykel, Prusoff, & Myers, 1975; Kaprio, Koskenvuo, & Rita, 1987). Several explanations for the increased vulnerability to suicide experienced by the widowed have been offered. Following the lead of Durkheim, several recent writers have focused on the loss of social support and social relationships as key factors in suicide of the widowed.

After some pioneering studies, conducted nearly two decades ago, F. Berardo (1970) suggested that the elderly widower suffers doubly because he loses not only his role in the family system, but through his retirement his role in the occupational sphere as well. He also pointed out that in our society the woman has assumed the responsibility for integrating the kinship group and maintaining contacts with friends and relatives over the years. As a result, she has the support of the kinship group when her husband dies, but the elderly widower is left totally alone. M. Miller (1979) has further noted that the loss of family role, combined with the loss of occupational role and the resultant downward social mobility, places the elderly widower in a particularly vulnerable position. Berardo (1968, 1970) describes the situation of widows and widowers as vague and unstructured, lacking clear guidelines for behavior, and lacking supportive interactions with friends, kin, and coworkers. E. Bock and I. Webber (1972), who also found older widowers to be at considerably greater risk of suicide than their female counterparts, describe the elderly male widower as much more socially and emotionally isolated than the older widow. Widowers were less likely than widows to have relatives living nearby in the community and to belong to social organizations.

Two other followers of Durkheim, A. Henry and J. Short (1954), have explained suicide in terms of the weakening of the relational system constituted by marriage; and Bock (1972) points out that "marriage not only integrates the individual into a close and meaningful association but also regulates him by requiring him to take the other person into account in activities and decisions" (p. 72).

Psychological explanations for the increased vulnerability of the widowed to suicide have focused on the negative psychological consequences of loss and bereavement. G. Winokur (1974) has called bereavement the "paradigm of reactional depression." R. Kastenbaum (1969) has described a phenomenon called "bereavement overload," in which an individual is psychologically overwhelmed by the loss of a significant love object. In a recent study, S. Bromberg and C. Cassel (1983) found that depression occurs in about 20 percent of widows and widowers during the first year after their spouses' deaths. Recognizing the significance of the loss of a spouse, T. Holmes and R. Rahe's research (1967) on their Social Readjustment Rating Scale gave widowhood a much heavier rating than any of the other events likely to occur in a lifetime.

Physical Illness

Physical health problems have been one of the most consistent and replicated findings associated with vulnerability and suicide in old age (Sainsbury, 1962; Dorpat, Anderson, & Ripley, 1968; Miller, 1976). Many aged suffer from painful, chronic, and often debilitating illnesses such as cancer, diabetes, Parkinsonism, diseases of vision and hearing, and strokes. The stress of illness in the aging body experiencing physiological and psychological changes as a result of the aging process, can markedly interfere with the body's ability to endure such stress (Osgood, 1985). Illness poses threats to life; to bodily comfort and integrity; to self-concept and future plans; to one's emotional equilibrium; and to the fulfillment of customary roles and activities in work, the family, and the community.

THE INSTITUTIONAL CONTEXT

The field of social ecology encompasses the study of how environment affects individuals' physical and mental health and social behavior and functioning. Many older adults are more dependent on their immediate physical environment to meet their needs. The environment can challenge and stimulate or inhibit personal growth and development in older adults.

Long-Term Care Institutions

There are more than 23,000 long-term care facilities serving over 1.5 million older adults. The average number of nursing home residents is expected to increase over 50 percent between 1989 and the year 2020 (Kramer, 1986). The institutionalized aged differ considerably from their counterparts living in the community, as they are much more likely to be female, unmarried, without family, old-old, white, poor, and physically or/and mentally impaired. In nursing homes, 72 percent of the population are female with women outnumbering men 2.5 to 1 (Harper, 1986, p. 4). Only 12 percent are currently married; 15 percent have never married. Eighty-four percent are 75 years or older and the average age is over 80. Ninety-five percent are white. The typical resident has three or four chronic conditions (Vladeck, 1980). Approximately 1 in 5 has a primary diagnosis of mental illness (Harper, 1986, p. 2).

Nursing homes are typical of the "total institution" defined by Erving Goffman (1960) in his well-known work on mental institutions. In total institutions all activity occurs in one physical location in the company of a large group of others. Rules and regulations govern everyday life. Privacy is at a minimum. Residents living in total institutions are told when to eat, when to sleep, and when to bathe by staff members who exert control over their lives. In such a situation, personal freedom and autonomy are greatly reduced.

Many older persons residing in institutions experience many of the same losses and stresses experienced by older people living in the community. They, too, are plagued by loneliness, depression, and alcoholism. However, nursing home residents also face a multitude of other losses, stresses, and problems associated with living in an institution, including loss of home and possessions, personal freedom, privacy, and independence. They may experience depersonalization, deprivation, and dehumanization. These factors place institutionalized older adults at risk for depression and suicide.

To date, little research has been conducted on suicide among elderly residents of long-term care facilities. Few studies have examined the extent and nature of overt suicide or attempted suicide in long-term care institutions. Even fewer studies have examined the nature and extent of what has been variously referred to as "hidden suicide" (Meerloo, 1968) or "indirect life-threatening behavior" (Nelson & Farberow, 1980). Intentional life-threatening behavior (ILTB) is defined as repetitive acts by individuals directed toward themselves that result in physical harm or tissue damage that could bring about a premature end of life. Examples include refusing to eat or drink, refusing medications, or refusing to follow specified medical regimens. One study conducted on the geriatric ward of a Veterans Administration medical center (Wolff, 1970) suggests that overt suicide does occur in long-term care facilities. Other studies have also revealed a fairly high incidence of ILTB in particular long-term care institutions (Mishara & Kastenbaum, 1973; Nelson, 1977; Nelson & Farberow, 1980). One of these studies (Nelson & Farberow, 1980) further suggests that some of the characteristics that are related to overt suicide are also factors in ILTB. The institutional study detailed in Chapter 3 examines the nature and extent of overt suicide and life-threatening behavior among residents of long-term care facilities.

THE STUDY

The prevention of suicide and other forms of self-destructive behavior among the institutionalized elderly is a major consideration because of its importance from humanitarian, professional, and legal points of view. The study reported in this book is the first large-scale national study of suicide in a population of institutionalized older adults. Findings allow us to identify the most at-risk groups of elderly and to highlight the major factors contributing to suicide in older adults in institutions.

Study Design and Methodology

The study described in this work employed a sample survey design. More than 1,000 administrators of long-term care facilities across the country were randomly selected and surveyed about their staff and facilities, and the incidence and type of suicidal behaviors that occurred among residents in 1984 and 1985. In addition, the study included a qualitative component consisting of four case studies conducted in facilities that had experienced instances of suicidal behaviors. To obtain in-depth information on particular factors related to suicide in each facility, staff and residents were observed and interviewed, and medical records of all residents who had engaged in any form of suicidal behavior in the previous five years were examined.

An Overview of Findings

Results of the study confirmed that suicidal behavior occurred in approximately 20 percent of the facilities surveyed. High risk groups of residents included white males and the old-old. Certain environmental factors such as size of facility, staff turnover rate, per diem cost, and auspices (public, private, and religious) were related to the occurrence and outcome of suicidal behavior. These and other findings are discussed in detail in the chapters that follow. Suggestions for suicide prevention based on these findings are also presented.

OVERVIEW

The book is divided into three parts. Part one examines various types of long-term care facility, including skilled nursing facilities, intermediate care facilities, and adult homes. Definitions of each are provided. In addition, the history of growth and development and characteristics of each type of institution are presented. The importance of the environment to physical and mental health of older adults is also explored in part one. A review of the literature on facility, size, privacy, cost, resources, and other specific environmental factors related to quality of life in institutions is included.

Part two highlights design, methodology, and findings from the national study of suicide in long-term care facilities. Based on study findings, profiles of aging residents at risk for suicide are constructed and presented. Case profiles of suicidal residents are included to provide a more personal account of suicidal behavior, and to illustrate important factors in the older individual's decision to end his or her life. Also included in part two are in-depth profiles of four long-term care facilities, highlighting environmental factors related to suicide among this population. Depression is a major factor in late life suicide. The last chapter in part two is devoted to a discussion of factors related to late life depression and recommended guidelines for recognizing signs and symptoms of depression in older institutionalized residents.

Part three focuses on suicide prevention. The first two chapters offer concrete suggestions on the treatment of depression in the elderly and the prevention of suicide in institutions. A wide variety of preventive techniques are highlighted, including drug therapy, electroconvulsive therapy (ECT), creative arts therapy, reminiscence, therapeutic touch, and environmental manipulations. The final chapter in this section considers the ethics of suicide and presents arguments for and against the right to die.

PART I

1

INSTITUTIONAL SETTINGS: THE LONG-TERM CARE CONNECTION

INTRODUCTION

Long-term care is a multi-billion dollar industry. Its tangle of public and private organizations operates at every level—federal, state, and local— stimulated by the burgeoning need for long-term care of the aging. Data from the *Inventory of Long-Term Care Places* (NCHS, 1986) show that in 1960, the number of long-term care facilities in the United States was just under 9,500; by 1986, these facilities numbered 26,380. About 5 percent of the elderly in the United States now live in nursing homes and other long-term care institutions. In 1977, the number of residents in long-term care facilities numbered just under 1 million. By 1986, almost 1.7 million lived in long-term care facilities (NCHS, 1986). The average cost per resident was $22,000 annually (Rivlin & Weiner, 1988). The long-term care industry currently employs more than 1,431,000 people, of whom more than 70 percent are practical nurses and nursing aides (Harper & Lebowitz, 1986).

In this century, the elderly population of the United States has undergone a dramatic increase, not only numerically but proportionately (Brody, 1977). Although most members of the expanding elderly population continue to function normally, even with chronic conditions, as a group they are highly vulnerable not only to isolation and poverty, but also to accidents, illness, and ensuing functional disability. Older adults may find themselves unable to handle normal daily routines or to manage life's complexities. The specter of dependency then looms—what B. Landsberger (1985) calls "demotion from independence."

Clearly, the rapid increase of the elderly has brought the nation face-to-face with our greater health care needs; but, ironically, the effort to meet those needs brings an equally bleak threat: the possibility that older adults will have to relinquish their independent adult identities.

Not only has the population of elderly increased, but the composition has changed and today includes a higher proportion of those 85 years or older. The oldest-old have significantly more health care needs than do those 60-84 years of age. A. Rivlin and J. Weiner (1988) point out that the segment of the elderly population 85 years and older is increasing at a faster rate than any other age group. They predict that by 2030 the proportion of functionally impaired oldest-old among nursing home residents will have reached 60 percent. Yet, as C. Harrington, R. J. Newcomer, C. L. Estes, and associates (1985) emphasize, "few public and private insurance dollars are being expended on long-term care . . . and new forms of care, particularly noninstitutional care, are needed" (p. 11).

The massive federal programs established in 1965 to ensure access to health care by the elderly through Medicare and by the poor and disabled through Medicaid called forth a phenomenal rush by the private sector into the nursing home industry. Seventy-five percent of all nursing homes and 85 percent of all residential facilities in 1986 were under for-profit ownership (NCHS, 1986). While some facilities provide excellent care, others are deficient. L. Lowy (1979) summed up long-term care arrangements in the United States as "fragmented and inadequate at best."

Whatever the quality of long-term care for the elderly, its cost is exorbitant, reflecting the escalation of total annual health care costs that is expected to reach $750 billion by 1990 (Rabin & Stockton, 1987). In fiscal year 1981, for example, hospital care, nursing home care, and physician care for the elderly population combined cost more than $71.6 billion (Kart, Metress, & Metress, 1988). Nursing home care is a close second to hospital care as an elder health care cost. Urgent questions about long-term care abound.

1. What does long-term care encompass?
2. What types of long-term care setting are available to the elderly?
3. Given the explosive growth of the long-term care industry, how should long-term care be paid for?
4. Who should pay?
5. What impact does the long-term care system and its cost have on an already stretched health care system?
6. What impact does institutionalization have on the growing population of older people?
7. What happens to the physical and mental health of old people when they are placed in long-term care institutions?

This chapter will describe the basic characteristics of the long-term care system and the principal types of setting within it and explain the existing payment systems for health care of the elderly.

THE LONG-TERM CARE SYSTEM

Long-term care has been defined as the range of services providing for the health, personal care, and sociopsychological needs of those whose ability to take care of themselves has been reduced by frailty, chronic illness or other functional impairments (Rabin & Stockton, 1987). Such services, viewed "as a system of interrelated components of national scope," form the nation's long-term care delivery system (Eustis, Greenberg, & Patten, 1984). Care is delivered through housing resources, or day care centers, or through nursing home and related residential institutions for the elderly. Levels of long-term care range from least to most supportive across a broad continuum: independent living (housing units for the elderly and disabled); supportive services (day care); protective, supervised, and/or custodial care (personal and board and care homes); assistive and supervisory care (intermediate care facilities); specialized professional care (skilled care facilities); and short-term convalescent care for selected patients (extended care/rehabilitative facilities) (Gelfand, 1988).

Although a prevailing public notion assumes that the structure of long-term care is the product of systematic planning for the complex needs of the aging society, in actuality it is a piecemeal system that has grown to monumental proportions. Its explosive, yet unplanned, expansion leaves increasing numbers of elderly Americans facing a bewildering muddle of facilities, with care erratically available and quality inconsistent.

One step toward a more rational and responsible public understanding of long-term care delivery is to make clear that all long-term care facilities are not nursing homes, even though intermediate care facilities and skilled care facilities dominate the long-term care scene. It is important to examine the existing continuum of housing options, paying attention to possibilities and drawbacks of each. Differences and similarities of a range of long-term care settings, moving from most to least independent, are examined in the succeeding pages: subsidized elderly housing; adult day care; board and care homes; and nursing homes, including intermediate care facilities (ICFs) and skilled nursing facilities (SNFs).

Subsidized Elderly Housing

While housing programs per se do not at first glance seem part of the long-term care continuum, the role played by public housing for the elderly should not be overlooked. Affordable and decent housing is a prerequisite for the elderly to remain in the community (Eustis et al., 1984).

Federally financed public housing has had a long and varied history from the National Housing Act of 1934 to the Community Development Act of 1974, which funded new or renovated existing units through the Department of Housing and Urban Development (HUD) until 1983 (Gelfand, 1988). The

Community Development Act also provided rent subsidies in units owned by private, non-profit, or public housing agencies for tenants who meet income-based eligibility requirements (Eustis, et al., 1984; Gelfand, 1988; Kane & Kane, 1987). Low-income households pay no more than 30 percent of their adjusted income, monitored annually, for housing operated by local non-profit public housing administrations (Kane & Kane, 1987).

Residents of subsidized rental units for the elderly and disabled must be functionally independent. Most are women, widowed or never married, living on restricted incomes. Although nationwide most are white, the ethnic composition differs with geographic location. The median age is about 82 (Richmond Redevelopment and Housing Authority, personal communication, 1989).

Subsidized housing is intended to provide clean, safe, affordable conditions where older adults can function independently. However, most public high-rises for community elderly provide no health services, which would raise operating costs and possibly diminish the independence of residents. These facilities also do not provide structures for encouraging aging residents to undertake health-preserving activities to maintain their independence. Inevitably, many tenants become functionally limited or ill, requiring, if not acute short-term hospital care, different living arrangements. If these individuals need indefinite nursing care beyond what can be provided in their homes, they are usually candidates for nursing home placement. Tenants are often distressingly unprepared to relocate to nursing homes or related institutions from their housing units.

Adult Day Care

As an alternative to institutionalization, adult day/health care is an integrated component of long-term care for the elderly. It is the service most frequently used by family caregivers of elderly adults (Rabin & Stockton, 1988). The concept of the day hospital originated in England with out-patient centers, first, for psychiatric patients in the 1940s, and then in the 1950s for geriatric patients. Geriatric day care centers opened in the United States in 1947 and 1949 under the auspices of the Menninger Clinic and Yale University, respectively. The movement has since appeared in most states (Gelfand, 1988).

Adult day/health care is not a senior center but "a program provided under social and/or health leadership, particularly if funded by Medicaid" (Gelfand, 1988). That is, it may be geared to social needs of adults who do not need twenty-four-hour institutional care, but who, because of their physical or mental limitations, cannot manage full-time independent living as defined by the Department of Health, Education, and Welfare (HEW) guidelines; or programs may focus on improving or maintaining good health; or they may use both approaches (Gelfand, 1988).

Objectives, staffing, and services vary among adult day care facilities across the country, depending on the specific model of care and on funding. Specific outcome criteria for goals or type of care are often lacking. In those centers covered by Medicaid, staffing requirements for health care needs of the elderly are set up. However, there are no federal guidelines for determining Medicaid eligibility (Gelfand, 1988). Increasingly, adult day care programs are operated by proprietary nursing homes, as a separate service located in one section of the nursing home.

Clientele are generally transported to the day care setting either by the facility's vehicle or by their caregivers, and they may stay for either a limited time (two to four hours) or for extended periods (ten or more hours), depending on the center's staffing and program. Clients engage in support group and activities programs, prescribed rehabilitative or restorative activities, or other programs. They usually receive prescribed medication from a qualified nurse. Unfortunately, because health professionals are often employed only part-time (perhaps no more than four hours per day), health care delivery may lack continuity.

Costs vary among day care centers, but average $24 to $35 per diem. In some states, Medicaid covers adult day care services (Rabin & Stockton, 1988), but most programs lack federal and state funding. Thus day care services must be paid for out-of-pocket by clients who use them or by their families.

A primary consideration for day care programs for those older people who require them is whether the care is worth the cost. Another consideration is the increase in clientele, requiring a greater level of services, and the disparity between that increased demand and personnel and service delivery (Harrington, Newcomer, Estes, & Associates, 1985). A serious criticism is directed at the sociopsychological support offered in adult day care; often programs and services appear to be more appropriate for children and have limited therapeutic value (Gelfand, 1988).

Board and Care Homes

Board and care homes go by a confusing number of names from state to state: foster care homes, adult care homes, sheltered care facilities, homes for adults, domiciliary, personal care, or community-care residences, or rest homes. A board and care home is more than a boarding home, yet less than a nursing home. The distinctive services it provides may include medication supervision, activities of daily living (ADL) and instrumental ADL assistance, laundry, houskeeping, transportation, money management, medical and other appointments, and community referral (Kane & Kane, 1987). However, such services vary widely. Basically, "a resident is provided a room, meals, assistance with activities of daily living, and some degree of protective supervision" at a pre-determined fee. A home houses "four or more adults who are not related to the board and care home manager" (R. Cohen, 1986, p. 7). Such residences can range in size from 1 to 300 or more beds.

Some states, but not all, license board and care homes. Their cleanliness and safety are regulated by either the Department of Health or the Department of Social Services in the locality. Of the 30,000 board and care homes in the nation, it is estimated that nearly 5,000 are unlicensed (Cohen, 1986; Kane & Kane 1987).

Board and care homes accommodate the chronically mentally ill, the disabled, and the elderly. Median age of residents is between 60 and 75 years; most are women. On the average, women residents are almost ten years older than the men (Cohen, 1986). Rates for board and care homes range from $250 to over $1,200 a month. They are not subsidized by Medicaid. The fees are paid, often on a sliding scale, out-of-pocket; for poor residents, the local Department of Social Services may pay all or part of the fees.

Board and care homes are usually in buildings that began life as hotels, hospitals, nursing homes, dormitories, or family homes. While many structures have been adapted to residents' physical requirements, e.g., those of the handicapped, many other structures have not. Consequently, socialization, mobility, and access to the outside world may be limited. Similarly, the quality of maintenance in board and care homes varies dramatically. The AARP cautions against using a home that has no service or regulatory relationship with other agencies. A comprehensive consumer guide to board and care homes may be obtained from the AARP (Cohen, 1986) or from local area agencies on aging.

Before choosing a board and care home, it is important to determine what services are covered under the rate; the manager's competence; how the home compares with other facilities in the area; what recourse one has in case of abuse, mismanagement or neglect; cost and whether or not payment is pro-rated or expected daily, weekly, or monthly; and what financial arrangements follow if the client is not satisfied with the home, or if the client should die (Cohen, 1986).

Nursing Homes History

Poor farms and almshouses, existing in the nineteenth and early twentieth centuries, estimated to have housed approximately 80,000 elderly; "homes for the aged," formed by charitable groups in small proprietary boarding houses for the old and indigent, were the beginnings of the nursing home concept in this country.

In 1935 welfare programs and Social Security payments for older citizens were enacted under the Older Americans Act; they did not, however, cover inmates of public institutions (Rabin & Stockton, 1987). After World War II, with major medical innovations and hospital acute care becoming more sophisticated, separate nursing homes were built to provide extended post-hospital recovery care that reduced in-hospital stays and costs; the proprietary nursing home industry was born. The explosive growth in the number and capacity of nursing homes since then has been prompted by the increased availability of public funds (Vladeck, 1980, p. 4).

Early attempts to license nursing homes met with very little success. Regulations were ineffective and monitored poorly, if at all; workers, from the administrator down were ill-qualified; and often, nursing homes were put in old houses and buildings not suited for comfort, therapeutic activity, or efficiency. In the mid-1950s, a new system of licensing nursing homes was enacted, but regulations remained extremely loose. As a result, thousands of facilities in every state in the nation still fail to meet minimal legal standards of sanitation, staffing, or patient care (Vladeck, 1980). Between 1950 and 1980 practices in most nursing homes were described as scandalous; and many facilities were exposed as nests of questionable fiscal behavior and patient care horrors.

Nursing homes are still burdened with an unpleasant public image, not unjustified, as places where older person must go to face death or a reduced version of life. The nursing home is seen as "their final coping place" (Jaeger & Simmons, 1970), where sickness and death prevail.

The Medical Model of Care

Traditionally, nursing homes have adopted a medical model in their care of older adults, focusing on disease states, etiology, treatment, technical interventions, and cure. This model, as described by C. Johnson and L. Grant (1985), is one-dimensional, hierarchical in structure, and limited in its scope of care for the elderly. Like hospitals, nursing homes organized around the medical model are replete with formal rules, regimentation, and routinization. Guidelines for care focus on illness rather than on the functional status, rehabilitation, and restoration of the person. Hence, the elderly resident is viewed as a "patient," which reinforces the societal misconception of the aged as ill. Medical intervention, rigorously geared toward cure rather than care, creates a "therapeutic nihilism which undergirds many of the approaches of nursing homes, despite the most humane goals" (Johnson & Grant, 1985, p. 19). To shape long-term care—whether in or out of institutions—on the medical model and make the physician the gatekeeper runs counter to current knowledge (Brody, 1977, p. 53).

The hospital is said to be the "workshop of the physician," but B. Vladeck (1980) describes the nursing home by contrast as "an entity based on the medical model without a physician." He points out that physician visits generally occur in harmony with the dictates of funding and accrediting agencies, and residents may or may not experience the "laying-on of the physician's hands during these visits." Psychosocial aspects of care are seldom planned for appropriately or evaluated.

The growth of the nursing home population and the increasing frailty of elderly residents indicate that more medical care is needed in nursing homes. However, Eustis and associates (1984) predict that, without effective surveillance, nursing home residents face an increased probability of mortality, declining function, reduced psychological and social well-being, and occurrence of preventable conditions like pneumonia and bedsores. Long-term care facilities have been mordantly described as tending to be "chronic disease hospitals for the physically and mentally impaired elderly, rather than care centers and homes for the ambulatory aged who are not self-sufficient" (Tobin & Lierberman, 1976, p. 235). Nonetheless, diminishing physical and psychological self-sufficiency need not mean diminished social function. S. Tobin and M. Lieberman (1976) caution, "the consequences will be dire if we revert to warehousing or storehousing these most needy elderly, and do not make every effort to provide life-sustaining social as well as physical supports" (p. 236).

Intermediate Care Facilities

Among the amendments to Medicaid programs introduced in the mid-1960s were those dealing with skilled nursing home care and intermediate nursing home care (medical care for which medical assistance is available). In response to the inability of skilled nursing care facilities to provide enough access to quality long-term nursing care for the elderly ill or to be a resource for basic health supervision (Glasscote & Beigel, 1976), the federal government recommended that intermediate care nursing facilities be made eligible for Medicaid funding. This not only endorsed the option of a less intense level of nursing care than continuous supervision by licensed personnel, it was an attempt to cut skilled care costs. The resulting legislation allowed nursing homes that were not meeting skilled care standards to re-certify many of their residents and facilities under "intermediate care" and thus avoid losing Medicaid payments. An era of abundant fraud and Medicaid abuse was inaugurated.

R. Glasscote and A. Beigel (1976) characterize the intermediate care facility as:

a health care institution, operated by a qualified administrator, and offering within the facility, physician and limited nursing services, recreational, and medical record services, as well as a well rounded program of supervised pharmaceutical, dietetic, social, and activities services that are all coordinated by a resident services director; and providing "as needed" either internally or from outside the facility, a professional rehabilitative service, and professional consultation to in-house services (p. 44).

Today, roughly one-half of the nation's nursing homes are classified as intermediate care facilities (Kane & Kane, 1987). They are distinguished from skilled nursing facilities by the levels of care provided. ICFs, and SNFs as well, are now required to address the biopsychosocial needs of their clientele, rather than deliver only the custodial care long identified as institutional. The state of Virginia, for example, decides on the appropriate level of long-term care for an individual using three factors: his or her medical needs, specific services required to meet their needs, and health care personnel required (Virginia Department for the Aging, 1988).

The "bed and body work" (J. F. Gubrium, 1975) of resident care (bathing, feeding, toileting, and making the bed) in most ICFs is done by nursing assistants, who must now undergo specific training to work in long-term care facilities (OBRA, 1987). Patients may also require supervised medication administration; help with meals, hygiene, or mobility; activities and restorative programs; or access to medical care for acute conditions.

Under the state's requirements, most older persons living in nursing homes qualify for an intermediate level of care. Care of this type, however, could be provided in sheltered care environments or hospital-based facilities, were there enough such facilities to meet the need. Yet most intermediate care is delivered within the confines of the nursing home.

Skilled Nursing Facilities

Skilled nursing facilities can be characterized as medical institutions that care for patients who are severely ill (Gelfand, 1988). Originally, SNFs were intended for the delivery of continuous nursing supervision, along with non-medical services; a stipulation of skilled care delivery has been that the client needs care by licensed nursing personnel at all times (Glasscote & Beigel, 1976). Glasscote and Beigel (1976), in their well-known field study of nursing and board and care homes, clearly summarized the function and organization of skilled nursing facilities: SNFs are required to provide specific services that require the "emergency and on-going services of a physician, nursing care, rehabilitative services, pharmaceutical services, dietetic services; and laboratory and radiologic services, dental services, social services, and activity services which may be contracted with outside resources" (p. 34). Twenty-four-hour nursing services are provided under the supervision of a registered professional nurse, by qualified nursing staff. Patient care plans are initiated on the patient's admission and updated regularly. Physician visits are mandated every thirty days within the ninety-day admission period and may, depending on the patient's condition, be reduced to sixty days (Gelfand, 1988). In homes with more than 120 beds, social work activities must be provided. SNFs are reimbursed for care under Medicare and Medicaid.

In 1986, nursing home residents numbered more than 1.5 million. According to the NCHS (1986) figures, over one-third are admitted directly from hospitals; an estimated 13 percent are transferred from other facilities in the long-term care system. The rest are admitted from their own or relatives' homes. Fewer than 50 percent of residents are fully ambulatory,

55 percent are impaired, and 33 percent are incontinent (D. Gelfand, 1988, p. 206).

The average nursing home resident is 82 years old. The number of those in the 75-84 age group in nursing homes has increased by 70 percent. Those 85 and over comprise nearly 36 percent of the nursing home population. Most nursing home residents (71 percent) are women, and this proportion increases with age. The ratio of women to men between the ages of 65 and 74 is three to one, for those 85 years and over, the ratio changes to four to one. Ten percent of residents have living spouses, 63 percent are widowed, and 22 percent never married. More than 60 percent of nursing home residents have few or no visits from significant others, and at least 50 percent have no living blood relatives (Gelfand, 1988; Eustis et al. 1984). Nonwhites comprise only 6.6 percent of the residents (NCHS, 1986). The profile of a typical nursing home resident is white, female, 82 years old, and widowed or never married, with chronic health conditions.

Most nursing home residents have multiple health problems. The most common are arteriosclerosis, heart condition, "senility," chronic brain syndrome, arthritis, and rheumatism (NCHS, 1986). There are more than 750,000 elderly, mentally ill nursing home residents in this country (Harper & Leibowitz, 1986). Emotional, behavioral and mental disorders frequently observed in nursing home residents include depression, confusion, wandering or restlessness, disorientation, agitation, lethargy, irritability, stress, mood swings, alterations in self-esteem, guilt, inappropriate dependence on staff, and paranoid delusion. It is surprising, in view of the data, that no psychiatrists or gero-psychiatric specialists in medicine, nursing, sociology, or psychology are employed full time by nursing homes. Such a situation presents serious problems for residents, many of whom are at increased risk for suicide.

PAYMENT SYSTEMS FOR ELDER HEALTH CARE

A long, arduous history attaches to Medicare and Medicaid, the two major programs covering medical care for the elderly. Both programs are administered by the federal and state governments, respectively.

Medicare

Title XVIII, the 1965 amendment to the Social Security Program of 1935, established Medicare as a federal insurance program for nearly all persons over 65 years of age, providing for acute hospital care, limited skilled nursing home care, physician's services, home health care, and some out-patient services. Medicare consists of two parts: *Part A*, a compulsory hospital insurance plan financed by Social Security, and *Part B*, a voluntary supplement paid for by the recipient for physician services, diagnostic testing, and select drugs. *Part A* coverage in nursing homes is limited (C. Kart, E. Metress, & S. Metress, 1988). In 1981 over 11 percent of the population had applied for Medicare (Gelfand, 1988), only 1.4 percent of nursing home residents in 1983 had Medicare coverage (National Center for Health Statistics, 1985a).

Medicare now covers less than one-half of the elderly person's medical expenses. In recent years deductibles, that is out-of-pocket payments for medical care by the elderly or their families, have soared. Medicare and Medicaid programs are based on the model of reimbursed care for disease-related illnesses, which has a bias toward institutional care rather than health maintenance care. Such a payment system creates a major obstacle to effective delivery of health care to the elderly. Medicare's focus on the medical care needs of older adults, negates their health promotion and maintenance care needs, and more often than not, older persons are more in need of the latter.

The Medicare system has long been the target of advocates for elder health care because of its mishandling by medical care agencies and medical professionals. Abuses in Medicare-supported nursing homes have long been identified (Vladeck, 1980; Eustis et al., 1984). After poor quality of nursing home care had been extensively publicized, increased regulation diminished many of the health and safety hazards. Nevertheless, serious problems still exist.

With limited regulatory controls, Medicare costs have risen rapidly. Reforms by the prospective payment system of 1983 set fixed fees for over 450 diagnosis-related groups (DRGs), with full payment under Medicare for treatment while hospitalized. One unfortunate consequence resulting from this recent policy is that hospitals are discharging elderly patients "sicker and quicker" to nursing homes and other institutions. Premature release of patients burdens staff of long-term care facilities, who may not have the advanced training for more intensive nursing care, and the likelihood of more misery for the elderly patient is apparent.

Medicaid

Title XIX is the companion amendment to Medicare under the Social Security system of 1935. Nearly 22 million persons used Medicaid to pay medical bills in 1981 (D. Gelfand, 1988, R. Kane and R. Kane, 1987). Medicaid is structured as a public assistance program run by the states under federal guidelines. Medicaid eligibility is not based on age, but on income requirements. Medicaid covers medical bills for certain low-income persons: those over 65, the blind, the disabled, members of families with dependent children, and certain other children.

The income and asset ceilings for Medicaid eligibility are painfully low; individuals who exceed the limits by even $1,000 may be able to afford health care only after they "spend down" their incomes and assets to "pauperized proportions and qualify as a member of the poor" as C. Kart, E.

Metress, and S. Metress describe it (1988, p. 311). Many older persons whose incomes, although meager, still minimally exceed a state limit for Medicaid fall through the health care cracks. They cannot themselves pay for medical care and prescriptions, yet they are shut out of Medicaid because they are not able to meet income eligibility requirements. Such individuals then fall into the category "non-compliant," the health care profession's label for their plight.

Funds quickly vanish when paying for costly nursing home care. Once resources have been virtually liquidated, the eligibility criteria for Medicaid benefits can be met. Once on Medicaid, nursing home residents are entitled to a monthly stipend of about $35 to spend as they like. In some nursing homes the stipend is obtained with difficulty. Even when residents are aware of the mandated stipend, they often find that $35 does not cover a month's personal needs. Because Medicaid programs are now subject to state cost constraints similar to those for Medicare, medical practitioners in nursing homes have become cautious about accepting Medicaid patients. Hence, the burden of care more and more frequently falls on families who are ill-equipped financially, physically, or psychologically to care for their elderly members. Eustis and associates (1984) have astutely observed that

while gerontologists, social policy makers, and some lawmakers view long-term care as encompassing the integration of community-based and institutional services, the reality is that there are no true linkages to acute, community, or chronic care for the elderly (p. 38).

2

ENVIRONMENTAL PERSPECTIVES
AND SOCIAL ECOLOGY

The belief has long been held that the environment directly affects health and disease. The Hippocratic writings note the direct causal relationship between changes of seasons, risings and settings of the sun, wind and temperature patterns, and other elements of the physical environment and the state of physical and mental health and disease in man. Social reformers of the eighteenth century advocated exposure to an optimum physical environment as a means of alleviating mental illness.

Influenced by such early ideas, many recent students of physical and mental health have argued that human behavior must be studied in the context of the physical and social environments in which individuals live and function because, as W. Ittleson, H. Proshansky, and L. Rivlin (1970) point out, it is the environment with its physical, psychological, and social components that surrounds and enfolds the individual. Human choice and action take place in socially bounded environments that set conditions under which people must operate, and aging is affected by these environments (Ward, La Gory, & Sherman, 1988, p. 1).

The new field of social ecology is defined in this chapter. Major environmental factors, which affect the older individual's quality of life in institutions, are highlighted, and some particular problems of living in institutions are discussed.

SOCIAL ECOLOGY

Social ecology is the study of the impact of physical and social environments on human beings (Moos, 1974). Researchers concerned with the relationship between human behavior and the sociopsychological and physical environment have produced a rich body of literature, which confirms the importance of the environment in enabling individuals to live and function optimally (Moos, 1976). The quality of the environment is important to the needs satisfaction of older persons. Successful interaction and adaption to the environment is necessary for optimal growth and development.

Certain needs are continuous and must necessarily be met throughout life. C. Beck, R. Rawlins, and S. Williams (1984) describe these needs as: maintenance of good physical and mental health, self-determination, dignity, freedom of choice, appropriate sensory stimulation, physical activity, social interaction, meaningful activity, and social status. All of these needs must be satisfied for the individual to achieve a sense of control and mastery within the environment. The well-known theory of environmental press developed by M. Lawton and L. Nahemow (1973) suggests that efforts to achieve optimal functional performance require a match between an individual's capabilities or competencies and the demand the environment makes on him or her. The term *capability* can be defined as a measure of high-level functional performance.

Competency refers to the person's state of biological health, sensorimotor functioning, cognitive skill, and ego strength. Persons with a diminished level of competence or ability to cope are dependent on and in need of a more supportive environment than are active, competent individuals. Such an environment includes physical aids and supportive physical design features. The theory implies that too much demand will result in fear, stress, and anxiety, whereas too little demand results in boredom, lethargy, and sensory and cognitive deprivation. Efforts to foster independence and improve affective state should match competencies of the older person with the demands of his or her environment.

A similar environmental theory, the theory of congruence (Kahana, 1982), is based on the concept of person-environment "fit," matching the types of need, in the case of older individuals, to the environment. This theory emphasizes the need to reach a proper fit between level of functioning/ competence of individuals and demands for environmental supports necessary to ensure optimal physical and mental health. When such an optimal person-environment fit occurs, a high level of individual well-being results. Research findings support E. Kahana's model. Studies of institutionalized aged persons have confirmed that a person-environment congruence in an institutional environment fosters autonomy, personalized care, and social integration, which results in higher morale and better adjustment of residents (Bennett, 1980).

Because the environment is crucial to health and well-being at all ages, particularly in aging, J. Kiernat (1983) has termed it the "hidden modality" in rehabilitative programs. Aging research has shown an even greater influence of the social environment on the health behavior of the elderly, who are more dependent for support on their immediate surroundings (Lawton,

1980; Lawton and Nahemow, 1973; Lawton & Simon, 1968; Kahana, 1982; Golant, 1984; Carp, 1976; Moos, 1974). Identity, connectedness, and effectance comprise the sociopsychological needs of older persons as described by Bengtson (1979). V. Bengtson (1979) defines *identity* as a personal sense of place in the world and a unique quality of human beings. *Connectedness* refers to the need to be a part of a social setting and a social group, a feeling of belonging. *Effectance* refers to a sense of control over one's life and one's environment, and the ability to make choices and influence change. The environment in which the older individual lives largely determines to what extent these needs are met.

In the process of aging, alterations occur in varying degrees from one person to another and at one time or another and in one environment or another. The elderly in institutions, who are most dependent on their immediate environments for social interaction, mobility, and personal care assistance, have been found to be the most vulnerable. Vulnerability can be attributed to functional deficits, lack of social supports, and limited control over surroundings and activities (George, 1980). For all of these reasons, environment can and does impact significantly on the personal life space of individuals living in institutions.

An individual's behavior is shaped, facilitated, or constricted by the environment (Lawton, 1980). Institutional environments may be conducive to challenge and stimulation, or they may promote relaxation and a sense of calm. All are necessary for optimal functioning and positive mental health. Individuals living in long-term care facilities can use the environment to engage in meaningful activities, work through the process of loss, or influence other people through their interactions. The next section highlights major environmental factors that affect the older individual's quality of life in institutions.

ENVIRONMENTAL FACTORS AND QUALITY OF CARE

A review of the literature on quality of care reveals some factors that affect quality of life, and patient/resident outcomes (i.e., morbidity, mortality, and happiness) in long-term care institutions. In one early study, B. Mishara and R. Kastenbaum (1973) observed changes in ILTB following the relocation of twenty-five elderly mental patients to a nursing home that offered a greatly improved physical environment. Six persons in the study were found to have extinguished ILTB after the move. The decrease in such destructive behavior was attributed to an improved environment.

Most studies of the impact of the environment on physical and mental health of older adults have been conducted in institutions. Key elements of the environment such as resources, facility ownership, size, cost, staff turnover, and privacy have been identified as exerting a major influence on quality of life and morale of residents in long-term care institutions.

Resources

S. Tobin's (1974) study of environmental factors, which influence quality of care in nursing homes, placed nursing homes on a continuum ranging from resource rich to resource poor based on three factors: organization, social service system, and health service system. Looking at the *organizational* dimension, resource-rich facilities tended to be corporately owned and required extra charges. Within the *social service system* dimension, the resource rich tended to be non-urban, located in affluent areas, with a large number of private paying residents. The *health service system* tended to have more residents referred by a physician, or hospital, and more residents whose care was reimbursable through Medicare. Ninety-five percent of the residents in resource-rich environments felt that their needs were being met, as compared to only 40 percent of the residents in resource-poor facilities who felt their needs were being met.

Facility Ownership

Facility ownership has been found to have an effect on quality of care. F. Elwell's (1984) study of 461 skilled nursing facilities in New York State, in which analysis of covariance was used to isolate the effects of ownership on quality of care, showed significant differences by type of owner. Government and voluntary institutions were superior relative to medical and personal care offered, allocated more money per patient day, and had a higher staff-to-patient ratio than did proprietary institutions. Elwell concluded that ownership is a very real issue in quality of care and deserves further consideration.

Examining data from the 1977 National Nursing Home Survey, S. Ullman (1984) similarly discovered that quality of care (as measured by length of waiting lists, skill level of the charge nurse, and provision of various therapies) appeared to be related to facility ownership. Church-related and non-profit corporate facilities exhibited a higher quality of care than did proprietary facilities. Non-profit facilities were also much more selective in their resident case mix. Interestingly, Tobin's 1974 figures indicated that nearly two-thirds of the 23,000 long-term care facilities were proprietary at that time.

Size

Size is another facility characteristic that has been shown to affect patient outcomes. The early work of S. Greenwald and M. Linn (1971) suggested that, as homes for the aged increased in size, patient satisfaction, activity, and communication declined. In another well-known early study of the effect of size on patient outcomes and quality of care, T. Curry and B. W. Ratliffe (1973), who studied twenty-six licensed proprietary homes in Ohio, found that residents in smaller facilities were less isolated and more sociable than residents in larger facilities. Residents in smaller homes had more friends in the facility, more monthly contacts with friends, and more total monthly contacts with relatives and family.

From their investigation of the literature on quality of care, C. Kart, E. Metress, and S. Metress (1988) determined that the institutions providing, in their terms, "the best" care are non-profit, small in size, wealthy in resources, and sociable, and the staff attitudes toward residents are positive (p. 336).

Privacy

Privacy is an integral part of individuality and the protector of autonomy. Without privacy, there is no individuality (Pastalan & Carson, 1970). Without privacy, autonomy is threatened by those who would intrude or choose to ignore the importance of privacy. "The autonomy that privacy protects is vital to the development and maintenance of individuality and consciousness of individual choice in life" (Pastalon and Carson, 1970, p. 90). Privacy also provides time for self-evaluation and creativity. In settings where people come and go freely, without thought to one's territory, time for reflecting and thinking is at a premium. Many of the elderly are more vulnerable to these types of loss of privacy than are individuals of other age groups.

Privacy has been identified as an important factor influencing patient outcomes. J. Koncelik (1976) reported differences in the behavior of nursing home residents as a function of the amount of privacy available. The researcher found that residents who perceived they had more privacy were better adjusted than were residents who perceived they had less privacy. When Lawton (1977) surveyed elderly residents of long-term care facilities, he found that approximately 50 percent of those residents sharing rooms desired a private room. In a longitudinal study of 193 elderly residents in long-stay institutions (Spasoff, Kraus, Beattie, Holden, Lawson, Rhodenburg, & Woodcock, 1978), only 16 percent of the sample were living in private rooms, and nearly half were in rooms with four or more beds (p. 283). Most researchers agree that the attainment of privacy is essential to maintaining positive self-regard, self-reflection, and autonomy and to providing emotional release in the institutionalized elderly (Windley and Scheidt, 1980; Tate, 1980; Louis, 1983).

Privacy is essential for suicidal patients, who suffer from low self-esteem and feelings of helplessness and hopelessness. Personal space needs are of prime importance in maintaining individual integrity, and while information related to the personal space needs of the elderly is limited, M. Louis (1983) found that intrusion into any patient's personal behavior space may weaken the individual's defenses and result in anger, refusal of procedures, or silence. Such responses can be detrimental to the elderly who have fewer resources to bolster such weakened defenses.

Staff Turnover

A shortage of professional nurses in long-term care facilities is not an uncommon phenomenon. Minimal professional nurse staffing and higher turnover rates are more frequent due to multiple factors: limited recruitment strategies, lack of status and prestige accorded other nursing specialties, inequities in salaries and benefits in comparison to other nursing specialties and professions, few role models in gerontologic nursing, and the perceived non-cost effectiveness (by administrative managers in long-term care institutions) in today's market economy for staffing increased numbers of nursing professionals (Eliopoulos, 1983). One recent study of turnover in long-term care facilities (Halbur, 1986) documented staff turnover rates between 55 and 75 percent in several states. In their analysis of secondary data R. Wallace and T. Brubaker (1984) found turnover rates from 50 to 150 percent.

Several studies have identified negative effects on residents of high staff turnover. Detrimental effects on patient morale, quality of care, and other patient outcomes have been noted (Kohn and Bianche, 1982; Kane & Kane, 1987; Knapp and Harrissis, 1981; Stryker, 1981). A study done by M. Kahne (1968) found that higher employee turnover rate in state mental hospitals negatively affected therapeutic treatment interventions and provoked noticeable stress, resulting in higher incidences of suicide. Another study conducted in long-term care facilities, showed similar trends (Kohn & Bianche, 1982). Personnel in institutions fill the roles of caretaker and often friend of the residents. It becomes difficult to adequately achieve quality of care in a constantly changing environment that requires residents to adjust to new faces in old familiar places. It is equally as difficult for residents to begin to know and trust staff members when they leave so frequently. Negative treatment outcomes resulting from the impact of staff turnover are entirely possible and probable.

Cost

In a labor-intensive industry such as long-term care, employee costs may be 60-70 percent of the operating budget (Halbur, 1986). Rapid staff turnovers, orientation costs in time and money, and reduced resources can directly affect quality of care.

Per diem cost has been shown to influence quality of care. One study revealed that facilities charging higher per diem rates provided better quality care (Ullman, 1984). The more expensive facilities provided better quality staff, quality therapies, and services than did those facilities charging less.

ON BECOMING INSTITUTIONALIZED

Long-term care institutions share common, clearly identifiable features, although the degree to which they may be classified as "total institutions" varies. Nursing homes are one type of total institution defined by Erving Goffman in his classic work on mental institutions. Goffman (1960) describes total institutions as "social hybrids, part residential community, part formal organization. These establishments are the forcing homes for changing persons in our society. Each is a natural experiment, typically harsh, on what can be done to the self" (p. 453). Total institutions as described by Goffman (1960) have the following characteristics in common:

First, all activities are conducted in the same place and under the same authority. Second, each phase of the resident's daily activity is carried on in the immediate company of a large batch of others, all of whom are treated alike, and are required to do the same thing together. Third, all phases of the day's activities are tightly scheduled, with one activity leading a prearranged time into the next, and the whole sequence of activities is imposed from above by a body of officials. Fourth, the various enforced activities are brought together into a single plan, purportedly designed to fulfill the official aims of the institution (p. 11).

Goffman (1960) further suggests that individuals who enter a total institution undergo both a "stripping" process and self-mortification. The person entering an institution, according to Goffman, is stripped of property, personal possessions, pets, and thus personal identity. Life-long habits and styles are abandoned for a scheduled and routinized existence dictated by strangers. The stigma of occupying a devalued state is known as "spoiled identity" (Goffman, 1963). With the loss of individuality, a sense of sameness occurs and individuals are stripped of the uniqueness, personality, and personhood that makes them who they are.

A consequence of institutional totality of the type that Goffman (1963) describes may be the lack of, or a diminished, self-determination in nursing home residents. Reduced self-determination, freedom, functional capacity, and competence often accompany growing old in a nursing home or institutional setting. Feelings of having no choice and feelings of loss of control lead to feelings of helplessness, which are psychologically debilitating. The nursing home resident becomes estranged from family, friends, neighborhood, church, and the outside world itself. Disculturation occurs when persons are stripped of the stable social arrangements of their homes and forced to accept a different set of values and attitudes associated with the institution.

Based on their study of several institutions for the aged, S. Tobin and M. Lieberman (1976) described institutionalization in these words:

The meaning of losses connected with giving up independent living is separation; the experience is that of abandonment, and reaction to it is extreme. Increasingly, the person becomes cognitively constricted, apathetic, unhappy, hopeless, depressed, anxious, and less dominant in relationships with others (p. 213).

Negative effects of institutional care have been classified into four general areas by R. Sommer and H. Osmond (1960): *deindividuation*, or a reduced capacity for thought and action, resulting from dependence learned in the institution; *disculturation*, emotional, social, and physical damage to the individual from loss of status and security and feelings of estrangement; *isolation* through loss of stimulation and contacts with the outside world; and *deprivation* and deadening of the senses.

Institutionalization can represent a loss of freedom and the physical separation from loved ones and home, perhaps forever. In their study of freedom and alienation in homes for the aged, C. Dudley and G. Hillery (1977) found that "conditional freedom," a form of deprivation freedom, was highest in nursing homes and other organizations with a rigorous institutionalized structure, and was closely related to alienation (normlessness, powerlessness, and isolation). Conditional freedom is defined by the authors as the recognition that a person's choices are prescribed by the social milieu in which they are operating, and are not solely a result of aging (p. 144).

Adaptation to institutional living is impeded by the emotional impact of separation and estrangement from family, friends, relatives, and the outside world. The serenity and protection often afforded to members of a family by others in the family no longer exist. Another factor cited by C. Bennett (quoted in Shuttlesworth, Rubin, & Duffy, 1982) is that in the institutional environment, privacy and freedom of movement tend to become lost, and interaction with friends and relatives strained and superficial. In addition, care provided by nursing home staff is all too often distanced and limited to material aspects, leaving humane treatment to chance (p. 200).

Residents of long-term care institutions are subject to suffering physical, social, emotional, and spiritual deprivation (Stotsky & Dominick, 1969). Deprivation is related to a lack of stimulation, social, recreational and occupational opportunities, adequate walking space within and without the facility, and space for social activities. In such situations, the elderly resident can easily become disoriented, disorganized, helpless, out of control, lonely, depressed, rejected, abandoned, unneeded, unwanted, and unloved.

One of the most traumatic losses of power is the loss of one's home (Hirst and Metcalf, 1984). Giving up one's home on entering an institution reinforces the reality that the legitimate power to control one's life is threatened (p. 75) and renders the person vulnerable to such other losses as abandonment, anxiety, loneliness, grief, anger and despair. In A. McCracken Knight's (1984) study of the emotional impact of possession loss, the author captured the response and feeling tone of two women who had given up possessions to move into long-term care residences: "You close your eyes, it's got to go" (p. 18). McCracken Knight (1984) concluded that a decrease in possessions accompanying relocation adds to the difficulty of the move by increasing the loss of continuity with life history and the loss of self-identity (p. 19). Persons who have always maintained control over their lives—who have, as H. Weber (1980, p. 55) terms it, "called their own shots—want control to the end, even to dying on their own terms. Perceived inability to maintain control over one's life, compounded by a diminished self-esteem, a sense of helplessness, and loss of power and decision making about one's life in the present and future, makes the person vulnerable and depressed, at high risk for suicide. Lowered self-esteem and powerlessness can undermine the coping abilities of older adults, and as F. Nietzsche has been quoted (R. Butler and M. Lewis, 1982, p. 80), "the thought of suicide gets one successfully through many a bad night."

Nursing homes, initially intended to enhance socialization and solidarity of residents, may in fact contribute to feelings of personal isolation and alienation. As D. Shomaker (1979) writes:

Nursing home existence was intended to translate collective lives into social solidarity, but fails to achieve such an end because survival and sociability grate against one another creating isolation. Therefore, the positive and identifiable ties that bind these people together are also the shadowy areas that divide them. There are those who argue that a nursing home was never intended to become a place where solidarity exists. If this is so, then the name becomes a paradox. "Home" then takes on the connotation that because one is incapacitated . . . the remainder of one's life . . . must be "lived" at "home" as a nonhuman with few shared values or sociability (p. 46).

Not only in the institutions studied by the authors, but in many more than we may care to admit, old people must live their remaining lives in very public places. Once institutionalized, they must share formerly private places such as bathrooms, bedrooms, and dining rooms, with persons they had never met prior to their move to the institution. Sleeping is often communal with one or more roommates. In the dining room, seats of choice become a rare commodity because residents are usually assigned by the nursing or dietary staff to eat with people they barely know and with whom they have little in common. This point was clearly made by one female resident when, having been told by the nursing staff that the nursing home was her home, she looked at the sea of unknown faces in the cafeteria and stated firmly, "This is not *my* dining room!"

The literature is replete with descriptions of the negative effects of institutional living as experienced by the old. Among those cited are dehumanization; deprivation; depersonalization; disculturation; loss of personal autonomy, control, and individual freedom; and loss of home, property, personal possessions, and money (Glasscote and Biegel, 1976; Gubrium, 1975; Johnson and Grant, 1985; Kastenbaum, 1964; Kayser-Jones, 1981; Landsberger, 1985; Denham, 1983; Davies and Knapp, 1981).

Specific environmental factors, discussed in this chapter, which can elicit or inhibit overt suicide, suicide attempts, or ILTB among residents of nursing homes and related facilities have been examined. Size of facility, facility onwership, staff-to-patient ratio, and other facility characteristics, that influence quality of care and/or patient/resident outcomes are likely to affect suicidal behavior.

The evidence presented indicates that suicide prevention among elderly residents in long-term care institutions can begin through the fulfillment of needs for freedom of choice, autonomy, privacy, and personal space. An enriched supportive environment, well-trained and caring staff, and a variety of recreational, social, and health-related services and resources should serve to extinguish self-destructive behavior in the vulnerable elderly in nursing homes.

Chapter 3 presents results of the first systematic, large-scale national study of patterns of suicidal behavior among residents of long-term care facilities based on the authors' research.

PART II

3

A SCIENTIFIC STUDY OF SUICIDE
IN INSTITUTIONS

The institutionalized elderly, more vulnerable due to functional deficits and lack of social support, are more dependent on their immediate environment (George, 1980) and often less able to exercise control over their environments and activities than community elderly. Frequently staff overindulgence and overprotection and personal loss of control in the immediate environment can evoke feelings of uselessness, personal inadequacy, dependency, helplessness, and depression. Factors such as these can place the older person at risk for overt or intentional life-threatening suicidal behavior. There is currently very limited knowledge of the extent and nature of suicidal behavior among the institutionalized elderly.

The study described in this chapter represents the first systematic, large-scale national study of patterns of suicidal behavior among residents of long-term care facilities. The study had two major aims: (1) to identify the most "at risk" individuals in long-term care institutions and (2) to identify environmental factors related to suicidal behavior. This chapter will describe the design and methodology of the study and present the findings.

STUDY DESIGN AND METHOD

The Sample Survey

For this study, a national computer-generated random sample of 1,080 institutions was derived from the National Master Facility Inventory obtained from the Long-Term Care Statistics Branch of the National Center for Health Statistics. The list is a comprehensive master list of all nursing and related care homes, which includes SNFs, ICFs, and personal care, or residential care, facilities in the United States. Board and care homes that have at least three beds and provide some sort of direct supervision of residents are included on the inventory.

A detailed written questionnaire, Survey of Facility Characteristics, and consent forms were mailed to administrators of each facility. The question- naire included items on the facility (size, location, ownership, cost, etc.); staff and residents (staff-to-patient ratio, staff turnover rate, etc.); and the number of overt suicides, suicide attempts, incidents of ILTB, and deaths from ILTB during 1984 and 1985. Overt suicide was defined as a recog- nizable, intentional act of self-destruction. Examples given included wrist- slashing, hanging, jumping out of windows (and from other high places), shooting, and asphyxiation. ILTB was clearly described in written form on the questionnaire and also in conversations with administrators and nursing personnel. ILTB was defined as repetitive acts by individuals directed toward themselves that result in physical harm or tissue damage and that could bring about a premature end of life. Examples of ILTB given included refusing to eat or drink, refusing to adhere to specified medical regimens, ingesting foreign substances or objects, experiencing serious accidents, and engaging in self-mutilation. Instructions on the questionnaire specified that ILTB must be regular and consistent over a long period of time and with serious consequences. Simply refusing to eat or drink occasionally was not sufficient to be defined as an ILTB. Similarly, such behaviors, when primarily related to a physical or cognitive condition, did not qualify as an ILTB. To be classified as an ILTB, a behavior had to be conscious and willful. Instruc- tions on the questionnaire specified that behaviors classified as ILTB would probably result in death just as surely as shooting or jumping

The questionnaire was pre-tested with a small sample of long-term care administrators in Virginia and adjusted before the initial mailing. A copy of the questionnaire is included in Appendix A. One telephone and two mail follow-ups to each institution resulted in the return of 463 (43%) completed questionnaires from administrators in all types of long-term care facility, from all regions of the country.

Responses were representative of the universe of long-term care facilities in the United States and no systematic bias was evident. Facilities differed in size (from less than ten beds to more than one hundred beds), setting (urban to small town), sponsorship/ownership (public to fraternal), cost (from under $20 a day to more $100), rate of staff turnover (from under 10% a year to more than 50% a year), staff-to-patient ratio (from five patients to more than eleven patients per staff member), and type or level of care (skilled to domiciliary and other care types/levels). Table 1 provides an overview of characteristics of the 463 facilities included in the study.

The total resident population was 30,269. Residents ranged in age from 22 to 91, with a mean age of 68 years. Seventy-eight percent of the residents were over 65 years of age, 16 percent were 40-65 years, and 6 percent were

Table 1
Characteristics of Facilities

CHARACTERISTICS	NUMBER	PERCENT OF TOTAL
Region of the Country		
New England	30	7.00
Mid-Atlantic	44	10.00
South Atlantic	77	18.00
East South Central	20	4.00
East North Central	89	20.00
West South Central	27	6.00
West North Central	60	13.00
Mountain	17	4.00
Pacific	84	19.00
No Response	15	
TOTAL	463	100.00*
Facility Setting		
Urban	136	30.00
Suburban	112	24.00
Rural	193	42.00
Small Town	14	3.00
Other	3	
No Response	5	
TOTAL	463	100.00*

CHARACTERISTICS	NUMBER	PERCENT OF TOTAL
Sponsorship/Ownership		
Public (federal, state, local)	85	19.00
Private	176	39.00
Proprietary	131	29.00
Religious	51	11.00
Fraternal	3	
Other	11	1.00
No Response	6	
TOTAL	463	100.00*
Bed Certification		
Skilled Care	105	24.00
Intermediate Care	169	39.00
Swing	9	2.00
Adult Home**	100	23.00
Domiciliary Care	22	5.00
Other	32	7.00
No Response	26	
TOTAL	463	100.00

Table 1 (Continued)

CHARACTERISTICS	NUMBER	PERCENT OF TOTAL	CHARACTERISTICS	NUMBER	PERCENT OF TOTAL
Facility Size (No. of Residents)			Per Diem Charge		
Under 10	76	16.00	Under $20	62	15.00
10 -- 50	154	33.00	$21 -- 49	183	44.00
51 -- 100	134	29.00	$50 -- 100	116	28.00
100+	99	21.00	Over $100	56	13.00
			No Response	46	
TOTAL	463	100.00*	TOTAL	463	100.00
Turnover by Facilities Per Year			Staff to Patient Ratio (All direct care staff)		
Up to 10%	209	45.00	Less than 1 to 5	286	77.00
11 - 25%	52	11.00	1 to 5 to 1 to 8	43	12.00
25 - 50%	66	14.00	1 to 8 to 1 to 10	13	4.00
Over 50%	136	29.00	1 to 11 or more	28	8.00
			No Response	93	
TOTAL	463	100.00*	TOTAL	463	100.00*

*Rounded.
**Called bed and board homes in some states.

under 40. Individuals under 65 years of age were paraplegics; quadraplegics; victims of multiple sclerosis, muscular dystrophy, or other physically disabling diseases; or mentally retarded. Eighty-nine percent of the residents were white while 7 percent were nonwhite. Twenty-seven percent were males and 73 percent were females (all percentages rounded).

The Case Studies

The qualitative component of the study consisted of four in-depth case studies conducted in facilities that had experienced some instances of suicidal behaviors, according to responses provided on the questionnaire. An attempt was made to choose facilities that differed in size, geographic location, auspices, and resident population. One facility was located in North Dakota and one was in South Dakota. One institution was in New England and another was located near Chicago.

In each facility, researchers observed the behavior of staff and residents; interviewed administrators, staff, and residents; and examined the medical records of residents who were identified by nursing staff as extremely depressed or who had engaged in suicidal behavior during the past five years. The researchers spent approximately three weeks in each facility. Observations and interviews were conducted during each shift. In two facilities staff members of the institution assisted with the gathering of data from medical records. In addition to gathering data in each institution, the physicians, psychiatrists, and mental health consultants who were seeing residents as patients were interviewed.

Staff who signed the university-approved consent form to participate in the study received a copy of the form. Semi-structured interview schedules developed for each of the various groups within the facility (administration, nursing, dietary, housekeeping, consultants, and residents) were used with consistency by all three researchers. The interview schedules elicited general information regarding title or position, credentials, educational level, philosophy of care, length of time in present position, and reason for working in long-term care. Questions were also asked regarding how many residents were considered depressed, suicidal, or had committed a suicidal act within the past five years (July 1, 1982–July 1, 1987); personal characteristics that may have led to depression, suicide, or a suicide attempt; factors or conditions in the particular environment that were considered depressing for people who resided there; mannerisms, patterns, physical condition, mood changes, or clues to suicidal behavior of persons who had completed or attempted suicide in that facility; and date of the event.

Residents who signed the consent form to participate in the study were asked, as they felt sufficiently comfortable, to share information about themselves and their lives and how satisfied they were with their lives at present. The semi-structured interview schedule for residents focused on past family relations, past employment and occupation history, reason for living in a nursing home, satisfaction with caregivers and the facility; and problems and concerns about life in the institution. Other questions were more specific, for example, "In your view, how many persons who live in this place would you say were depressed? had ever indicated they thought about ending their lives? a particular person that comes to mind?" Another focused on the resident's feelings, eliciting such responses as "angry, depressed, lonesome, sad, what's the use, and wish I were dead." A third question asked whether the resident had ever been depressed, when, for how long a period, and some of the things that were happening at the time. The fourth question dealt with a sensitive issue: Have you ever felt like doing something to end your life? while living in this facility? any particular reason? how would this be done? what made you change your mind? have you had these thoughts in the past month?"

The medical record form was used to collect data on those residents who were identified by nursing home staff as engaging in suicidal behavior or as deeply depressed in the past five years. Using a structured medical records form to record data, the following types of information were obtained from each record: demographic data, which included date admitted, payment method, annual income, gender, birth date, religion, number of living children, and other living relatives; frequency of visits from family and friends; interaction within the institution; participation in facility activities and church.

More specific information focused on past hospitalization(s) for psychiatric illness or alcoholism (when, how long, and for what), ILTBs (type and date of each occurrence), past history of suicidal attempt(s) (type and date of each occurrence), consistent notations of depression or pain within two years of suicidal acts, description of overt acts (e.g., wrist-slashing, shooting, jumping, hanging, or asphyxiation), description of ILTBs (e.g., refusing medication, food, and fluids and over what time period), serious accidents; ingesting foreign objects/substances; and self-mutilations (date, time of day, and outcome of the act—lived/died). The third section focused on adjustment to institutional life in the first six months, number of residents in the room, functioning status, clinical diagnosis, and medication regimen.

The researchers developed a form to obtain data about the environment, including questions regarding the metropolitan area; institutional data such as floor plans, mission statement, philosophy, goals, objectives, and history; information on the relationship of the facility to the community, i.e., agency affiliations, volunteer activities, and publicity; and questions about possible future changes, such as expansion, bed availability, programs, and certificate of need.

Observations at each facility were concerned with interactions of people and their environment. Observations were made on all shifts, units, areas of the facility, and other aspects of the physical environment; staff behavior;

resident behavior; and activities. Participation in everyday operations and routines of the nursing home was not the intent of the researchers.

Data Analysis

Suicide rates per 100,000 were calculated for each form of suicidal behavior in 1984: overt completed, overt attempted, ILTB died, ILTB lived, total died, and total suicidal behaviors. Rates were calculated for males and females, whites and nonwhites. Descriptive analyses using frequency distributions were performed to determine the most commonly chosen methods of overt suicide and ILTB and the extent to which each resident engaged in each type of suicidal behavior. Chi-square techniques were used to determine whether or not significant differences existed between observed and expected patterns of suicidal behavior by gender, age, and race. Chi-square techniques were used to test whether or not any facility characteristic, such as size or per diem cost, significantly determined whether suicidal behaviors occurred in the institution and whether deaths from such behavior occurred. Facilities that reported some suicidal behavior were compared to facilities that reported none. Facilities that reported some deaths from suicide were compared with facilities that reported none.

Field data collected in the four institutions were content analyzed for major themes. This information highlighted major factors contributing to suicidal behaviors in elderly residents. Data collected in the field studies also aided in the construction of environmental cases.

Findings from the Quantitative Analysis

A total of 294 residents (1 percent of the total sample of 30,269 residents) engaged in some type of suicidal behavior. Of the 463 facilities in the sample, 84 reported at least one instance of suicidal behavior (overt or ILTB) in the two years of 1984 and 1985. Eleven facilities experienced nine or more instances of suicidal behavior (overt or ILTB) in the same two-year period. During the same period, an additional seven institutions reported five or more incidents; many other facilities experienced one to four incidents of suicidal behavior.

To examine the scope of the problem of suicide in long-term care facilities, rates per 100,000 were calculated for 1984 for each category of behavior: overt completed, overt attempted, ILTB died, ILTB lived, total died, and total suicidal behavior for the total sample, for males and females, and for whites and nonwhites. Rates reported are for individuals who are age 60 and over. These rates were compared to reported rates for community elderly when possible. Rates for community elderly calculated and reported by the National Center for Health Statistics reflect the rate for those who are 65 years of age and over and are available for 1980 and for 1983 by gender and

Table 2
Suicide Rates per 100,000 in 1984

Suicidal Behavior	Rate for Community Elderly, 1983	Rate for Total Institutionalized Sample*
Overt Completed	19.2	15.8 (N = 5)
Overt Attempted	--	63.3
ILTB Died	--	79.1
ILTB Lived	--	227.8
Total Died (ILTB & Overt)	--	94.9
All Suicidal behaviors		386.0

*N = <20
-- = not calculated.

race. Calculated reported rates for community elderly reflect statistics only for those who have died and probably only those who engaged in overt behaviors. The reader must use caution in interpreting these rates because many of the rates are calculated on a sample size (N) of less than twenty. Tables 2, 3, and 4 present the suicide rates for all residents, for males and females, and for whites and nonwhites for each type of suicidal behavior. When appropriate, the rate reported for community elderly 65 years and over is given for purposes of comparison.

The suicide rate per 100,000 for overt completed suicide for the institutionalized elderly in the study is somewhat lower than the suicide rate reported for elderly living in the community in 1983. Several factors could account for the lower rate in the institutions. Accurate reporting and recording are not always the case in such facilities. Suicides may be "covered up" and reported as "death from natural causes" or "accidents" to avoid stigma and scandal for the facility. Presumably, elderly persons living in institutions are more highly supervised than elderly persons living in the community and thus cannot as easily take their own lives. Finally, it is possible that some deaths from ILTBs may be reported for the community dwelling elderly. However, when deaths from ILTBs and overt suicide are considered, the rate for the elderly persons living in instutions is more than four times higher than the reported suicide rate for those elderly persons living in the community.

Rates by gender and race are roughly comparable to rates reported for the community dwelling elderly in 1980. The suicide rate for institutionalized

Table 3
Suicide Rates per 100,000 by Gender in 1984

SUICIDAL BEHAVIOR	ELDERLY MALES IN COMMUNITY, 1980	INSTITUTIONALIZED MALES*	ELDERLY FEMALES IN COMMUNITY, 1980	INSTITUTIONALIZED FEMALES*
Overt Completed	34.8	35.8 (N = 3)	6.0	8.6 (N = 2)
Overt Attempted	--	131.3 (N = 11)	--	38.7 (N = 9)
ILITB Died	--	131.3 (N = 11)	--	60.3 (N = 14)
ILITB Lived	--	274.5	--	210.9
Total Died (ILITB & Overt)	--	167.1 (N = 14)	--	68.9 (N = 16)
All Suicidal behaviors	--	572.8	--	318.6

*N = <20
-- = not calculated.

Table 4
Suicide Rates per 100,000 by Race in 1984

SUICIDAL BEHAVIOR	ELDERLY WHITES IN COMMUNITY, 1980	INSTITUTIONALIZED WHITES*	ELDERLY NON-WHITES IN COMMUNITY, 1980	INSTITUTIONALIZED NON-WHITES*
Overt Completed	28.6	17.8 (N = 5)	6.3	0
Overt Attempted	--	53.4 (N = 15)	--	166.0 (N = 4)
ILITB Died	--	78.3 (N = 11)	--	0
ILITB Lived	--	220.6	--	207.8 (N = 5)
Total Died (ILITB & Overt)	--	96.1	--	0
All Suicidal Behaviors	--	370.1	--	373.8

N = <20
-- = not calculated.

Table 5
Suicidal Behavior and Outcomes

BEHAVIOR	NUMBER	PERCENT
Type		
ILTB	249	84.69
Overt Suicide	45	15.31
Total	294	100.00
Outcome		
Survived	228	77.50
Died	66	22.45
Total	294	100.00*

*Rounded

males is considerably higher than the rate for females for all suicidal behaviors. Males are more likely than females to engage in overt suicidal behavior and to die from their suicidal behavior. Suicide rates for elderly males in the community are also considerably higher than the rates for females. Suicide is more of a white phenomenon both in the community and in institutions. Institutionalized whites are much more likely to engage in overt suicidal behavior than are institutionalized nonwhites. They are also much more likely to die from suicidal behaviors.

Over 80 percent of those residents who engaged in any form of suicidal behavior engaged in ILTB. Less than 20 percent engaged in overt suicidal behavior. More than 75 percent of all those engaging in some type of suicidal behavior (overt or ILTB) lived; 22 percent died. Table 5 presents the results of analysis of types of suicidal behavior and outcome (survived or died) of such behavior. Whether older individuals engaged in some type of ILTB or in overt suicidal acts had virtually no effect on outcome. Eighty percent of those choosing overt methods survived; 77 percent of those engaging in some form of ILTB survived. Table 6 displays the results of analysis of suicidal outcomes by type of behavior.

Wrist-slashing, jumping, hanging, shooting, and asphyxiation were the methods used most often by elderly residents in long-term care facilities to commit a suicidal act. The most commonly chosen method of overt suicide was wrist-slashing (49%), followed by shooting (18%) and asphyxiation (13%). The most widely used form of ILTB was refusal to eat or drink (43%), followed by refusal of medications (40%). Across all age groups, only twenty individuals (8%) chose self-mutilations and serious accidents. Table 7 displays the

Table 6
Suicidal Outcomes by Type of Behavior

BEHAVIOR	NUMBER	PERCENT
ILTB		
Survived	192	77.0
Died	57	23.0
Total	249	100.0
Overt		
Survived	36	80.0
Died	9	20.0
Total	45	100.0

results of analysis of most common method of overt suicide and ILTB among residents.

Using chi-square we were able to analyze differences in type of suicidal method by gender, age, and race. No statistically significant differences were found in the type of method used (overt or ILTB) between whites and non-whites ($\chi^2 = 0.288$, df = 1, $p = 0.5917$). When we compared men and women and individuals of different age groups, however, we did find differences. Men were much more likely to choose overt methods of suicide, whereas, women resorted to ILTBs ($\chi^2 = 3.086$, df = 1, p = 0.079). Sixty-nine percent of women engaged in ILTBs, as compared to 31 percent of the men. Those under 60 years and the young-old were much more likely to use overt methods; the old-old were more likely to engage in ILTBs ($\chi^2 = 21.4$, df = 3, $p = 0.001$). In fact, 61 percent of the ILTBs were committed by those 75 and over. Only 14 percent of the ILTBs were committed by those persons under age 60.

Analyses revealed no statistically significant differences in particular type of overt suicidal behavior by gender, age, or race. No differences in particular type of ILTB were found by gender or race; however, differences by age group did appear. We categorized ILTB into two types: active and passive. Active ILTB included self-mutilations, serious accidents, and ingesting foreign objects or substances. Passive ILTB included refusing to eat or drink and refusing medications. Analyses revealed that the old-old are much more likely to engage in passive forms of ILTB (69%) than are the young-old, and those under age 60 (31%). The young-old and those under 60 are much more likely to engage in active forms of ILTB (73%) than are the old-old ($\chi^2 = 35.1$, df = 3, $p = 0.001$). Only 3 percent of the active (ILTB) behaviors are performed by those in the oldest-old age category.

Table 7
Method of Suicidal Behavior

BEHAVIOR	NUMBER	PERCENT
Overt		
Wrist-Slashing	22	48.89
Shooting	8	17.79
Asphyxiation	6	13.33
Jumping	5	11.11
Hanging	4	8.89
Total	45	100.00*
ILTB		
Refusing to Eat or Drink	106	42.57
Refusing Medications	100	40.16
Ingesting Foreign Objects/Substances	23	9.24
Serious Accidents	12	4.80
Self-Mutilations	8	3.21
Total	249	100.00*

*All figures rounded.

We were then interested in finding out who was more likely to die and who was more likely to survive after engaging in some type of suicidal behavior (overt or ILTB). Chi-square analyses revealed no statistically significant differences in outcome by gender or race; however, we did find differences by age group. Even though the old-old were more likely to engage in ILTBs rather than in overt suicidal behavior, they were much more likely to die (77%) than were the young-old (17%) or those under age 60 (6%). The young-old were more likely to die from their suicidal actions than were those under 60 (χ^2 = 21.16, df = 3, p = 0.001).

Finally, we were interested in finding out what particular facility characteristics or staff/patient characteristics were related to suicide in the institution. Chi-square analyses revealed two environmental characteristics

Table 8
Annual Staff Turnover and Total Suicidal Behaviors*

Annual Staff	Suicides			
Turnover	None		Some	
	No.**	%***	No.**	%***
Up to 10%	189	50	20	24
11 -- 25%	35	9	17	20
25 -- 50%	54	14	12	14
Over 50%	101	27	35	42
Total	379	82	84	18
No Responses (0)				

$*\chi^2 = 23.04$, df = 3; p= <.001
**Total N = 463.
***Rounded.

related to suicide. Each made a significant difference in whether or not any incidents of suicidal behavior were experienced. Staff turnover and size of facility (number of residents) were important predictors of suicidal behavior. Those facilities experiencing a high turnover in staff were statistically significantly more likely to experience some form of suicidal behavior (overt or ILTB) than were those facilities with low staff turnover ($\chi^2 = 23.04$, df = 3; $P < 0.001$).

Ninety percent of those facilities that had a staff turnover rate of less than 10 percent a year experienced no suicidal behavior and 10 percent experienced some instances of such behavior. By contrast, in facilities experiencing staff turnover of 50 percent or greater, only 75 percent reported no suicidal behaviors and 26 percent reported some behaviors. Results of the analyses are displayed in Table 8.

Size of resident population was the other facility characteristic associated with suicidal behaviors in the institution. Largely populated facilities were significantly more likely to have some incidence of suicidal behavior (overt or ILTB) than were small facilities ($\chi^2 = 8.62$, df = 3, $p < 0.05$). Of those facilities with under 10 residents, only 7 percent experienced any suicidal behavior, compared to facilities with over 100 residents, of which 22 percent experienced some suicidal behaviors. Results of the analyses are displayed in Table 9.

Two other facility characteristics were significantly related to whether or not residents died from suicidal acts. Per diem cost and auspices (public,

Table 9
Size of Resident Population and Total Suicidal Behaviors*

Size (number of) residents)	Suicidal Behaviors			
	None		Some	
	No.**	%***	No.**	%***
Under 10	70	19	5	6
11 — 49	121	32	33	39
50 — 100	109	29	25	30
Over 100	78	20	21	25
Total	378	82	84	18

No Responses (0)

$*X^2 = 8.615$; df = 3; p= <.05
**Total N = 463.
***Rounded.

private, religious, and other) were both significant. Death from suicide (overt or ILTB) was much less frequent in high cost facilities than in those that charged less for their services ($\chi^2 = 8.02$, df = 3, $p < 0.05$). Facilities that charged over $100 per day, the most expensive institutions, reported no deaths from suicide. By comparison, of those facilities charging less than $20 per day, only 4 percent experienced some deaths from suicide. Of those facilities charging $20–49 per day, 9 percent experienced some suicidal behaviors. Results of the analyses are displayed in Table 10.

The type of facility, or auspice under which the institution is managed, was also a factor in whether or not deaths occurred from suicide. Public and private facilities experienced significantly fewer deaths than did religious or other facilities ($\chi^2 = 7.14$, df = 3, $p < 0.10$). Results of the analyses are displayed in Table 11.

Findings from Qualitative Analysis

Data collected in the four institutions highlighted several factors related to suicide in this population. Many who lost the will to live and took active steps to end their lives or quietly gave up and refused to eat or drink or take their medications had experienced one or more major losses shortly before engaging in a suicidal act. Loss of a spouse or child were important factors, as was loss of a pet. Loss of physical function—particularly loss of hearing or eyesight, loss of speech, or loss of ability to walk—was devastating to many. Often, these types of loss were the result of a stroke. As one man,

Table 10
Per Diem Cost and Total Number of Deaths by Suicide*

Cost Per Day	Deaths by Suicide			
	None		Some	
	No.**	%***	No.**	%***
Under $20	60	16	2	7
$20 - 49	168	43	15	52
$50 - 100	104	27	12	41
Over $100	56	14	0	0
Total	388	93	29	7
No Responses (46)				

*X^2 = 8.015, df = 3; p <.05.
**Total N = 463.
***Rounded.

Table 11
Type of Auspice and Total Deaths by Suicide (overt and ILTB died)*

Auspice	Deaths by Suicide			
	None		Some	
	No.**	%***	No.**	%***
Public	79	19	6	20
Private	171	40	5	17
Religious	46	11	5	17
Other	131	31	14	47
Total	427	93	30	7
No Responses (6)				

*X^2 = 7.143; df = 3; p= <.10
**Total N = 463.
***Rounded.

who had earlier attempted suicide, put it, "I'm no good to anybody. I can't drive. They took all of my money for this place. I can't even go fishing with my boy, and fishing was the only thing I really loved after Martha died. I wish I could just sneak out of this place one time and get my pole and tackle and get in the boat and fish all day long. But, I can't even drive and they sold my boat, too. I took the operation on my legs a few years ago 'cause they gave me a ninety-percent chance of dying. Well, that's why I took the blame thing. And wouldn't you know it's my luck. I didn't die and here I am. I'm no use to anybody. I can't do nothing now but just sit and stare out the window. I'd be a whole lot better if I was to die."

When individuals are no longer able to dress, bathe, and engage in toileting behaviors without assistance, it is particularly humiliating and dehumanizing. The loss of personal dignity and self-esteem was a major loss related to suicide. Many suicides occurred relatively soon after a hospitalization for a serious disease.

Loss of cognitive function was also a factor. When it is impossible to remember people, places, and dates, and when misplacing glasses, teeth, purse, and other items become regular events, the impact on the formerly competent, independent adult is difficult to bear. One older woman, who was extremely depressed and was a possible candidate for a future suicide, reported painfully, "I'm no longer in control. My daughter has taken over everything now. I can't even remember my brother and my sister's birth dates. What good is someone like me to anybody?"

Loss of money, home, car, land, farm, and personal possessions results in feelings of powerlessness and dependence. Such losses strip one of his or her pride, status, and dignity. These losses were particularly devastating for males. Researchers discovered that suicide in males was more likely to occur after the auction of the family farm or some other major financial loss.

Depression was a major factor in suicide. Frequent notations of crying, listlessness, fatigue, loss of appetite, and somatic complaints appeared in the medical records of suicides. Staff and other residents also frequently identified those who had taken their lives as "sad," "down," "withdrawn," and "depressed."

Feelings of rejection, abandonment, and loss of love were common among residents identified by staff as "very depressed" and possibly suicidal. Many noted loss of family members or no visits from family as a major factor producing feelings of rejection and abandonment. As one young aide put it, "This is a terrible place to spend the holidays. Many here have no family or family don't come to visit. The staff are talking about spending time with their families when they get off work. It must make them feel so bad."

In one institution, moving residents was problematic, and several residents who committed suicide had experienced one or more physical moves in the year preceding their death. As staff at the facility recognized, moves are very disruptive and disorienting for older adults. With each move there are changes in staff, bathing and eating routines, and roommates. Many older individuals have a very hard time adjusting to such changes.

These and other factors that increase the risk of suicide among residents of long-term care facilities are discussed in greater detail in Chapter 4.

APPENDIX A: SURVEY OF FACILITY CHARACTERISTICS

INSTRUCTIONS:

Responses to the following questions in this survey should pertain to "CURRENT STATUS" in regard to your facility. By current status we mean that the information you provide is based on the date upon which the questionnaire is completed.

Please complete all questions in the survey as fully and accurately as possible. Complete confidentiality is assured. Your institution's identity will be removed from the form before any analysis is begun, so it will not be possible to identify your answers.

1. In what year did the facility open?   19___

2. What is the total square footage of the facility? _____ sq. ft.

3. How many miles from your facility is the nearest big city or Standard Metropolitan Statistical Area (SMSA), which is a city of 100,000+. (If your facility is located in a large city or SMSA please use the symbol 0) _____.

4. How would you describe your setting?

   [ ] URBAN
   [ ] SUBURBAN
   [ ] RURAL
   [ ] OTHER(PLEASE SPECIFY)

5. Would your facility be categorized as

   [ ] non-profit   [ ] for profit

6. Would your facility be categorized as (Please check all that apply):

   [ ] PUBLIC
           State [ ]   Local [ ]   Federal [ ]   County [ ]
   [ ] PRIVATE
   [ ] PROPRIETARY
   [ ] RELIGIOUS
   [ ] FRATERNAL
   [ ] OTHER (PLEASE SPECIFY)

7. Is your facility medically affiliated with a hospital?

   [ ] YES   [ ]   NO

8. Is your facility certified for:

   [ ] MEDICARE
   [ ] MEDICAID
   [ ] BOTH MEDICARE AND MEDICAID
   [ ] OTHER (PLEASE SPECIFY)

SURVEY OF FACILITY CHARACTERISTICS

9. How many residents are currently residing in your facility? _____

10. How many residents resided in your facility in the calendar year 1985? _____

11. How many residents resided in your facility in the calendar year 1984? _____

12. How many of the facility residents are currently included in each of the following payment categories?

    PRIVATE PAY
    MEDICAID
    MEDICARE
    PRIVATE INSURANCE
    OTHER (PLEASE SPECIFY)

13. What is the bed capacity of your facility at this time? _____

14. How many beds in your facility are currently licensed as:
    (Please include each category in your response if appropriate)

    SKILLED
    INTERMEDIATE
    "SWING"
    ADULT HOME
    DOMICILLARY
    OTHER (PLEASE SPECIFY)

15. What is your present average per diem charge for each resident?
    _____

16. At the current time what is the average resident length of stay in your facility? _____

17. How many deaths occurred in your facility in the calendar years:
    (Please include all patients who were transferred to a hospital and diagnosed as dead on arrival)
                                  1984 _____ (total)
                                  1985 _____ (total)

18. Currently how many of the residents in your facility are placed in each of the following units?

    PRIVATE ROOMS
    TWO BED ROOMS
    THREE BED ROOMS
    FOUR BED ROOMS
    OTHER (PLEASE SPECIFY)

SURVEY OF FACILITY CHARACTERISTICS

19. As of today how many residents in your facility are: (Fill in the number)

    MALE _____(total)   FEMALE _____ (total)

    Caucasian _____   Caucasian _____

    Non-Caucasian _____   Non-Caucasian _____

20. At the present time what is the average age of all residents residing in your facility? _____

21. How many residents are currently diagnosed as having each of the following conditions? (If an individual has more than one diagnosis, indicate this under each category that applies)

    ALCOHOLISM   _____
    BUERGER'S DISEASE
    (Thromboangiitis Obliterans)   _____
    CANCER   _____
    COGNITIVE IMPAIRMENT/SENILITY   _____
    DIABETES MELLITUS   _____
    DRUG ADDICTION   _____
    HEART DISEASE   _____
    LUNG DISEASE   _____
    MENTAL ILLNESS OR EMOTIONAL
       DISTURBANCES
    PARKINSONISM   _____
    OTHER NEUROLOGICAL DISEASES,
    i.e., MULTIPLE SCLEROSIS   _____
    DEMENTIA   _____

22. At the present time how many residents are:

    INDEPENDENTLY AMBULATORY
    (no human or mechanical
    assistance required)   _____

    AMBULATORY WITH ASSISTANCE
    (wheelchair or other
    adaptive device, and/or
    human assistance)   _____

    NON-AMBULATORY   _____

23. Of your current resident population, how many are able to complete their normal activities of daily living? (for example: feeding/eating, bathing, toileting, grooming):

    INDEPENDENT OF ANY HELP   _____

    NEEDS SOME HELP WITH
    SOME ACTIVITIES   _____

    NEEDS FULL HELP WITH
    ALL ACTIVITIES   _____

SURVEY OF FACILITY CHARACTERISTICS

24. How many of the following positions are currently occupied full-time (40 hours per week) at your facility.

   REGISTERED PROFESSIONAL NURSES   _____
   LICENSED PRACTICAL/VOCATIONAL NURSES   _____
   NURSING ASSISTANTS/TECHNICIANS/AIDES/ORDERLIES   _____
   PHYSICIAN/MEDICAL DIRECTOR   _____
   OCCUPATIONAL THERAPISTS   _____
   PHYSICAL THERAPISTS   _____
   RECREATIONAL THERAPISTS   _____
   SOCIAL WORKER/SOCIAL SERVICE   _____
   NUTRITIONIST   _____
   ACTIVITIES DIRECTOR   _____
   OTHER (PLEASE SPECIFY)   _____

25. Is the Medical Director/Principal Physician employed:

   [ ] FULL-TIME   [ ] PART-TIME

26. What is your current nursing staff to patient ratio, excluding students, volunteers, and other part-time caregivers from your calculations: Number of nursing staff   _____
                      Number of patients

27. How many of your staff in each of the following categories terminated their employment during the last 12 months?

   REGISTERED PROFESSIONAL NURSE   _____
   LICENSED PRACTICAL NURSE   _____
   NURSING ASSISTANTS/TECHNICIANS/AIDES/ORDERLIES   _____

28. At the present time are there volunteers who help out in the facility?

   [ ] YES   [ ] NO

29. Is there a current and ongoing activities program in your facility? (For example: exercise, music, pet therapy, etc.)

   [ ] YES   [ ] NO

30. Do residents currently participate in organized facility activities?

   [ ] YES   [ ] NO

31. Do residents currently participate in activities outside the facility? (For example: trips, cultural activities, clubs, church, etc.)

   [ ] YES   [ ] NO

32. At this present time how many residents in your facility participate regularly, at least once a week, in these organized facility activities? _____

SURVEY OF FACILITY CHARACTERISTICS

INSTRUCTIONS:

The responses to the following questions in this survey pertain to
"CURRENT STATUS" in regard to your facility. By current status we mean
that the information you provide is based on the date upon which the
questionnaire is completed.

Please complete all questions in the survey as fully and accurately as
possible. Complete confidentiality is assured. Your institution's
identity will be removed from the form before any analysis is begun, so
it will be impossible to identify your answers.

OVERT SUICIDE is defined as a recognizable, intentional act of
self-destruction. Examples of overt suicide include: slashing the
wrist, hanging, jumping out of windows and from other high places,
shooting, and asphyxiation.

We are interested in information regarding residents who have attempted
and successfully committed each of these forms of overt suicide in your
institution during the last two calendar years (1984-1985).
Specifically, we want to know the number of residents in each of the
following categories who have either attempted or completed each form of
overt suicide: men (caucasian, non-caucasian) and women (caucasian,
non-caucasian) and exact ages of all who attempted or successfully
completed each form of overt suicide.

The format on the reverse side of this page is designed to facilitate
easy transfer of information from your medical records to categories of
information just described. The following example, given for one form
of overt suicidal behavior, illustrates the manner in which your
information should be recorded on the form.

E X A M P L E
1985
OVERT SUICIDAL BEHAVIOR

SHOOTING

	Attempt	Complete
MEN (TOTAL)	0	3
Caucasian	0	3
Non-Caucasian	0	0
Ages	70	79
		75
		84
WOMEN (TOTAL)	2	1
Caucasian	1	1
Non-Caucasian	1	0
Ages	84	88
	83	

1984

OVERT SUICIDAL BEHAVIOR

	WRIST SLASHING		JUMPING		HANGING		SHOOTING		ASPHYXIATION	
	Attempt	Complete	Attempt	Complete	Attempt	Complete	Attempt	Complete	Attempt	Complete
MEN (TOTAL)										
Cauc.										
Non-Cauc.										
Ages										
WOMEN (TOTAL)										
Cauc.										
Non-Cauc.										
Ages										

1985

OVERT SUICIDAL BEHAVIOR

	WRIST SLASHING		JUMPING		HANGING		SHOOTING		ASPHYXIATION	
	Attempt	Complete	Attempt	Complete	Attempt	Complete	Attempt	Complete	Attempt	Complete
MEN (TOTAL)										
Cauc.										
Non-Cauc.										
Ages										
WOMEN (TOTAL)										
Cauc.										
Non-Cauc.										
Ages										

For this study, <u>INTENTIONAL LIFE-THREATENING BEHAVIOR</u> (ILTB) is defined as repeated self-destructive behavior(s) by individuals, which result in physical harm, tissue damage, or could bring about a premature end to life. Examples of ILTB(s) include: non-adherence to important medical regimens; refusal to eat and/or drink; ingestion of foreign objects/substances; refusal of medication; self-mutilation; and regularly having serious "accidents". These less overt means of self-destruction could, eventually, have as lethal a result as the more overt forms of suicidal behavior.

We are interested in information regarding residents in your facility who have engaged in each of these types of indirect life-threatening behaviors and either survived or died as a result of such behavior during the last two calendar years (1984-1985). Specifically, we want to know the number of residents in each of the following categories who have either survived or died from engaging in each type of indirect life-threatening behavior: men (caucasian, non-caucasian) and women (caucasian, non-caucasian) and exact ages of <u>all</u> who engaged in each form of such behavior.

Intentional Life-Threatening Behavior(s) of this type must be regular, consistent, and with serious consequence(s) over a specific length of time. Simply refusing to eat or drink once or twice a week, month or year, may not constitute or qualify as Intentional Life-Threatening Behavior (ILTB). However, the individuals repeated non-acceptance of food or drink for two or more weeks at a time, <u>does qualify</u> as (ILTB). Repeated behavior of this type would probably result in death. We realize that providing this information does require a subjective amount of judgement on the part of the person completing this form.

Since specific types of ILTB would be documented in some manner in the resident's medical record, we have designed the format on the reverse side of this page to facilitate easy transfer of information from these medical records to categories pertaining to this study. The following example, given for one form of indirect life-threatening behavior, illustrates the manner in which your information should be recorded on the form provided.

E X A M P L E

1984

<u>INTENTIONAL LIFE THREATENING BEHAVIOR</u>

SERIOUS "ACCIDENTS"

	Survived	Died
MEN (TOTAL)	2	1
Caucasian	2	1
Non-Caucasian	0	0
Ages	80	78
	74	
WOMEN (TOTAL)	0	1
Caucasian	0	1
Non-Caucasian	0	0
Ages		84

1984
INTENTIONAL LIFE THREATENING BEHAVIOR (ILTB)

	REFUSAL OF MEDICA-TION/MEDICAL REGIME		INGESTING FOREIGN OBJECTS/SUBSTANCES		REFUSAL TO EAT/DRINK		SERIOUS "ACCIDENTS"		SELF-MUTILATIONS	
	Survived	Died	Survived	Died	Survived	Died	Survived	Died	Survived	Died
MEN (TOTAL)										
Cauc.										
Non-Cauc.										
Ages										
WOMEN (TOTAL)										
Cauc.										
Non-Cauc.										
Ages										

1985
INTENTIONAL LIFE THREATENING BEHAVIOR (ILTB)

	REFUSAL OF MEDICA-TION/MEDICAL REGIME		INGESTING FOREIGN OBJECTS/SUBSTANCES		REFUSAL TO EAT/DRINK		SERIOUS "ACCIDENTS"		SELF-MUTILATIONS	
	Survived	Died	Survived	Died	Survived	Died	Survived	Died	Survived	Died
MEN (TOTAL)										
Cauc.										
Non-Cauc.										
Ages										
WOMEN (TOTAL)										
Cauc.										
Non-Cauc.										
Ages										

SURVEY OF FACILITY CHARACTERISTICS

Your contribution to increasing knowledge about the nature and extent of suicide in long-term care facilities is valued. A benefit of contributing is in the potential for developing interventions which could reduce the incidence of this mental health problem.

In the space provided below, please add any additional information, not requested in the questionnaire which you consider of further importance to the study.

Your participation is very much appreciated. Thank you.

4

ENVIRONMENTAL PROFILES

Along with the qualitative component of the research project, the researchers conducted medical record analyses, observation, and in-depth interviews over a period of three weeks with staff and residents in each nursing home. Four case studies are reported in this chapter. Each case presents a brief historical overview, physical description of the facility and area, statement of philosophy of care, and profile of residents and staff.

THE FOUR INSTITUTIONS

New England Health Care Center

Located in the heart of Connecticut, New England Health Care Center is in a town of approximately 52,000. The area was originally settled in 1639 but later became a bedroom community to the capital, Hartford. The fertile land along the Connecticut River was the site of the first westward migration of English settlers from Massachusetts Bay Colony.

In the 1870s, Italians, Germans, French, English, Canadians, Poles, Lithuanians and Czechoslovakians arrived to work in booming textile and manufacturing industries. By 1910, three out of every ten people were born outside of the United States. The population growth rate continued to be high during the 1950s and 1960s, and is now twice that of New England as a whole. Most of the recent immigrants are of Hispanic background from Puerto Rico and Jamaica. Today, Connecticut is the most densely populated state with the second highest per capita income of over $16,000. The Hartford area is home to more than fifty insurance companies and continues to mass produce military equipment including aircraft engines and propellers, guns, and other products such as optical instruments, ball and roller bearings, machining tools, and silver, copper, and brass products.

Churches, schools, parking lots, shopping centers, and open areas of greenery reduce the feeling of crowding often experienced in an area of such high population density. There are children in apartments near the Health Care Facility, and their voices can be heard from any of the outside areas of the home as they play in the nearby pool. The community does not appear wealthy; instead it reflects the efforts of solid middle-class workers, the backbone of the American economy.

The concept and philosophy under which New England Health Care Center operates is holistic. It is owned by a non-profit religious group and is one of several facilities being developed in the Northeast and Florida. The ministry is the result of a vision by an Irish Catholic priest who felt a divine command to care for the elderly and sick and approached his order for their permission to carry out his work. The Missionaries of the Holy Apostles granted special approval for the development of a choice of health care services in the community.

A network of health care professionals and pastoral counselors provide personalized programs of care for the patients. Much emphasis is placed on individualization. Five levels of care—home health, supervised apartments, skilled nursing care, intermediate nursing care, and hospice—are provided within the organization, but not all levels are currently available in each location. The goal of management is to provide comprehensive care in a manner that ensures dignity and respect for the person. Residents may move within levels of care according to their need. The center's philosophy, found in official statements in brochures, reflects its founder's belief that "caring is more than a personal choice . . . it is a divine command from the Lord."

New England Health Care Center is licensed by the State Department of Health as a skilled and intermediate care facility, consisting of eight fully equipped private rooms, and eighty-six semi-private rooms with adjoining baths. Potential residents may wait two or more months to enter the nursing home. Sixty-five percent of the residents are covered by the Department of Income Maintenance, which sets rates for long-term care on an annual basis, prospective reimbursement. Daily charges for care in the facility ranged from $78 to $83. The Medicaid reimbursement rate for 1986 and 1987 was approximately $69 per diem.

Located in a high-density residential area one block from a major east-west local artery, New England Health Center is shaped like two *H*'s placed side by side, but with a short center leg. It sits on a carefully manicured lawn facing a thirty-year-old shopping center and parking lot. Trees separate the rear of the facility from an adjacent apartment complex. Flowers, appropriate for the season, and shrubs line walks and frame the entrance with brilliant colors during the summer. All rooms have an outside exposure window. At the end of the *H* crossbar on each east-west plane is a large solarium, which is completely glass enclosed. Here the residents gather for unit group activities.

The entry doors of New England Health Care Center open into a large waiting room covered by an impressive cathedral ceiling. Offices flank both sides of the room; among them, the shared offices of the chaplin, recreation coordinator, placement coordinator, and social worker. Partitions between offices only partially extend to the ceiling thereby reducing the degree of privacy in each area. The reception area is covered by dark carpet and furnished with large colonial furniture in earth-tone plaids. Current magazines and newspapers cover the tables. Several shelves of books—current titles, paperbacks, and *Reader's Digest Condensations*—line one wall. A variety of ceramic pieces, displayed in glass-covered cabinets on an adjoining wall, are available for purchase.

Behind the reception area is a small chapel where prayer services are conducted. Across the hall is the business office where the financial activity of the nursing home takes place. Residents can withdraw money from their accounts as needed for independent purchases. Nearby, an in-house store, operated by the residents and designated as the "local gathering spot," is open daily to encourage socialization among residents, staff, and visitors, who can purchase soft drinks, coffee, pastries, and candy there.

Halls are bright, with well-polished light tile. Dark handrails, thought to be depressing, have been replaced with a lighter wood. Wallpaper with large, colored flowers has been replaced with a smaller floral design that is pale pink, blue, and yellow on a green background. A slight odor of disinfectants can be detected in the wing where residents are bedbound, but no urine odor can be identified.

The main or center corridor of the building leading to the dining room is lined on either side with a dental office, the business office, therapy rooms, a beauty shop, the kitchen, laundry, employee lounge, and areas for turbines and electrical equipment. The dining room, the hub of activities, is the least-attractive area in the facility. Its furnishings, including a few broken wheelchairs, appear old and worn looking. The room displays a collection of "left overs" in the area. Because many functions take place in the dining room, it can easily be transformed into a theater-style open area and decorated for whatever occasion.

Two of the three nurses' stations are located just outside the solarium. Between the solarium and nurses' station are storage areas for the medication room and nourishments, a bathroom for staff, and an isolation area for soiled linens. Caged parakeets chirp near the nurses' stations. Their songs and noise provide a homelike atmosphere. This area is large enough that residents often crowd the intersecting hallways in wheelchairs, geri-chairs (rarely used), and special adaptive wheelchairs. All residents are up, dressed, and encouraged to ambulate with the assistance of walkers, canes, wheelchairs, and each other. No one stays in bed unless prescribed by a physician or a nurse. Because it is an area of activity, many of the residents have special times and places when they meet, chat, observe, and comment on the comings and goings. The watchers and gossipers of the center could always be found in this area.

Resident rooms line both sides of the halls in a north-south direction from the third nurses' station located in the center of the cross-hall. Nurses' stations are placed midway between sixteen patient rooms in either direction. State law stipulates that there be no more than twenty-five patients per unit, so the nurses' stations divide the six units. Semi-private rooms are furnished with a bed, chair, dresser and closet for each resident. If possible, a chair is brought from home. Other possessions include pictures, clothing, pillows, and wall hangings such as crucifixes. Wherever possible, residents can choose their roommates.

Activities are provided in the mornings and afternoons. Current plans call for more activities after dinner and on weekends. The resident council helps plan some activities. Activities include music appreciation groups, sensory stimulation, exercises, reminiscing, sports such as soft racquetball and bowling, a rhythm band, word and trivia games with prizes for the correct answer, sing-alongs, ceramics, a newsletter written by and for the residents, current events discussion, poetry, pet therapy, tea or coffee groups, new food and recipe-tasting groups, and men's groups, mass and rosary weekly as well as Protestant services, fashion shows, and other special events. Activities away from the facility include picnics, outings to local parks, and just driving around the area where many of the residents spent their lives.

An analysis of residents shows an average age of 80.2. Thirty-six of the residents ranged in age from 91 to 100; two residents were over 100 years of age. Seventy percent of the population were women. All were white and ethnically diverse. Many spoke English as a second language. In addition, 16 percent were married, 63 percent widowed, 7 percent divorced, and 14 percent single. Many residents had multiple diagnoses; however, the diagnoses most frequently identified included cerebrovascular disease (30%), organic brain disease (13%), fractures (11%), Alzheimer's disease (4%), cancer (6%), gastrointestinal (GI) bleeding (7%), chronic lung disease (6%), and diabetes(4%). Approximately 30 percent of the residents required total care including feeding.

From a religious prospective, 80 percent of the residents were Catholic and 20 percent were Protestant, the majority of whom were Episcopalians. There were no Jewish residents.

The administrator for New England Health Care Center was appointed in March of 1983. A director and assistant director of nursing; a social worker; a medical director; an admissions/discharge planning nurse; an activities director; a chaplin; a business office administrator; and dietary, maintenance, and housekeeping directors make up the health care management team. In addition, consultants provide services on contract to the facility and to residents as requested by the physician, the staff, and the family. These include dentist, physical therapist, registered dietician, registered medical records librarian, optometrist, podiatrist, pharmacist, clinical social worker, psychiatrist, speech pathologist, and respiratory therapist. Each consultant conducts one inservice per year for the facility and reviews, evaluates, and establishes policies in conjunction with the health care management team and administration, in accordace with state requirements.

The Connecticut regulatory code requires that there be at least one registered professional nurse (RN) on each of three eight-hour shifts. New England Health Care Center staffs the day and evening shifts with six RNs, and three RNs on the night tour. Additional RNs include one infection control nurse and a staff development coordinator. Twelve nursing aides are required from 7 A.M. to 9 P.M., and six from 9 P.M. to 7 A.M. daily. Staffing for the facility includes twenty-one aides on the day tour, eighteen for the evening tour, and ten for the night tour. Each aide provides care for ten to fourteen residents. Staff turnover has been minimal in all areas but nursing where turnover has averaged 60 percent for the past three years. A seventy-two-hour nursing aide training program is provided by the facility as an incentive to retain staff and to ensure high-quality resident care; however, high-quality care requires, at the least, minimal numbers who are well versed in care of aging persons. The increasing turnover rate of nursing staff is most problematic for the nursing home.

Aliwippa Nursing and Convalescent Center

Aliwippa Nursing and Convalescent Center (ANCC) is located in a small rural community in Illinois, one of many small cluster communities that border each other in the Prairie State. The community of Aliwippa, incorporated in 1859, boasts a population of nearly 5,800. The citizenry are second-, third-, and fourth-generation farming families who express pride in their community and its historical roots. It was in the "good old days" that cattle, raised by local farmers, were railroaded to the Chicago stockyards. Many of the residents of ANCC fondly recall the excitement of the cattle roundups and the trips to the "big city," but the roundups and stockyards belong to a bygone era. Corn, wheat, and soybean crops—the major industries in this rural area—now cover the countryside, and small industries provide additional employment for many of the farming members of the community. In contrast to an earlier time in Aliwippa's history when railroads transported people and products to their destinations, private vehicles and commercial trucking are the main modes of transportation today.

A firehouse, police station, library, post office, city hall, hospital, and newly renovated grand opera house occupy the central city of Aliwippa. Scattered throughout the city are at least ten houses of worship of various religious faiths; three elementary schools; a junior and senior high school; a vocational school; two nursing homes, including ANCC; and numerous gas stations, family businesses, small industries, restaurants, bars, and stores. Three community colleges are located within a twenty- to forty-mile radius in the surrounding towns or within commuting distance from Chicago.

Historically, ANCC is situated on the site of the old residential home and hospital in the city's older residential area. Initially, the mansion and the land were donated to the town by a wealthy family for use as a home for the aged. Later, a prominent physician purchased the mansion for the community's first hospital, a thirty-three-bed facility, which continued its operation until the late 1960s. It was then used as a skilled care facility for community elderly until its closure in 1971. The present two-story, L-shaped brick structure was erected on this site and admitted its first resident in 1975.

ANCC is the only brick building on a tree-lined street; it is three blocks from the heart of the city amid large two-story frame residences, built in the early 1920s. Original owners, or descendants of original owners, currently occupy these dwellings. A spacious lawn, numerous shade trees, shrubbery, and small vegetable and flower gardens surround ANCC. A few tables, chairs, and benches are strategically scattered across the lawn. Propped on the main bench is the center's welcoming sign. The patio is colorfully decorated with hanging plants, a swing, and a few rocking chairs. There are no fences.

The facility, one of sixteen owned by a private, proprietary chain, is licensed for 120 intermediate care beds. ANCC currently operates on an 80/20 reimbursement rate under public aid (Medicaid). Eighty percent of resident care is Medicaid funded, while the remaining 20 percent is derived from private payments. The average per diem rate per capita is $48 or $1,448 per thirty-day month. Medicaid reimbursement for resident care averages $36 per day. The average length of stay (LOS) in this facility is twelve months.

The building, deceiving from the outside, has been altered by an additional extension, juxtaposed between the two wings of the L-shaped structure, to provide offices for the administrative personnel, the beauty parlor, and a large lounge used for church services and staff meetings. Two more thirty-bed units on the second floor accommodate residents who require "heavy care" (Arling, Nordquist, Brant, & Capitman, 1987). Not uncommonly, most residents share rooms. Two three-bed rooms and three private rooms surround the nurses' station on each floor. Bedrooms are furnished with personal hygiene equipment, a bed, nightstand, and lounge chairs for each resident. A dresser, clothes closet, bathroom, and window air-conditioning unit are shared. Nursing stations and day areas, where many residents spend their time, are small, congested, poorly lighted, and heavy with traffic. A large dining room, kitchen, laundry, and maintenance room are located in the basement. An elevator transports residents to and from the dining area, which also serves as the activity center. A small space beyond the dining room is often used for rehabilitative/restorative care. Tile floors throughout the building are clean and waxed to a low luster.

Nurses can be identified by their white attire, while non-professional staff wear various colored shirts, depending on department. Nurses pass medication and perform most of the personal care. Many of the residents dress, or are dressed, in street clothes, while others remain in hospital gowns.

Activities are attended primarily by those residents who can interact reasonably well with their environments and who are mobile. Highlights of the program include bus excursions through the countryside, trips to town for a meal, or to Chicago to watch the Bears play football. The dining room serves as the activity room for bingo, exercises, games, and Friday afternoon "happy hour," a favorite with residents and staff. Hymn sings and Sunday services, depending on pastor availability, are usually held in the lounge. Children and adults from the community entertain during the holidays. Few on-the-unit activities are provided for the many who remain there. A cat lives on the first level of the building and is cared for by three of the residents.

The average age of all residents in the center is 78 years, although many of the oldest-old are visible throughout the facility. Thirty-two of the 110 residents in the facility at the time of the study were men. One was nonwhite. Not surprisingly, the majority (seventy-eight) of the residents were women. Two of these women were nonwhite. The oldest resident celebrated her 104th birthday during the time of the study.

Heart condition is the primary medical diagnosis (60 percent) among residents, followed by dementia and other cognitive impairments (30 percent). The remaining 10 percent include lung disease, cancer, alcoholism, and emotional disturbances. More than 50 percent of the residents ambulate with the assistance of others or adaptive equipment, 38 percent are independent in ambulation, and the remaining 12 percent are unable to ambulate. All ADL are accomplished independently by 20 percent of the residents, while 40 percent require assistance with some ADL. The remaining 40 percent require full assistance with all ADL.

ANCC employs at minimum five registered and five licensed practical nurses and forty aides, orderlies, and technicians for all shifts. The social service worker, dietary manager, and maintenance manager are employed full-time. Other personnel include the administrator, director of nursing, assistant director of nursing/rehabilitation nurse, part-time activity director, part-time psychosocial coordinator, full-time business manager, and medical records clerk. Hourly rates for nursing aides-in-training are less than the national minimum wage. Their wage scale increases to minimum wage and slightly above after completion of the nursing assistant course. For LPNs, earnings begin at $6.50 per hour, while RNs earnings begin at $7.50 per hour. A benefits package covers only those fully employed. Understandably, staffing and retention are major concerns, since a "300 percent" staff turnover occurred during 1985-1986. Staff turnover is readily apparent in the nursing assistant classification. In 1986, twenty nursing aides/orderlies, three RNs, two LPNs terminated employment with ANCC. Five additional nursing personnel left one week prior to the study. By the summer of 1987, more than seventeen nursing staff terminated their employment. Given this deficit, even the basic activities of daily living are minimally managed by an already over-burdened staff. Because the major part of direct patient care in the nursing home is performed by nursing assistants, the turnover rate has serious implications for patient care delivery in this facility.

To ensure minimal licensed staffing levels, agency personnel are used to fill slots throughout the nursing home. The drawbacks to employing agency nurses in long-term care facilities are lack of continuity in care, lack of attachment prevalent among residents and agency staff, and increased budgetary constraints. Establishing relationships with residents is often hurried and is not always a priority activity. The attitude of new orientees hired to fill nursing assistant jobs is revealed in the following statement: "We wash 'em, get 'em up, feed 'em, put 'em on the toilet, diaper 'em, and put 'em back to bed. That's all we get paid for." While these attitudes are not generally pervasive throughout the center, they present further concern for the quality of care provided the person in residences.

The Highlands

The Highlands is located in a small city in the North Dakota, equidistant from the two largest cities in the state and nestled in a valley where two major rivers meet. Referred to as the "Pride of the Prairie," the city, now populated by 31,000 inhabitants, was initially inhabited by native Americans. Immigrants from Germany, Norway, Sweden, and Denmark later flooded the city when the railroad opened the Dakotas and the Homestead Act made available free, rich, and harvestable land. Many of the older local residents, some of whom now live at The Highlands, are of immigrant stock, having come to the area as farmers or railroad personnel. These are a strong and fiercely independent people, who survived the Great Depression and endured the difficulties of prairie life, including its harsh winters and severe draughts. Miles and miles of open space and wheat fields have formed the backdrop against which these residents have lived their lives.

Today the city in which The Highlands is located is both a major trade center and an agricultural center for the Midwest. It is also the home of the largest state college, as well as a Catholic university, a state mental institution, two hospitals, four nursing homes, thirty-eight churches, eleven elementary and secondary schools, radio and television stations, modern shopping centers, and convention facilities.

The Highlands, a 64-bed nursing home, originally owned and operated by a Protestant denomination, opened in 1962, with a minister as its administrator. In 1967, additional construction expanded the facility to 104 beds. The facility was sold by the church in 1976 to a for-profit corporation organized by the son and grandson of the minister/administrator of the original nursing home. In 1980, the organization's new construction increased the bed capacity to 140. A 2,000-square-foot chapel was added in 1982. The current administrator of The Highlands is the grandson of the original minister/administrator. His father is the assistant administrator.

The facility is licensed to provide skilled and intermediate nursing care to its residents. One hundred sixteen beds are allocated for skilled nursing care, while twenty-six are designated as intermediate care. Approximately 80 percent of the 140 residents in the facility are receiving Medicaid benefits. Almost all share a room with at least one other resident. Many residents share a room with two or three others. The per diem cost at The Highlands is $60 or $1,800 per month. Two physicians visit residents monthly. The facility has no affiliation with a hospital.

Located in an older residential area of the city, The Highlands is a large one-story brick building surrounded by a beautifully manicured lawn and many colorful flower beds. The tall, white steeple and cross adorning the top of the new chapel are prominent features towering above the facility. Adjoining the original structure are several brick apartment buildings, also owned and managed by The Highlands, where older individuals who are able to live independently reside. Many occupants who become too sick or frail to care for themselves independently move into the nursing facility.

The nursing home has five wings of rooms. One wing is reserved for residents covered by Medicare. Two of the older wings contain smaller rooms, fewer bathrooms, and older equipment than do the newer wings. Two nurses' stations, a central dining room, an activity room, and a day lounge are situated in each wing. The institution resembles a hospital in many respects. Nurses wear white uniforms and shoes. The long hallways are covered with linoleum. Resident units in all wings are equipped with a metal bedside table, with urinal, bedpan, basin and water pitcher. There is a pungent odor of urine and antiseptics, particularly in the wings where residents are more ill. Many residents are clothed in hospital gowns throughout the day. Routines are well established.

Most resident activity occurs in and around the dining room or day lounge. The day area is sparsely furnished with a vinyl couch and two or three vinyl chairs, a small card table and four chairs, and a television set, which plays continuously throughout the day and evening. The day lounge, located directly across from a nurses' station, permits easy view and access to residents. Outside the day lounge, along the wall next to the nurses' station is a popular area for many residents who spend their day sitting on chairs and benches watching activities in the hall and around the nurses' station. Another major gathering place is the centrally located dining room. Residents begin to line up for their meals an hour or more before mealtime, and often remain long after the meal has ended, sitting, watching, talking, and waiting.

Recreational and social activities are group oriented, and part of daily life for approximately 15 percent of the residents who participate regularly in scheduled activities. Church services and Mass are held weekly. Approximately 10 residents participate in a bell choir and practice weekly in the chapel. A favorite among the residents is the monthly birthday party honoring those whose birthdays fall during the month. Singers and other musicians periodically come to entertain the residents. During the Christmas season, a children's group comes to sing carols and distribute gifts. Exercise classes and Bingo are among the other favorite activities in the facility. Shopping outings, fishing trips, and picnics away from the facility are offered less frequently, but some residents can and do participate in these activities. There is no pet therapy program included in the monthly activities.

The residents of The Highlands are primarily female (70 percent) and white (99 percent). The average age is 82 and many are 90 years and older. The oldest resident is 101 years of age.

Over 40 percent of the residents are diagnosed as having a major cognitive impairment, mental illness, or emotional disturbance. Only 15 percent of the residents are able to ambulate independently and perform normal tasks of daily living without assistance. Most need some assistance with these activities. Approximately one-third of the residents need full assistance with all daily living activities.

In addition to the administrator, assistant administrator, and director of nursing, The Highlands employs sixty-three full-time staff members including four RNs, nine LPNs, a social worker, an activity director, and forty-eight aides/orderlies/technicians. The institution does not employ a medical director or principal physician. Most of the day-to-day care of residents is provided by aides or technicians, many of whom have high-school educations or less. Staff members participate in a brief orientation period before beginning work on the resident care units. Full-time aides and orderlies are paid the minimum wage; others, employed on a part-time basis, receive no overtime pay for extra hours worked. Each aide or orderly is responsible for approximately ten residents per shift. The staff turnover rate in 1984 was 75 percent.

The majority of the aide's work is "bed-and-body work." Aides and orderlies awaken residents, clean, groom, bathe, feed, turn, and assist with their toileting needs. For the most part, RNs and LPNs pass medications, chart, do paperwork, and, at times, assist with unit activities. Although the mission statement in the official staff handbook gives priority to the emotional and spiritual needs, as well as physical needs, the bulk of staff time is spent on meeting residents' physical needs—keeping residents clean, dry, well fed, and well groomed. There is little time in the busy schedule to meet the socioemotional needs so necessary to maintain some degree of normalcy in daily living—just to chat, play a game of checkers, or help with dressing.

Lutheran Home

Lutheran Home, is located in South Dakota in a city of approximately 26,000 inhabitants, which is referred to as "The Pheasant Capital of the World." The city was first inhabited by native Americans and later populated by farmers and railroad workers coming from Scandinavia, Germany, Russia, and the British Isles in search of fortunes in the new frontier. Nestled in a fertile river valley and surrounded by glacial lakes, this prairie village has grown in the last 100 years into a bustling railroad hub, which serves a major Midwestern trade and service center. A regional agricultural center, the city has grain terminals, livestock sale barns, and several well-known farm implement dealerships. Today the city, located at the intersection of two major interstate highways, is a busy convention and cultural center. Within the educational system of this particular state, the city is endowed with the largest public university, as well as a noted Catholic college, fourteen elementary and secondary schools, two hospitals, four nursing homes, one mental health center, thirty-eight churches, and seventeen parks.

Opened in 1969, Lutheran Home is owned and operated by the American Lutheran Church. This home is the third of its kind built and operated in South Dakota under the auspices of that denomination. The first of the three institutions owned and operated by the Norwegian Lutheran Church opened in a nearby city in the early 1900s, supported by contributions from local congregations. In the 1950s, a corporation consisting of twenty-three local congregations as its members was established, and the second Lutheran Home was built in an adjacent city. In 1982, eleven congregations formerly with the original corporation, pulled away from the parent corporation to form one independent organization. Lutheran Home is now owned and operated by this new independent corporation under the auspices of the American Lutheran Church.

The Christian heritage and religious influences are apparent in the Lutheran Home. The administrator, a former parish minister, operates the nursing home based on his strong economic and accounting background. He views the purpose of the church's involvement in long-term care as "the mission of the church, following the command of Christ, to care for the needy, the old, the widowed, the sick . . . and to give the very best care we can give with compassion and love." The director of nursing, the wife of a minister, describes the mission of Lutheran Home similarly, "We are here to provide care and to meet the physical and socioemotional needs of residents in a Christian manner." Part of her work as nursing director is to ensure that staff members treat residents with kindness and compassion, and to refrain from being verbally, physically, or emotionally abusive to residents of the home.

The institution employs a chaplain who serves Lutheran Home for mass and recitation of the rosary regularly in the chapel on the premises. Much of his time is spent meeting the spiritual needs of residents. Prayers are offered before meals and religious music is played over loudspeakers in the facility at different times during the week. Memorial services paying tribute to deceased residents are attended by residents, staff, and family members.

The nursing home, an eighty-six-bed facility, is licensed as a skilled nursing facility. Supervision of care management is provided by registered professional nurses twenty-four hours a day. The facility is not supported by or affiliated with a hospital or medical center. The average cost per day is $50, or $1,500 per month.

Lutheran Home, a 28,000-square-foot, one-story red-and-yellow brick structure, is located in a residential area off a major artery and across the street from a low-income housing project. Many of the aides and orderlies who work at Lutheran Manor live in these apartments. The facility is surrounded by a well-maintained lawn and many large shade trees. Connected to the building and accessible from within the facility are newly constructed sheltered care apartments. These one-, two-, and three-bedroom units, built in 1986, were designed to preserve the independent functioning of older adults for as long as possible, and to offer low-cost housing for older adults who are maintaining their independence. Some apartment dwellers have spouses in Lutheran Home; some may themselves eventually become residents of the nursing home.

Located within the facility are seventy private or semi-private rooms; two nurses' stations, one at each end of the facility; a pharmacy; a therapy room; an activity/crafts room; a beauty shop; a chapel; resident and visitor's lounges; a library; and a large, central dining room for residents who are able to eat independently. Apartment dwellers wishing to take their meals in the central dining room are provided transportation. A small dining area is provided for "feeders," residents who need the assistance of staff to eat. In addition, there is a day care center for children, many of whom are children of staff members of the facility. Staff and residents can be seen eating on the large outdoor patio in the center of the home, watching children at play near the area.

Social and recreational activities are at the core of life at Lutheran Home. A coffee hour, provided each afternoon, is attended by most of the residents. Every month residents' birthdays are celebrated with a dinner in their honor. Daily devotions are conducted each morning; Bible study is held weekly.

Other activities at Lutheran Home include piano music, singing, German songfests, rhythm band, Bingo, bowling, movies, arts and crafts, picnics, shopping trips, and other outings away from the facility, which are attended frequently. Residents spend most of their time in various activities or in the dining area.

Most of the residents of Lutheran Home are female (80%), and all are white. The majority (70%) are Protestant and many are Lutheran. Parallel to the population of the community, many are of Scandanavian, German, or Russian descent. The average age of residents is 86 with many over 90 years of age. Approximately one-third of the residents have been diagnosed with a cognitive impairment/senility or a mental or emotional illness. Approximately 10 percent can accomplish the normal tasks of daily living without assistance. Move than half of the residents need full assistance with eating, bathing, grooming, and toileting. Residents admitted within the last five years are older, sicker, and more frail than were the residents admitted in earlier years.

Lutheran Home employs two full-time and three part-time RNs, three full-time and seven part-time LPNs, and fourteen full-time and thirty part-time aides/orderlies/technicians. The home fills staff vacancies with summer employees, some of whom are nursing students from the local college. Students leave the nursing home after graduation and prior to the beginning of school semesters, which creates a serious staffing shortage. During 1984, the staff turnover rate reached nearly 50 percent, which is lower than the national average (75%) for long-term care facilities. Each aide or orderly is assigned the direct care for approximately eight to ten residents, depending on the shift assigned. Frequently, staff may be assigned to give care to more than eight to ten residents per shift.

INSTITUTIONAL PROBLEMS

Although the four facilities differed in several ways, they shared some environmental problems in common. Among these were high staff turnover rates; problems related to food and problems characteristic of institutions such as regimentation, rules and regulations, communal living, and other environmental factors discussed in this section. The first of these is staff turnover.

Staff Turnover

Each facility experienced extremely high turnover in staff, especially among aides and orderlies. Several factors account for increased turnover rates among nursing staff. It is not uncommon for aides and orderlies in nursing homes to have less than an eighth-grade education. They lead fairly transient lives, moving from place to place and from job to job. The work can be demeaning and demanding, often requiring heavy lifting and bathing incontinent residents. The pay is low and the benefits are poor. A heavy resident care load places increased responsibility on non-professional staff, often not sufficiently trained for this type of employment. High staff turnover creates severe shortages in staff. Those who remain are frequently overworked and overtired from the demands of working double shifts and long hours, filling vacant positions on all shifts. Often there are no accommodations for staff during their break times or during shift change while they are waiting to begin a second shift. In one facility, staff voiced strong complaints about the inadequate break area, which was small, with no air-conditioning and inadequate lighting; it was located across from the laundry area.

Staff turnover presents special problems for administrative staff and residents alike. Persons in administrative positions are constantly faced with a shortage of workers that, in turn, creates training problems for new staff. Regulatory issues surrounding staff-to-patient ratios are a constant source of concern for administration. The high turnover rates pose serious difficulties for residents who must adjust to new faces and personalities, new work styles, disruptive routines, and the loss of former confidantes and friends. Staff shortages result in unattended needs of residents. Call lights go unanswered, residents are inappropriately attended, and very little time, if any, remains for nurses, aides, and orderlies to meet the socioemotional needs of residents. Activities such as chatting or engaging in a game of checkers is viewed as "goofing off" or "wasting time" by top-level managers. When a staffing shortage occurs among registered or licensed practical nurses, the charting and paperwork demands fall on those who temporarily fill in, agency nurses unfamiliar with the facility or nurses on swing shifts who are already overburdened. Little time is available for priorities other than passing medications or handling crises when they occur.

One of the more difficult aspects of administration within one particular facility was the newness of many of the key players in management positions. In one institution, the administrator, a former social service worker with the facility, assumed the pivotal position within months of completing administrator training. The director of nursing, in the position for two months, rose up through the ranks over many years and, by virtue of default, became the head of the largest department with major responsibility for care delivery. A new activities director, hired on a part-time basis, came up with many creative ideas, but found implementation cumbersome because of time constraints, the overwhelming needs of the residents, and the marginal staffing of the facility. A maintenance manager, who was recently added to the staff, had limited experience in a nursing home environment and little familiarity with mechanical equipment necessary to operate the department smoothly. Because cost is a prime factor in determining what "frills" can remain in the budget, the physical therapist position, recently vacated, remained unfilled.

Staff at all levels expressed frustration between what they wished to do for and with the residents and what they could do in the limited time available. Many took jobs in long-term care because they genuinely loved older people and wanted to spend quality time with them. High turnover rates and constant shortages of staff resulted in minimally meeting the physical needs of residents, the "bed-and-body work," with little or no time left for human contact and affection.

Food

Food is a major source of concern among residents of institutions, and the situation was no different in the four facilities studied. "Monotonous and boring," "bland and tasteless," were terms used to describe the food. Others more dramatically referred to it as "slop"! Many residents were on special diets and could have no salt, sugar, or seasoning on their food. Institutional cooking seldom allows for meeting the special likes of each individual. Cost constraints did not allow for certain more expensive foods such as steak or shrimp. Ethnic foods, such as strudels or other German, Polish, Swedish, or Norwegian foods, were not included on the menus. Residents had limited choice in what they wished to eat, and many received items they simply did not like. While some fresh, in-season foods were prepared, few salads were planned, and food was not always attractively served. In the words of one resident, formerly a professional cook in a well-known Chicago restaurant, "If I see one more green bean on my plate, I'll toss the tray!"

Many residents in the institutions viewed mealtime as the major highlight of their day. Eating meals was the one activity that most residents participated in outside their rooms. As a result, issues and concerns related to food remain tremendously important in the lives of the residents.

Institutional Living

Many of the environmental problems described here are related to institutional living. Institutions by their very nature have rules and regulations, regimens and routines. Life is fairly structured and regimented, with little room for expressions of individuality. Residents are forced to live together, eat together, and in most cases, share sleeping space together. There is limited freedom and choice in matters pertaining to eating, bathing, and sleeping arrangements. Residents are afforded little privacy, and most life is lived in public among strangers. As residents have attested, institutional living is much different from life in one's own home and family setting; it is not really "home," and to some it will never be "home."

Lack of privacy was a major problem for residents. Many shared bathrooms with at least one other person, and sometimes two or three others. Staff and other residents entered rooms, often without first knocking. This generation of elder residents, who are not accustomed to displaying their bodies, were frequently bathed or assisted in toileting in the presence of roommates or other residents using public facilities. Few places were available or accessible to residents to be alone and to enjoy complete privacy. Many of these residents had lived on large farms surrounded by many acres of land and few visitors. In the institutional setting, they are devoid of personal possessions and furniture, have limited lifespace, and are expected to interact with total strangers.

Another problem faced by residents of these facilities was loss—loss of freedom, independence, personal autonomy, control, and identity. As one resident expressed it, "I get so tired of being told what to do. They even tell me when to go to bed, or to the bathroom." Or as another described it, "At home I was my own boss. I got up when I wanted, and I did what I wanted when I wanted. Here, somebody else calls the shots." Another resident, irate at the staff's approach with him, commented that "the least they could do for a blind man is to introduce themselves and tell me what they are going to do to me." He would strike out when he heard voices of particular staff coming close to him. Rather than accommodating his sensory loss, the resident had been prescribed antipsychotic medication, in the event that he became "belligerent" and difficult to manage.

In these facilities, staff often serve as surrogate families because the family support system had diminished significantly. They are trusted to shop, handle resident finances, partake of the resident's food gifts, and become an essential part of the resident's life. A resident, who had placed her trust in a staff member "like my own daughter," was upset for many days because the staff person had taken money from her purse, then lied about it. Conversely, other staff members have taken residents to their homes for holiday festivities, or for a trip around the countryside, or to a favorite restaurant to provide the support needed.

For many living in these institutions time passes slowly. Residents no longer work, vote, drive, or get out. Some referred to their new "home" as a prison. Others referred to it as a cage. Many saw the institution as a place to die, the "last roundup," as one resident described it. Others passively adapted to the structured environment.

Residential Moves

Moves within the institution were problematic for residents in three facilities. In one facility, residents were moved with repeated frequency from room to room and from floor to floor. Movement within the facility was generally promoted by ineligibility for Medicare benefits, when the resident was re-evaluated and transferred from ICF to SNF or SNF to ICF status, or when roommates were incompatible. Incompatibility, however, was not always the impetus for change in all facilities. Often moves were impromptu and involuntary, with no pre-planning involved or resident input sought. Fear of reprisal, the stress of another loss, the adjustment to new surroundings that must occur in order to adapt, had an impact on the coping abilities of these individuals. Three of the residents had moved into one of the facilities less than three weeks before. Moves such as these can prompt changes in behavior as manifested in anger and resentment, docility, withdrawal, increased dependency, and depression. Because staff communication does not always follow translocation moves within the institution, residents are at risk for alterations in care management, changes in treatment regimens, and potential safety hazards.

Several residents who committed suicide had experienced one or more physical moves within the year preceding their death. As staff at one facility recognized, moves are very disruptive and disorienting to older adults. With each move, residents must contend with changes in faces and places, bathing and eating routines, new roommates, and physical location. Friends and acquaintances are left behind and new relationships are expected to develop. Older persons frequently find adjustment to these changes difficult, and may just "give up." Some degree of functional loss, either physical or sociopsychological can occur with unexpected changes in the environments of the vulnerable elderly. In some cases, death may even result from the move.

5

PROFILES OF "AT RISK" INDIVIDUALS

INTRODUCTION

Based on data reported during the course of the initial study, research efforts were expanded in 1987 to complete three-week community studies in each of four consenting nursing homes in which suicide had been reported in the original research. Nursing homes participating in the community study were located in New England and the Midwest. Data for this study were collected through observation, interviews with staff and residents, and families, when available. Retrospective analyses of the medical records of all suicides for the years 1981-1985 were completed.

This chapter reports eight case studies chosen to invite the reader to understand the psychosocial elements of aging that contribute to self-destructive behaviors in older residents in long-term care facilities. These cases illustrate the complexity of the problems experienced by the aged and the multiple pathways to self-destruction. Case illustrations have been re-constructed from interviews, participant observations, and medical record data collected in the nursing homes involved in the study. The cases typify suicidal behaviors found among residents who died from engaging in overt suicide or intentional life-threatening behavior in long-term care institutions. Names, places, and dates, have been changed to protect the anonymity and privacy of persons and research sites.

Various types of suicidal behavior and outcome are found among the cases. The first two illustrations are examples of suicide attempters. The last of the profiles illustrates overt suicidal behavior. The intervening cases present individuals who engaged in some form of ILTB and died as a result of those acts.

"AT RISK" INDIVIDUALS

Rocky

Rocky, a 66-year-old divorced, white male veteran, was admitted in 1984 to a large skilled care facility in the Midwest. Prior to this admission, he had been treated in the nearby Veteran's Administration Medical Center for a pulmonary condition, multiple injuries resulting from a series of falls, and a fractured hip. Assessment of his health status revealed limited mobility, unsteady gait and balance, and a visual deficit resulting from cataracts. Due to his acute condition, no corrective surgery for cataracts had been performed. Shortness of breath on limited exertion was compounded by a lengthy history of smoking, a habit that he was unwilling to relinquish entirely. He alternated between oxygen therapy and medication to relieve the shortness of breath, but continued cigarette smoking to satisfy his habit, and to "alleviate my anxiousness about life. If I quit smoking, I might as well die." Rocky, a thirty-year veteran of World War II and the Korean conflict, spent most of his nursing home life in a wheelchair.

As the fourth eldest of eight siblings, Rocky was withdrawn from school in the seventh grade to help meet the demands of farm life and a growing family after his older brothers left to join the army. In his growing years, he was particularly close to his mother, a very religious follower of the Baptist faith. He described his father as a stern man, and a man who saw the farm as his whole life. Rocky said, "This was his life but not mine." He left home at seventeen to join the service, "just like my brothers did. I figured the other kids coming up were old enough to take over."

During his army career, Rocky married and divorced three times. He had four children, but had no contact with two of his children since they were infants. The development of the parent/child relationship between Rocky and his remaining children was not particularly strengthened over the years. One of the children visited occasionally, the other, seldom if at all. "If my children don't have time for me when I am well, they sure as hell don't have time for me when I am sick!"

Rocky described his retirement from the service, and his third divorce as traumatic events in his life, which he tried to solve with booze. Although he drank while he was in the service, Rocky referred to his last twenty years of retirement as his alcoholic years. "I became an alcoholic, and drank all my money away. There wasn't a whole lot for me to live for, really. I surprised myself and did [live]." The injuries Rocky sustained prior to his admission to the nursing home were the result of a drinking episode. "I don't know which is worse to go through, then or now," referring to the physical and psychological pain and discomfort of past experiences and his adjustment to the "rules and regulations" of the nursing home environment. "God, I don't want to be here, but it's not fair to the family to expect them to take me."

Rocky's first year in the nursing home was a difficult one for him and for the staff. He would have frequent episodes of epigastric distress with nausea and vomiting, or would refuse food for three or four days at a time, claiming swallowing difficulties. He remained in bed for prolonged periods, complaining of severe muscle, joint, and low back pain for which a narcotic/analgesic was prescribed three to four times daily over an extended period of time. "It just made me feel—better." He was angered and disappointed because of his placement in a facility so far away from both home and his mother, who was old and ill and in a nursing home in his home town. Depression was, as Rocky described it, "frequent and strong" to the point that, on numerous occasions, Rocky openly discussed committing suicide and described how he would accomplish the act of hanging, using a belt or bed sheet.

After a long adjustment period, Rocky made small strides toward some resolution of feelings of anger, frustration, and loss of control. He tolerated open relationships with certain of the nursing home staff and a few select residents. He adopted the role of spokesman for the "corridor residents" who sat near his room. Rocky described his new role: "I try to make everybody happy, and now I can say what I think. Some folks don't like that. They say I shoot my mouth off, but it doesn't matter anymore. There are those [residents and staff] whom I have helped who see me in a different way, and that feels good. Helping other people helps me take my mind off my troubles, and to keep myself in control. That doesn't mean I don't get depressed; I do, but I have learned to handle my feelings a little better through helping and believing."

Rocky's spirituality was manifest in his "finally finding some religion." He kept his Bible within reach at his bedside at all times, "and I pray when I get in trouble like that [thoughts of suicide]. Other folks here [in the nursing home] have these same thoughts too, but I tell them—and myself— to hang on and pray hard. Still, it's real difficult because you get so depressed, there just doesn't seem to be any other way to handle the tremendous loneliness you feel."

Janice

Janice, an 84-year-old white, widowed female, had recently been transferred from the hospital, where she was treated for an acute arthritic flare-up and a cardiac condition, to a 140-bed facility in a medium-size city in South Dakota. Her past history revealed that, on the strong urging of her sister, Janice left her home of forty years in California to be near her. She spoke longingly of San Francisco, the place she called home, where long-term relationships with friends and relatives had been established, and where memories of her life with her husband, now deceased, began.

Prior to her retirement, Janice had been active in nursing for more than four decades and had made many friends during her professional life. She and her husband chose to have no children; they were a close and loving couple and engaged in most activities together.

Physically, she suffered shortness of breath and chest pain associated with recent cardiac involvement, severe joint pain resulting from arthritis, and seriously limited vision related to glaucoma and cataracts. The arthritis had been under control in California, where it was warm and dry, but living in the cold Midwestern climate had activated the condition. Her social life was limited because there were neither the cultural events she had been accustomed to nor the companionship of former friends to attend such functions. She was extremely lonely and unhappy in her new environment, vehement about her dislike of the Dakotas, and bitterly resentful of the move.

Janice blamed her nephew, her sister's son, for admitting her to the nursing home "just to get rid of me." She expressed strong feelings of anger and resentment toward both of them. She painfully related the story of how they convinced her to sell the home she loved so dearly and move east where she lived in her own apartment for a short time. Then her relatives "dumped" her in the nursing home, sold her furniture and possessions, and rented her apartment without telling her. The stress and losses she experienced were devastating. The loss of her apartment and furniture represented a loss of cherished possessions, independence, and personal control. As Janice put it, "I thought my heart would break. I knew I would never go home again."

When she first arrived in the new city, she managed well through community services. She received Meals-on-Wheels and had a personal care attendant who cleaned and ran small errands five days a week. She ate well and maintained an average weight of 180 pounds for her large frame. After moving to the nursing home, she lost more than 50 pounds, physically resisted being taken to eat meals served in the dining room, and adamantly refused them in her room. She informed the staff she was uncomfortable eating in a large dining room with strangers, many of whom "dribble, drool, scream, holler, and soil. Who could eat with people like that around them? In my opinion the food is just like hog slop."

Janice experienced two apparent heart attacks, one during her hospital stay and one while in the facility, which left her with shortness of breath and frequent chest discomfort. Walking was difficult for her because of her breathing difficulties and joint pain. The staff's plan for Janice was to increase her walking distance for short periods each day. Each time the staff appeared to walk her, a major battle ensued. She cried, screamed out in pain, and finally resorted to striking out and kicking. Her behavior was not understood by the staff who "avoided this nasty, spoiled old woman like the plague." Janice described her new home as a prison and likened it to an institutional life sentence. As she perceived it: "They torture and torment me here until I am out of my mind. How can you live in a place like this? I have never gone through such misery and pain in my life, nor have I subjected others to such treatment in all my days of nursing. All of them are just cruel and uncaring here."

Weight loss became more apparent and Janice grew physically weaker. She related that she was so tired and weak, she could barely get up in the morning. She slept poorly at night, and attributed her lack of sleep to a lumpy mattress and gnawing pains in her legs. The staff pointed to depression as the culprit.

After just a few months, the feelings of loneliness, helplessness, social isolation, depression, and loss of functional ability became emotionally burdensome. She cried frequently, stayed in her room days at a time, and refused to interact with staff or other residents. She had not attended any of the activities in the facility because "they were for children"; she had neither listened to her radio nor watched the television. Because her vision was so limited, she was unable to read, her favorite pastime.

Openly communicating her thoughts, Janice at one point stated, "If they [the staff] insist on walking me to dinner or to the shower room, I'm going to drop dead. I just pray for God to take me away. I'm so tired I just want to die. The girls here don't care about me. I don't want to live anymore. I wish every day that I could die." Some of the staff members were afraid that Janice would take her own life, but no preventive intervention was initiated to circumvent this. She sat alone in her room, extremely limited in auditory and visual stimulation, away from others, in a dark and lonely world of silence. The sense is that it will only be a matter of time until Janice takes active measures to end her own life or quietly resigns herself to a slow and painful death from starvation and dehydration.

Dan

Dan was an 85-year-old college graduate who had lived a fulfilling and active life in the Midwest. As a former Federal Housing Administration (FHA) district supervisor and a prominent civic leader in his community, he was respected and well liked. He was actively interested in the local college, traveled extensively throughout the country and the world with his wife, Lillian, and could always be counted on to speak on a wide variety of topics.

An unfortunate incident that became "the beginning of the end" for Dan occurred at a community picnic. Engrossed in conversation with a friend as they were walking along a knoll, he tripped and fell over a log, incurring severe damage to the spinal cord. After a lengthy hospitalization, he was transferred to a 120-bed nursing home in the community. At first, Dan adjusted well to the facility and was actually looking forward to being there. Determined to rehabilitate himself to walk again, he dutifully attended physical therapy and exercised to the extent possible, given his condition. His wife and children were devoted to him, visiting often and providing support and encouragement. He remained actively involved in achieving his goal, and periodically accompanied his family to their weekend cabin.

However, instead of regaining mobility, Dan became progressively weaker, and less able to move about. Therapy was simply not enough to overcome the spinal damage he had sustained. Compounding this were the other medical problems that resulted. Orthostatic hypotension, muscle cramping, chronic urinary tract infections, and painful bladder spasms only added to the chronic pain from the fall itself. Still, he never missed a therapy appointment, in the hope that he would walk again one day.

Dan's spirit and hopes were broken in a dramatic fashion during one of his physician's visits. Responding to his complaints about the lack of progress and apparent physical decline, the physician looked at Dan squarely and said a bit impatiently, "Mr. W———, I'm afraid that you will never walk again on your own. I thought you already understood that." Despite his awareness of the physical decline, Dan was completely unprepared for what he heard. He had viewed his problem as temporary in nature, one that would be eventually resolved with continued therapy. The physician left the room abruptly, leaving Dan alone to deal with the shock and disappointment of the news.

The thought that he, a man of pride and independence, would have to depend on others for the rest of his life was just too much for Dan to bear. From that point on, he deteriorated rapidly, withdrawing from physical therapy because he felt that it was pointless if he wasn't going to get better anyway. He became severely depressed, expressing feelings of worthlessness and uselessness. He commented to a staff member "You could kill me. You could help this process along."

He rarely left his room, and when asked to join an activity, he often responded, "Why are you bothering with someone like me? Just leave me alone." As his condition worsened, he often became confused and paranoid, yelling to a visitor or nurse, "You're all out to get me—get away so I can sleep." His motivation for living was clearly shattered. He eventually confined himself to bed, refused all medication, stopped eating altogether, and became severely dehydrated. On March 20, 1986, two years after his admission to the nursing home, Dan died.

Sadie

Sadie, aged 79 and widowed, was described as an intense, but pleasant person. A former supervisor with the local phone company in a New England city, Sadie retired after the death of her husband, to tend her home and to spend more time with her grown children and grandchildren, her only living relatives. Sadie was active in civic affairs, maintained her interests in reading, handwork, and current events, and managed her life independently for fifteen years after her husband's death.

The children, noticing subtle changes in behavior, admitted Sadie to a nursing home. Sadie, perceiving herself as able to manage in her own surroundings, was bewildered and angered by the family's insistence that she go to a nursing home—"your new home," as her son referred to it—against her wishes.

Admission assessment revealed an adequately nourished, alert, knowledgeable individual who was functional in all areas of ADL. A pre-admission history revealed that Sadie experienced occasional urinary leakage, which she managed at home. The physician had been treating her for cardiac irregularities, borderline hyperglycemia, hypertension, arthritis, and possible Alzheimer's disease. Facial pain, exacerbated by tension and irritability, was relieved by Motrin. Nitroglycerine was prescribed for chest pain as needed. The medication regimen remained unchanged after admission.

Because she seemed to be adjusting well to the routine, Sadie was moved to a permanent double room with a roommate for company. Within weeks Sadie was unable to eat her meals. When staff expressed concern about her diminishing appetite and limited intake, she responded, "I'm too angry with my son to eat. When he comes to take me out of here, I may; otherwise, I don't care whether I ever eat." Sadie accused the family of pulling a fast trick on her. Increased irritability, severe facial pain, and a fall ensued during this period, accompanied by social withdrawal and requests to be left alone. Sadie was hospitalized after episodes of vomiting and weakness. Passing out on the unit occurred with frequency. Following hospitalization, she was increasingly tense, communicated little, and refused to leave her room for meals or activities.

Sadie attempted unsuccessfully to leave the nursing home with her few prized possessions. Unable to do so, she asked for the "big pill" and stopped accepting most medications. Finally, she confined herself to bed, spat out food and medicine and refused to open her mouth. Dependence on nursing staff for ADL increased. The family, confronting Sadie with concern about the consequences of her actions, stated, "If you don't eat and take your medicine, you could become very ill again, or worse, die!" Smiling, Sadie rejected the family's concern.

Institutional life seemed literally intolerable for her at that point. Confusion, physical deterioration, and ultimate refusal of all treatment culminated in the development of respiratory complications. The family requested a "no code." Sadie died six months after leaving her home.

Jake

In 1986, Jake, a 91-year-old retired railroad conductor, and Gertrude, his wife of sixty-three years, moved from a small rural Midwestern town, to a nursing home in a large city far removed from their home. Although they would have preferred the closeness and familiarity of the town in which they had lived for over fifty years, there were no long-term care facilities available to them there. Gertrude's health was failing and Jake was unable to provide for her needs in their home.

Jake and Gertrude shared a small room in the institution and were constant companions, spending each day together in some activity. They were inseparable. The couple often took short walks, that is, when Jake could persuade his spouse to accompany him. They often were observed holding hands as they strolled around the grounds. The nursing home staff described Jake as an affable, healthy, happy person always ready for a joke. Less than three months after the couple's admission to the nursing home, Jake's emotional and physical well-being changed noticeably. To Gertrude's disappointment, he chose not to accept the children's invitation to Thanksgiving dinner, complaining of severe headache and stomach pains. This was not the first such episode since his admission. Over the holidays, headaches, abdominal pains, nausea, loss of appetite, changes in stool, and sleep disturbances occurred. Jake was hospitalized for three weeks with a diagnosis of peptic ulcers.

After discharge to the nursing home, Jake became more anorexic and physically deteriorated, appearing thin, pale, and despondent. "Why doesn't the Lord take me?" he cried frequently. He and Gertrude were soon moved to a wing for less functional residents. It was then that Jake clearly exhibited signs of giving up. He became less mobile, spoke very little, engaged less and less in activities of daily living, and rarely left his room, preferring to lie in bed and repeat to himself, within earshot of Gertrude, "I want to die. I just want to die." Jake and Gertrude moved several more times within the nursing home after his initial hospitalization because of increased dependency needs. His adjustment to each new surrounding became more difficult and was often incomplete.

This once acutely alert gentleman became confused, disoriented, and more depressed. Still painfully able to utter the despair that was now a part of him, Jake would cry aloud, "We're so sick, why does God make us live so long? We're no good to anyone. Our families are so far away. We can't enjoy anything now. It's cruel for God to keep us alive." At times, Gertrude responded to Jake's cries with anger and unpleasantness, as she perceived the absolute hopelessness of their situation. Often she would sob aloud, "I'm so homesick and lonesome!" The staff expressed sadness in seeing this once-loving couple of sixty-three years reduced to fear and bitterness. Jake focused on his nihilistic obsessions: "I can't fight this any more. I'm finished. I just want it to be over." He chose not to have his family visit, stopped eating and drinking entirely, and refused all medication and social contact. He slept most of the day, and at night he would either scream or pray, or both. Jake was transferred to the local hospital where attempts to administer intravenous fluids and medications were unsuccessful because of Jake's determination to intervene and remove the IVs. In light of his deteriorated condition, the family agreed to a "no code" status and, two weeks later, his battle finally won, Jake died.

Irene

Irene was a person of exceptional beauty. When introduced, she was dressed in a pair of tight-fitting black slacks, which enhanced her shapely figure, and a bright purple silk blouse, a birthday gift from her friends. Her snow-white hair was perfectly in place, and her makeup impeccable. She had just returned to the facility from an evening out with some younger friends. The smile on her face and the sparkle in her eyes reflected the excitement of a teenager returning from a date. She was open and charming, an unforgettable individual. Because of her youthful fifties presence, one could barely believe that Irene, a widow, was 81 years old and had raised eleven children on a farm outside the city. She had lived in the nursing home approximately one week and went there at the insistence of the family.

The last time the interviewer saw Irene alive, just two months after their initial meeting, she was barely recognizable. Her appearance was disheveled, her face pale and sunken, and her lips a bluish color, she rapidly paced back and forth near the pay phone. A healing laceration was observed over her left eye.

Recovering from the painful shock of seeing Irene in this state, the interviewer asked what was going on with her and how could she help. With a look of recognition, she replied: "I can't go on like this anymore. I feel like a caged animal. If I don't get out of here soon, I am going to die!" It was obviously difficult for her to decide to call her son, a professor at a nearby university, to beg him to take her out of the nursing home. She did call but there was no answer.

Irene's overall health state had seriously deteriorated. Before her admission to the nursing home, she had been able to manage her own health regimen and to keep late onset diabetes and hypertension under control. At the time, however, she was recovering from a mild heart attack. She had also suffered from congestive heart failure. Shortness of breath during this anxious episode was moderate to severe. Oxygen and more than twenty medications had been prescribed for her.

Notations in the medical record and interviews with staff members revealed that Irene was a very lonely and depressed person, and at one point had attempted to end her own life by refusing to eat, drink, or take the medication. Frequent expressions of loneliness, feelings of family rejection and abandonment, and periods of crying were also noted. A more in-depth examination of the medical record and interviews with staff and with Irene uncovered pertinent factors that contributed to depression and suicidal behavior. Chief among these was family rejection. Irene had spent her entire life caring for her children. She had given up the dream of teaching school in deference to devoted motherhood. Times had been very difficult for Irene and her family. A hard worker, she scrubbed other people's homes, took in laundry and sewing, made clothes for the children from the discards of others, and helped her husband farm their land, often working from dawn to dusk, to help make ends meet.

A few of Irene's children completed college on their own, all married well and were financially independent. She was proud of her oldest son, a professor in a local university. Neither the children nor the grandchildren visited Irene very often during her residency in the nursing home. Ironically, one of her granddaughters was employed by the facility, but seldom visited her grandmother. Irene felt totally rejected and abandoned by the children she devoted her life to. "I just want to be wanted. When you get old, your family just forgets you and you have no purpose in life anymore. Eleven children and no place to go in the end."

Another major factor contributing to Irene's depression and suicidal ruminations was her financial situation. The loss of the family farm was the most devastating loss she and her husband had suffered. Financial loss was severe and they never recovered. She was destitute after her husband's death and was ashamed and embarrassed that she was forced to live on welfare to meet expenditures. Because she was unable to afford many new clothes, she made do and ate little to avoid gaining weight. As a Medicaid resident in the nursing home, she received less than $35 a month for necessary expenditures and had little left over for extras. Unless her friends treated her to a night out, she could not afford that luxury she so enjoyed. As she put it: "I hardly ever have a nickel to my name. Who wants to waste their time and money on a poor old woman? Not even the children. I have nothing to leave them in my will. They must be ashamed of me now."

Irene had much of which to be proud. A creative, resourceful, and independent woman and successful wife and mother, she had managed to clothe and feed her family and contribute to their education. Reduced to dependent status in the nursing home, with many rules and regulations, she could not adjust to the loss of independence, freedom, and personal autonomy. She viewed herself as trapped and likened her feelings to those of a caged animal, stating, "If they make me stay here, then my life is over. I might just as well be dead."

Recognizing the seriousness of Irene's situation, the family was contacted, but they refused to take responsibility for Irene or to help in any way. During the last two months of her life, Irene gave up hope of ever leaving the nursing home or of seeing her family. One of the last statements she made to the interviewer was, "I don't have much to live for now. I sit and cry myself to sleep every night and pray that I will die. When I awaken, I cry again. It's hopeless." She fell shortly before her death, was admitted to the skilled care unit for treatment, and died of congestive heart failure.

Boyd

Boyd, age 60, an electrician by trade, was brought to the facility with terminal lung disease. Three years prior to his admission, he had retired from his job to care for his spouse who died of cancer a short time later. To cope with his grief and sadness he turned to alcohol. Because the alcohol problem worsened, four of his children rejected him and did not reconcile their differences until three weeks before his death.

Boyd was of Italian descent, had lived in America most of his adult life, spoke halting English, but easily made his wishes known. He would complain vehemently about the food to the family, but never to the staff. He took meals in his room, even when he was feeling well. He was territorial and difficult to get along with, a loner who isolated himself from activities and other involvement with the center. However, he adored his grandchildren, and there was noticeable improvement in his behavior when they visited.

Boyd's suicide was slow, and, over time, successful. There were four episodes of refusing to eat, which lasted from one to three weeks. During this time he also refused medication, with the exception of medicine for pain. Nausea and vomiting became common occurrences. He verbalized that "this was not an easy way to die." He did talk to a trusted few of the staff about death, frequently asking, "When is it going to be over?" Most of the reflective notes about his behavior were documented on the night shift. One entry noted, "Death would be painful and suffocating; I would rather die quickly."

A permanent tracheostomy was performed to facilitate Boyd's breathing. In an effort to provide more independence in self-care, he was instructed in the care of the tracheostomy; however, he frequently used poor technique in its care and management. Boyd was also known to have put foreign objects into the stoma, and frequent bleeding had been noted. He refused to be suctioned for several weeks at a time, and ultimately had the equipment removed from his room. He remained on antibiotics almost continuously, and progressive use of bronchodilators and pain medication were added to the list. In addition to his refusal to eat, Boyd had been observed on several occasions attempting to smoke while receiving oxygen. He declined to discuss his behavior, stating that it was his own business.

Two episodes of significant skin tears occurred, which Boyd declined to discuss or have examined. Interventions to halt these self-destructive behaviors were not entirely successful.

As Boyd's condition worsened, he refused suctioning, refused to use the oxygen, and required more medication to relieve the pain. A do-not-resuscitate order was placed in the medical record at his request. One morning he did allow a nurse to suction him for the first time in five days. Three days later, he died in the hospital. Boyd had begged not to go to the hospital because he was certain that he would be placed on a respirator, which did occur. His sons made the difficult decision to have the respirator removed in the final moments of his life.

Lenny

Lenny, a 78-year-old bachelor, was a former high school teacher and was well-known in the community for his professional contributions and accomplishments. Lenny had made a comfortable salary, and maintained financial independence during his adult life. After his retirement, Lenny made his home with his younger sister, his only living relative. Both maintained active and independent lifestyles, shared in the financial operation of the home, and participated in community functions. In 1986, Lenny was hospitalized for a minor stroke, and with prescribed therapy, regained the use and control of his lower extremities. Six months after hospitalization, Lenny had resumed near-normal activities; by the end of the ninth month, he was able to drive his car short distances. One of Lenny's main enjoyments in life was to drive his car, to exercise his "freedom." With the exception of a slight speech impediment, Lenny considered his recovery complete. Unexpectedly, in the spring of 1987, Lenny's sister determined that it would be the best thing for both of them for Lenny to move to a nursing home to be properly cared for after the stroke. With protests, Lenny reluctantly agreed to a trial stay.

Tall, handsome, and well-groomed, Lenny walked slightly behind his equally well-groomed sister into his future home, a long-term care facility in a small Midwestern city. The staff described him as an angry man. A series of events shortly after his admission confirmed their observations. The sister had taken Lenny's car keys to protect him from harm. An argument ensued and Lenny lashed out loudly, "That's [the keys] a man's independence. Take that away and you take his whole life away." To no avail he begged his sister to take him home to live.

Lenny became more angry and suspicious when his sister drove to the nursing home in a new car two weeks after his admission. Thereafter, his sister's sporadic visits usually ended in arguments. Tentative plans for dinner or for a ride were postponed or canceled. Lenny's rejection was manifest in feelings of loneliness, frustration, and anger. These feelings and behaviors increased in frequency, and depression surfaced. Increased dependence on others was apparent to the staff. Agitation and depression became more severe after a move from a private room on the intermediate care unit to a four-bed room on the skilled care unit. To Lenny, the move symbolized a further loss of independence, personal control, privacy, and freedom.

Although Lenny experienced other moves during the year, the move to the four-bed room was particularly traumatic. Lenny objected vehemently to living with persons whom he disliked and to his limited privacy. If a resident who was disoriented wandered into his room, or if his roommates occupied the bathroom when he needed it, Lenny would become enraged, often throwing a urinal at his roommate. Lack of sleep contributed to his irritable behavior.

Lenny became actively suicidal. Acquiring a razor blade from an unsuspecting aide, he cut his wrist, but failed in the attempt. Lids of tin cans were not effective to accomplish the act. Suicidal thoughts such as, "Just give me a revolver so I can end it all" or "Open the back door and throw me in the trash barrel" were repeatedly verbalized.

The nursing home team responded by placing Lenny on twenty-four-hour nursing observations and increasing the dose of Doxepin at night. Haldol was increased to twice daily. Xanax was prescribed at the hour of sleep to relieve anxiety. However, Lenny's deep and continuing depression affected his eating, sleeping, and overall function. When a meal was served to him, Lenny would respond "To hell with this, it's time to shove off anyway." Food and fluids were adamantly refused. Vulnerable, Lenny developed pneumonia and died, five months after his admission.

CASE ANALYSIS

The individual profiles portrayed in this chapter are representative of many older residents of long-term care facilities who suffer losses, loneliness, and depression. Functional incapacity, loneliness, loss of control, lack of a strong family support network, limited visitation by friends and family, and social withdrawal are crucial elements that can lead to depression and suicidal ruminations among the institutionalized elderly. These elements, compounded by a diminished self-esteem, a sense of helplessness and hopelessness, and loss of power in decision making about one's life in the present and in the future, renders an older individual in the institution at high risk for suicide.

Loss

Loss, a theme common to each of the profiles presented here, is a major factor contributing to suicide among residents in long-term care facilities. Significant losses include loss of spouse, friends, pets, money, control, independence, physical mobility, and sensory/perceptual losses. When Janice, Sadie, Lenny, and Irene moved to their respective institutions, the loss of their home, possessions, freedom, independence, autonomy, and privacy were forfeited. For Janice, the loss of her apartment and furniture represented a loss of independence and personal control. The loss of personal possessions, those extensions of themselves—their identity—was especially devastating for them. Accustomed to being in control of his own lifestyle over the years, Jake found that the freedom, autonomy, and control necessary to maintain and preserve person-environment balance in his new surroundings were gone. A sense of powerlessness combined with diminished self-esteem can adversely affect the older person's ability to cope. Diminished coping ability and the impact of multiple stressors leave the elder at risk for depression and suicide.

Depression

Among the profiles presented, environmental stress seems to be a primary factor in precipitating depressive symptoms. To maintain self-esteem, individuals must have maximum control over their lives. When older adults are helpless to control significant events in their environment, feelings of lowered self-concept and self-esteem result. Lowered self-esteem goes hand in hand with depression. Depression frequently masks itself in somatic complaints, guilt, and a depressed mood in elderly persons.

Rocky, Janice, Dan, Sadie, Jake, Irene, Boyd, and Lenny were victims of depression. Somatic, or masked, complaints, common in many elderly who are depressed, cannot be taken lightly under such conditions. Unfortunately, these symptoms are not always recognized as indicative of elderly depression, perhaps because it is falsely assumed that symptoms expressed by the older adult are normal concomitants of aging. What is critical to understanding suicide in older persons is that depression, often masked and unrecognized, is a precursor to overt and indirect life-threatening behavior.

Feelings of hopelessness, worthlessness, loss of love and concern permeated the daily lives of these persons in the institution; suicidal ideation was clearly expressed. Seldom was an anti-depressant prescribed, a psychological consult requested, or group or individual counseling initiated. However, anti-psychotic medication was the prescribed drug of choice to control behavior. Increased social withdrawal and isolation characterized their final days.

Family Dynamics

Family rejection, abandonment, and lack of informal supports are important factors contributing to suicidal behavior among residents of long-term care facilities. Many of the residents portrayed here perceived themselves as having no family from which they could receive support. In fact, many of them did not. Families were either far away, unable to make the commitment, stressed by their own problems, or did not wish to become involved or burdened with the extra responsibility, possibly related to earlier unresolved conflicts. In the profiles of at risk elderly, clearly, these individuals experienced feelings of separation, rejection, and abandonment by their families—Lenny and Janice by their siblings; Sadie, Jake, Rocky, and Irene by their children. Feelings of abandonment, anxiety, despair, and loss fluctuated in intensity, often more than they could cope with at this crucial time in their lives.

Often families must deal with their own guilt at having made the difficult decision to place their family member in a nursing home. Withdrawal and avoidance may be their means of coping with the situation. However, as a social system, neither the elder nor his or her family can be treated in isolation.

Physical and Functional Loss

Loss of physical function, especially seeing, hearing, speech, mobility, and ability to perform ADLs may contribute to a sense of helplessness and loss of control for many elders such as Dan, Boyd, Irene, Jake, Lenny, Rocky, Janice, and Sadie, all of whom suffered major physical losses. It is often a humiliating and dehumanizing experience when individuals are no longer able to feed, dress, toilet, and bathe themselves. Because of functional deficits, these elderly persons became most vulnerable to loss of control. In Rocky's case, his physical incapacity prompted overt and covert anger, and he resorted to periods of refusing food as one means of controlling his life— or death. Dan's motivation for living was clearly shattered. He became severely depressed, and expressed feelings of worthlessness and uselessness. Irene's anxiety affected her ability to function and aggravated her already compromised cardiac status. Jake, Sadie, and Lenny's deteriorating physical status prompted moves within the nursing homes, and to and from the hospital, moves not under their control, which affected their self-image as capable adult individuals.

Moves

Frequent moves within and out of the facility serve to increase personal and psychological pain for vulnerable individuals. Like other residents, Jake, Sadie, and Lenny experienced multiple moves within the facility. With each new move, they were confronted with new roommates, new staff, and new routines. Moves such as Jake, Sadie, and Lenny experienced further reduced their life space, and reinforced a lack of belonging and a strong sense of insecurity. Sharing space with another human being, a stranger, can increase anxiety for persons accustomed to living alone. Privacy, a scarce commodity in institutional settings, is essential to maintaining positive self-regard and autonomy in the environments of the elderly.

The lack of consistency and continuity within the facilities made adjustment more difficult. Lenny, for instance, reacted to the moves in a desperate and drastic manner by exhibiting irrational behavior. Many moves are made at the convenience of staff, without the active involvement and consent of the elder. Withholding control significantly contributes to helplessness, hopelessness, depression, and intentional life-threatening behavior.

In summary, factors that contributed to the decision to stop living are common to those elderly residents who contemplate or complete suicide. Loss, depression, social isolation, social withdrawal, family abandonment and rejection, and physical moves within their environment all occasion difficulty, as has been demonstrated throughout this chapter. Emotional pain is often more than the vulnerable older person can endure, and the will to live under these circumstances rapidly disintegrates in many elderly in long-term care institutions.

PART III

6

LATE LIFE DEPRESSION

Depression is the most common mental disorder of later life (Blazer, 1982). Depressive symptoms occur in 30 percent to 65 percent of individuals over the age of 60 (LaRue, Dessonville, & Jarvick, 1985). Depression is the major precipitating factor in suicide among the elderly. Suicide is the most serious negative consequence of depression; however, there are many other negative consequences. Depression frequently causes severe emotional pain that can decrease social and physical activity, increase insomnia and anorexia, and reduce functional abilities. Unfortunately, depression in the elderly is often unrecognized and untreated.

Organically based major depression, also referred to as primary depression, results from various biological and chemical changes in the brain and nervous systems or from changes in the endocrine system. Situational or reactive depression, on the other hand, is an emotional response to various losses, stresses, changes, and other external events experienced by adults in late life. Another important distinction in the depression states is between primary and secondary depression. Depression may be the major illness or may occur secondary to other illnesses or to the effects of various medications. The latter is referred to as secondary depression.

This chapter will examine the biological basis of major depression, the psychosocial factors in reactive depression, and the illnesses and drugs that contribute to the development of secondary depression. Diagnosis of late life depression will be the focus of the last half of this chapter. Signs and symptoms of depression will be highlighted. Different methods of assessment ranging from laboratory tests to standardized scales and assessment instruments will be discussed briefly.

BIOLOGICAL FACTORS

Biogenic Amine Theories

Some biological theories of depression attribute the higher incidence of depression in late life to changes in neurotransmitters involved in brain activity. J. Schildkraut (1965) suggests that some depressions result from a deficiency of catecholamines (especially norepinephrine) at important receptor sites in the brain. As individuals age, the synthesis of catecholamine proceeds at a slower rate.

Other studies have focused on the neurotransmitter, serotonin. G. Brown, F. Goodwin, J. Ballenger, P. Goyer, and L. Major (1979) and H. Van Praag (1982) have found abnormally low levels of activity of a serotonin metabolite in the spinal fluid of depressed individuals. The aging process results in decreases in the concentration of certain adrenergic neurotransmitters in the brain, notably serotonin, norepinephrine, and dopamine. Aging also results in decreases in acetylcholine, a cholinergic transmitter. These organic changes place the older adult at increased risk of suffering a major depression.

Endocrine Theory

Another major biological theory is the endocrine theory of depression. "Depressive illness results from disorders in connections between the pituitary gland, the hypothalamic nuclei of the brain, and endocrine organs, such as the thyroid and adrenal glands" (Melville and Blazer, 1985, p. 16). Age-related changes associated with depression include diminished thyroid function, decreased hypothalamic function, alterations in gonadal functions, and diminished response of the pituitary gland to hypothalamic releasing factors.

Secondary Depression

Depression may be secondary to illnesses such as Parkinsonism, thyroid disease, brain tumor, pernicious anemia, and cancer of the pancreas. Certain medications may also cause depression in older adults. The following are examples: female hormones, corticosteroid analgesics, anti-hypertensives, anti-inflammatory agents, antianxiety agents, antipsychotic agents, cancer chemotherapeutic agents and anti-parkinson drugs. Because older adults are more likely than younger adults to suffer from some of these illnesses and are also more likely to take a variety of drugs, they are more vulnerable to secondary depression.

Figure 1
Theoretical Model of Aging and Suicide

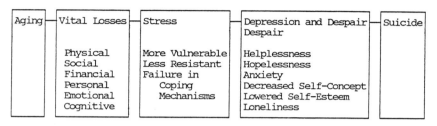

From N. J. Osgood, <u>Suicide in the elderly: A practitioner's guide to diagnosis and mental health intervention</u>. Rockville, MD: Aspen, 1985, p. xliv.

PSYCHOSOCIAL FACTORS

Most psychosocial models of depression emphasize two major factors: loss and stress and inability to cope with stress. Most older depressed individuals are suffering from reactive depression, an emotional response to the losses and stresses of aging. A theoretical model of the relationship between aging, depression, and suicide is presented in Figure 1.

Loss

In his seminal work *Suicide*, E. Durkheim wrote that egoism is said to be accompanied by "collective currents of depression and disillusionment," and by "miserable weariness and sad depression" (1951, pp. 214, 225). Although he primarily emphasized social forces as causes of suicide, Durkheim recognized and noted the intimate connection between losses in the social realm and those in the psychological realm. S. Freud (1917), the father of psychological explanations of suicide, contended that the loss of a loved one results in feelings of abandonment and rejection, which may swell into anger directed against the lost loved one. Loss results in a particular state of mind in the individual. In an attempt to kill the memory of the lost loved one, suicide may result.

Old age has been described as the season of losses. Many older persons lose vital social roles in the worlds of work, family, politics, and community, with concomitant losses of income, power, status, and prestige. Physical losses such as declining health, painful chronic debilitating illnesses, losses of limbs, hearing, or eyesight occur as well. Others experience significant personal losses, such as the death of a spouse or close friend. The last stage of life often becomes a series of good-byes as older friends and relatives die one by one. Faced with such losses, the older person lives in an ever-contracting social world, increasingly cut off from verbal and physical contact.

Loneliness and severe depression often accompany the multiple losses suffered by great numbers of elderly. Many older persons experience a sense of emptiness and meaninglessness and lose motivation for working, playing, and living. In late life there are fewer social roles and opportunities open to individuals. Similarly, the process of making friends and developing intimate relationships is more difficult as the years go by.

The losses of people, goals, and social roles lead to sadness and mental pain. Older adults at risk usually seek new sources of satisfaction; however, if they fail to find new people, goals, and roles to replace those that have been lost, then feelings of anxiety, despair, helplessness and hopelessness, may dominate them.

According to J. Belsky (1984), losses shake people's confidence in their abilities to control their environments and to satisfy their personal needs. As a result, individuals who experience losses feel incompetent and inadequate. Self-esteem suffers and a sense of helplessness results in decreased activity as they come to view any activity as useless in effecting change. Institutionalized individuals face additional losses, which contribute to depression. Many residents of institutions become estranged from family, friends, neighborhood, church, and the outside world. They suffer physical, social, emotional, and spiritual deprivation (Stotsky & Dominick, 1969). In such situations these individuals can easily become disoriented, disorganized, helpless, lonely, and depressed. They may feel anchorless, rejected, abandoned, unneeded, unwanted, and unloved, adrift from home and family.

Stress

According to Marvin Miller (1979, p. 25), "whether an older person is able to resolve a suicidal crisis or succumbs to self-inflicted death is very much a function of the ability to cope with stress." A stressor is anything that implies or causes threat or trauma to an organism. External stressors include such events as retirement, widowhood, and relocation. Internal stressors refer to changes in bodily or mental function or to disease within the organism. Losses, whether real, threatened, or imagined, are stressors that require adaptation, flexibility, and resiliency if persons are to cope successfully and survive. Multiple losses suffered by members of the aging population increase stress at a time of life when they are least resistant and least able to cope. Impaired ability to cope with stress has been noted as a major characteristic of the aging process by C. Eisdorfer and D. Wilkie (1977), L. Jarvick (1975), and A. Welford (1962).

Many residents in institutions experience multiple losses and stress. In addition to physical, social, and personal losses experienced by older adults, many more residents also face losses of home and possessions, freedom and independence, personal autonomy, dignity, and respect. The stress of adjusting to physical moves and new environments place these residents under additional stresses. In the 1940s R. Spitz (1946) described a type of anaclitic depression in infants who lost their mothers as "failure to thrive." More recently D. Blau (1980) has suggested that the decline and death of certain older persons soon after entering a long-term care institution could also be a form of anaclitic depression.

Loneliness

Artists, poets, novelists, and songwriters have all commented on the agony, anguish, emptiness, and fear of loneliness. Loneliness is a negative emotional state that implies alienation, lack of close emotional ties, less than optimal social interaction and reinforcement, and feelings of rejection, isolation, and marginality. In describing the emotional state of loneliness, W. Sadler and T. Johnson (1980) note that it is a condition in which "we feel left out, cut off, lost, forgotten, unwanted, unneeded, and ignored" (p. 38). A review of the literature reveals that loneliness is linked consistently with depression (Bragg, 1979; Russell, Peplau, & Cutrona, 1980; Schultz & Moore, 1982; Weeks, Michela, Peplau, & Bragg, 1980; Young, 1982).

Many older adults, especially those who have lost a spouse, a child, and close friends, suffer from loneliness. Institutionalized residents are more likely to be widowed and devoid of family relations. This factor, coupled with moves to strange new environments from familiar neighborhoods and surroundings, increases the risk of loneliness and depression in this population.

Self-Esteem

Confronted with the many losses and stresses of growing old, individuals may lose their sense of personal identity and suffer from a decline in self-esteem, changed self-concept, and a sense of meaninglessness in life. R. Kastenbaum (1964) discusses old age not only as an unexpected event but also as a profound misfortune in which individuals are faced with difficult tasks of explaining to themselves and others how it came to pass that they are not what they used to be. Such individuals experience what Kastenbaum refers to as the "crisis of explanation"; for these persons, growing old brings a very negative self-evaluation and loss of self-esteem; they can not accept or explain the new old self and, therefore, they lose their earlier identities.

Self-hatred and low self-esteem are at the root of suicidal behavior. When the discrepancy between performance and ambition is very great, as is often the case in late life, the resultant carrot-and-stick situation further hastens negative changes in self-concept. Changes in appearance that accompany the aging process negatively affect the person's self-image and include wrinkled skin, graying hair, memory changes, slowed reaction time, easy fatigability, loss of stamina, uncertainty of gait, greater vulnerability to infections and chronic illness, and reduced keeness of all five senses. Overemphasis on youth and beauty in the culture further contributes to negative self-concepts and diminished self-esteem of aged individuals.

Residents of institutions who are told when to eat, sleep, bathe, and engage in activities suffer even greater losses in self-esteem than those who live independently. Many who have lost functional abilities and must depend on the use of walkers or wheelchairs remain in bed or require assistance with eating, bathing, and personal self-maintenance; they feel degraded and stripped of personal dignity. Their self-esteem and self-concept suffer, and, in many cases, these individuals lose their personal identities as they become integrated into impersonal bureaucratic systems.

Helplessness and Hopelessness

Two major factors have been recognized as contributing to depression and suicide among the aged (and those of other ages): helplessness and hopelessness.

The theory that depression is an ego state in which the feeling of help-lessness is the basic underlying dynamic was first put forth by E. Bibring in 1953. Helplessness is defined by M. Seligman (1975, 1976) as a state in which individuals experience an inability to control or predict significant life events and suggests that it is the core of all depression. He notes that "the depressed patient believes or has learned that he cannot control those ele-ments of his life that relieve suffering, bring gratification, or provide nur-ture—in short, he believes that he is helpless" (1975, p. 92). The aged are the most susceptible to helplessness, according to Seligman, because they have experienced the greatest loss of control. Similarly, R. Schulz (1976) argues that the loss of job, income, physical health, work, and child-rearing roles results in increased helplessness and depression in the aged. S. Ap-pelbaum (1963) and E. Stengel (1964) have also identified the basic feelings of helplessness as a factor in elder suicide.

Helplessness and hopelessness often go hand in hand and can result in suicidal behavior in the aged at risk. Karl Menninger (1938), whose classical work continues to exert a major influence on the study of depression and suicide in the aged, characterized suicides in the older population as a result of the wish to die. In emphasizing the wish to die as a major motive in elderly suicide, Menninger identified hopelessness as a major contributing factor. M. Farber (1968) similarly conceived of suicide among the aged as a desperate response to hopeless and intolerable life situations, when he wrote, "Suicide occurs when there appears to be no available path that will lead to a tolerable existence. . . . It is when the life interest is one of despairing hopelessness that suicide occurs" (p. 17). Farber defines hope as the rela-tionship between a sense of personal competence and life-threatening events. A. Kobler and E. Stotland (1964), who studied successful suicides, point directly to a loss of hope as the precipitating factor, noting that "suicide occurred in each case when, and only when, all significant hopeful relationships were broken" (p. 11).

Those who have analyzed suicide notes of individuals of various ages have found that the elderly express a sense of hopelessness and "psychological exhaustion" in their notes (Cath, 1965; A. Darbonne, 1969; Farberow & Shneidman, 1970). They are tired of life and tired of living. They have given up. The sense of rage and anger that is often expressed by younger people in their notes is absent from the notes of older individuals. Many of the suicidal individuals we encountered in the institution expressed their feelings as "exhausted, tired of living and all used up."

S. Kierkegaard (1941) referred to despair as a "sickness unto death." Similarly, Miller (1979) has described the crossing of what he calls the "line of unbearability" as the primary factor in elderly suicide:

Lying dormant within all of us is an extremely personal equation which determines the point where the quality of our lives would be so pathetically poor that we would no longer wish to live. This "line of unbearability," as it might be called, usually exists only subconsciously and we are therefore not normally cognizant of it. However, when we actually find ourselves in an intolerable situation, even for the first time in our lives, we become conscious of our "line of unbearability." Once the line of unbearability is crossed, a crisis is triggered. Those who still maintain hope cry out for help. Those who don't, kill themselves quickly and with determination (p. 8).

The multiple losses of aging render the elderly more vulnerable to stress, while at the same time depleting their resistance to stress and their coping mechanisms. Faced with multiple stresses and decreased ability to cope, older persons are often left helpless to alter their life situations. The resulting sense of despair and hopelessness produces a lowering of self-concept and self-esteem in the helpless old. The situation of many elderly is "like a closed room in which one is subjected to excruciating and relentless emotional and physical pain, a room in which the one door leading out is labeled SUICIDE" (Maris, 1981, p. 315).

ASSESSMENT

Careful assessment is essential to accurate diagnosis of depression in older adults. A variety of assessment tools are available to the practitioner, including behavioral assessment relying on the *Diagnostic and Statistical Manual of Mental Disorders (DSM III-R)* (American Psychiatric Association, 1987), medical and social histories, laboratory tests, and depression rating scales and other standardized instruments. This section will discuss the clinical diagnosis of depression, focusing on signs and symptoms, and major distinguishing features as specified in *DSM III-R*. Important aspects of history taking will also be discussed. Laboratory tests that can aid in detection of depression will be described. Depression rating scales and standardized instruments used to determine the level of depression will be the focus of the last part of this chapter.

Clinical Diagnosis of Depression

According to Freud (1917) the distinguishing features of melancholia are profoundly painful dejection, loss of interest in the outside world, inability to love, absence of all activity, and self-condemnation. Depressed people picture themselves as worthless and morally despicable. Clinical depression includes a feeling state of low spirits, dejection, sadness, unhappiness, and a dysphoric mood. Slowed thinking and decreased purposeful physical activity accompany the mood change, and there is a loss of pleasure or interest in all or almost all usual activities or pastimes (American Psychiatric Association, 1980). Depressive delusions; pessimistic thoughts; guilt; self-blame; low self-esteem; feelings of hopelessness; negative attitudes and other beliefs about self, the world, and others; and negative cognitive states also characterize the individual who is clinically depressed (Beck, 1967). Hypochondriasis is another major element in late life depression, expressed in various physical and somatic complaints and increased attention to one's body (Busse, 1970; T. Brink, 1979; Steuer, Bank, Olson, & Jarvik, 1980). Changes in volition, the constant striving and impulses within an individual, occur with depression. Persons who are depressed withdraw from more demanding activities and experience apathy and lethargy, a "paralysis of will" that can lead to almost total immobility (Blazer, 1982).

Symptoms of depression are of five major types: emotional, cognitive, behavioral, physical, and volitional.

Emotional symptoms include sadness, dejection, apathy, grievous unhappiness, emptiness, and lowered life satisfaction.

Cognitive symptoms include depressive delusions, pessimistic thoughts, self-blame, feelings of helplessness and hopelessness, memory loss, self-criticism, guilt, a sense of personal failure, worry, slowed thinking, confusion, and feelings of uselessness and worthlessness.

Behavioral symptoms include slowing of physical movements, agitation, hand wringing, restlessness, hostile behavior, lack of attention to grooming and self-maintenance, reduction in activities, and withdrawal from family and friends.

Physical symptoms include loss of appetite and weight, loss of libido, sleep disturbance fatigue, tachycardia, constipation, headaches, muscle/skeletal pain, stomach distress, and backaches.

Volitional symptoms include paralysis of will, immobility, apathy, regression, social withdrawal, and giving up.

Table 12, developed by D. Blazer, (1982) displays some of the major signs and symptoms of depression in the elderly individual.

To qualify as a major depressive episode, according to the *DSM III-R*, an individual must exhibit either depressed or dysphoric mood and four or more of the following symptoms for at least a two-week period: (1) disturbed appetite, accompanied by weight loss or gain; (2) insomnia or hypersomnia; (3) decreased energy level, accompanied by sustained fatigue; (4) psychomotor agitation manifested by pacing and restlessness; (5) loss of interest or pleasure with or without loss of libido; (6) self-reproach, unworthiness, or guilt; (7) diminished ability to think, concentrate, or recall; (8) preoccupation with bodily functions; and (9) suicidal thoughts with or without fear or suicide attempts. The *DSM III-R* does not differentiate cognitive or affective symptoms of depression between young and old.

Depression tends to take a slightly different form in the elderly than in other age groups (Zung, 1980). W. Zung characterizes depressed elderly persons as being anxious, preoccupied with physical symptoms, fatigued, withdrawn, retarded, apathetic, inert, disinterested in their surroundings, and lacking in drive. Numerous other studies have shown that apathy, withdrawal, and functional slowness are common symptoms of depression in the older group. Table 13, developed by Blazer (1982), highlights elements of depressive states more common to older and younger individuals.

The careful taking of medical and psychosocial history is critically important to assessing depression in the older adult. The history should focus on past and present medical illnesses, behavioral symptoms, and family relationships. History of psychiatric illness or hospitalization is particularly important. History of alcoholism is also essential. A sexual history, often overlooked, may indicate recent loss of libido. The history may be gathered from past medical records, as well as from interviews with clients and family members.

Routine laboratory tests can aid in the detection of depression. Blood tests should be done, including, a complete blood cell count, thyroxine level determination, and electrolyte testing. Anemia or covert infection can be noted in the complete blood cell count. More specialized laboratory tests can detect deficiencies in vitamin B^{12} and folic acid (Blazer, 1982). An electroencephalogram can reveal changes in the brain and detect local lesions or the presence of drug-induced abnormalities (Wang, 1980).

Two psychoendocrinologic tests can be used to diagnose depression. The *TRH Simulation Test* measures the level of thyrotropin (TSH) secreted in response to infusion of thyrotropin-releasing hormone (TRH). Those who are seriously depressed will have a blunted response. The *Dexamethasone Suppression Test* (DST) tests the body's response to a synthetic steroid, taken orally, that within twenty-four hours can suppress secretion of cortisol. Seriously depressed individuals will demonstrate test values elevated above the normal of 5 mcgms/ml (Melville & Blazer, 1985).

Table 12
Symptoms and Signs of Late Life Depression

Symptoms	Signs
Emotional: Sad, dejected, decreased life satisfaction, loss of interest, impulse to cry, irritable, fearful, hopelessness, helplessness, failure, emptiness, loneliness, uselessness. Negative feelings toward self.	Appearance: Stooped, sad hostile, crying, whining, anxious, irritable, suspicious, uncooperative, socially withdrawn.
Cognitive: Low self-esteem, self-criticism, pessimism, suicidal thoughts, ruminations, doubt of values, concentration and memory difficulty. Delusions; uselessness, blame, somatic, nihilistic. Hallucinations; auditory, visual, and kinesthetic.	Examination: Weight loss, confusion, clouding of consciousness, mood variation, bowel impaction.
	Severe cases: Drooling unkempt appearance, ulcerations of skin or cornea due to picking, decreased blinking.
Physical: Loss of appetite and libido, fatigable, initial and terminal insomnia, frequent awakenings, constipation, pain restlessness.	Psychomotor retardation: Slowed speech, Movements, gait, minimal gestures.
Volitional: Loss of motivation, inability to get going, "paralysis of will."	Severe cases: Muteness, stupor, semicoma, cessation of chewing, swallowing, blinking.
	Psychomotor agitation: Pacing restlessness, hand wringing, picking at skin, constant motor activity, grasping at others.
	Unusual behavior: Suicidal gestures, negativism, refusal to eat, drink, aggressive outbursts, falling backwards.

Source: Adapted with permission from D. G. Blazer, Ed., Depression in Late Life. St. Louis, Mo.: C.V. Mosby, 1982, p. 24. Copyright 1982 by C. V. Mosby.

Table 13
Elements of Depressive States Common to Older Versus Younger Age Groups

More Common to Older Age Group	More Common to Younger Age Group
o Decreased life satisfaction loss of interest[a]	o Sadness, dejected mood
o Withdrawal from social environment[b]	o Use of term depression to identify feeling state
o Sense of emptiness[b]	o Feelings of guilt, self-blame
o Pessimism about future[ab]	o Low self-esteem
o Cognitive symptoms (especially slowed thought, poor concentration)[a]	o Appetite loss
o Rumination over problems	o Suicidal thoughts, discission
o Poor physical health[ab]	o Suicidal gestures, incomplete attempts
o Recent bereavement[ab]	o Use of suicide threat for manipulation
o Pseudodementia	
o Sleep difficulty[a] if severe insomnia[b]	
o Somatic complaints (especially digestive, pain, cardiac)[a]	
o Hypochondria[a]	
o Agitation[b]	
o Weight loss	
o Loss of motivation	
o Vegetative signs (especially constipation)	
o Completed suicide	

Source: Adapted with permission from D. G. Blazer, Ed., Depression in Late Life. St. Louis, Mo.: C.V. Mosby, 1982, p. 24. Copyright 1982 by C. V. Mosby.

[a]Also common in late life with depressive state.

[b]Associated with increased suicide risk in the elderly.

Disruption in the normal sleep cycle characterizes depression and can be detected using the sleep electroencephalogram. The total period of rapid eye movement (REM) sleep may be reduced by as much as 50 percent in depressed individuals (Coble, Kupfer, & Shaw, 1981).

Assessment Instruments and Scales

Numerous scales and checklists have been developed to assess depression or factors associated with depression in the elderly. Extensive information on rating scales for depression is available in the review of rating scales by I. Waskow and M. Parloff (1975). Before presenting a brief review of some of the most popular scales used by clinicians, it is important to offer the following caveats regarding the use of rating scales and checklists to diagnose depression in the elderly. The reader should keep in mind that the majority of scales have not been developed or normatively standardized or validated on older populations and, therefore, may not adequately assess depression in this particular age group. Rating scales and symptoms checklists should never replace good clinical assessment and should only be used in conjunction with a thorough intake interview with client and family, appropriate laboratory tests, and clinical diagnoses.

One scale frequently used to assess depression was developed in the mid-1970s by the Center for Epidemiologic Studies. The *Center for Epidemiologic Studies Depression Scale (CES-D)* is a short, easily administered self-report measure. The *CES-D* is comprised of twenty items that assess symptoms of depression. Each item, with the exception of numbers 4, 8, 12, and 16, is scored on a range of zero to four, with higher scores indicating more impairment, for which scoring is reversed. The total summed score ranges from zero to sixty. The most widely used cutoff point for depression is 16 (Jenike, 1983). N. Krause (1986) factor analyzed the *CED-D* and discovered three theoretically meaningful factors: depressed affect, somatic and retarded activities, and positive affect.

The *Beck Depression Inventory (BDI)* (Beck, Ward, Mendelson, Mock, & Erbaugh, 1961) is another popular scale. The *BDI* consists of twenty-one multiple-choice items. For each item the respondent must choose among four statements representing increasingly severe instances of the depressive symptom. Item scores range from zero to three; with zero representing the absence of the symptom and three being the most severe. Total score ranges from zero to sixty-three. Adequate reliability (Gallagher, Nies, & Thompson, 1982) and concurrent validity (Endicott & Spitzer, 1978; Gallagher, Breckenridge, Steinmets, & Thompson, 1983) have been established for the *BDI*. A modified version of the *BDI*, the *Geriatric Depression Scale* (J. Yesavage and T. Brink 1983) is particularly useful, since it eliminates somatically oriented questions and employs an easy to understand yes/no answer format rather than the four-point answer scale of *BDI*.

Hopelessness is a major factor in late life depression and has been identified as a significant factor in suicide (Kovacs, Beck, & Weissman, 1975). A. Beck has also developed a scale to measure hopelessness, "a system of negative expectancies concerning one's self and future" (Beck, Weissman, Lester, & Trexler, 1974, p. 861). The *Hopelessness Scale (HS)* is composed of nine items about attitudes toward the future structured in a semantic differential format and eleven items that were drawn from a pool of pessimistic statements made by psychiatric patients who were judged by clinicians to appear hopeless. Factor analysis yielded four factors: feeling about the future (encompassing feelings of hope and enthusiasm), loss of emotion (including faith and good times); feelings of wanting to give up and not wanting to try anything, and future expectations (including anticipations of what life will be like, a dark future, etc.).

Evaluation of mental function is of prime importance in assessing depression in older adults. Depressed older individuals demonstrate considerable

Table 14
Characteristics Commonly Distinguishing Pseudodementia from Dementia*

Pseudodementia	Dementia
Short duration of symptoms	Long duration of symptoms
Strong sense of distress	Often unconcerned
Many, detailed complaints of cognitive loss	Few, vague complaints of cognitive loss
Recent and remote memory loss are equal	Recent memory loss is worse than remote
Attention, concentration often good	Attention, concentration usually poor
Memory gaps common	Memory gaps unusual
"Don't know" answer common	"Near miss" answer common
Emphasizes disabilities, failures	Conceals disability, emphases accomplishments
Makes little effort to perform tasks	Struggles to perform tasks
Does not try to keep up	Uses notes, calendars to keep up
Performance varied on similar tasks	Consistently poor performances on similar tasks
Pervasive affect change	Affect shallow, labile
Social skills lost early	Social skills retained
Orientation tests: "don't know"	Orientation tests: mistakes unusual or usual
Behavior incongruent with severity of cognitive problem	Behavior compatible with severity of cognitive problem
Symptoms not often worse at night	Symptoms often worse at night
Prior positive psychiatric history common	Prior positive psychiatric history not common

Source: Adapted with permission from C. E. Wells and G. W. Duncan, Neurology for Psychiatrists. Philadelphia: F. A. Davis, 1980, p. 93. Copyright 1980 by F. A. Davis.

fluctuation in their mental abilities. A mental status examination consists of evaluating the following: orientation and consciousness, mood and affect, motor behavior, perception, thought processes and content, and memory and intelligence.

Mental function may be examined through direct observation, careful interviewing, and the use of formal testing. The *Mini-Mental State Examination (MMSE)*, devised by M. Folstein and colleagues (1975), is a good short form examination that tests orientation, memory, and intelligence. These tests need to be administered at more than one point in time to accurately assess mental functioning.

A major problem in accurately diagnosing depression in older adults is determining whether the person who appears to perform poorly on mental status measures is suffering from depression or organic brain disease. Often symptoms of depression are mistaken for dementia; consequently the depression is not treated. Pseudodementia, which presents with disorientation, confusion, poor intellectual function, and symptoms of dementia, is common in depressed elderly adults. As Melville and Blazer (1985) note with respect to pseudodementia, "Although its etiology is not entirely clear, the condition may be related to apathy, inattention, and distractibility, combined with decreased sensory and neuro-biological adaptive abilities" (p. 30).

Actually, depression and pseudodementia differ on several dimensions notably duration and time of occurrence of symptoms, type of memory loss, change in affect, and behavioral change. Table 14, adapted from Wells and Duncan (1980), illustrates characteristics that distinguish pseudodementia from dementia.

Accurate diagnosis of depression is just the first step. To decrease the risk of suicide for residents of long-term care facilities, depression must be treated. Depression is eminently treatable. In the next chapter we will discuss a variety of treatment modalities ranging from electroconvulsive therapy and pharmacological treatments, to psychotherapy and the use of creative arts therapy.

7

TREATING LATE LIFE DEPRESSION

Depression is a major underlying factor in most geriatric suicides. Therefore, it is essential to accurately identify and effectively treat depression in elderly individuals. Underlying factors in late life depression and methods of assessing depression in older adults were discussed in Chapter 6. Treatment is the focus of this chapter.

Antidepressant therapy and electroconvulsive therapy are two medical treatments for depression that are effective with older adults. In addition to these medical treatments, various psychosocial therapies are also effective. Psychotherapy, reminiscence and life review therapy, creative arts therapy, and support group therapy all are useful treatment modalities. Psychosocial nursing interventions such as one-on-one nursing and therapeutic touch will also be discussed.

ANTIDEPRESSANT THERAPY

A number of different psychotropic medications are available to treat late life depression, particularly when severity and duration of signs and symptoms are accompanied by compromised functional ability in the elderly. These include antidepressants, lithium, minor tranquilizers, and stimulants. Physicians prescribing these medications need to be aware of the special problems associated with each drug when treating an elderly population.

Tricyclic Antidepressant

Tricyclic antidepressants are thought to act on central monoamine pathways, particularly at noradrenergic and serotonergic sites, to facilitate synaptic transmission. Agents differ in their relative selectivity for the two aminergic systems, hence failure of treatment with one does not always imply failure with a second. Imipramine, desipramine, amitriptyline, doxepin, and nortriptyline are all effective agents (Blazer, 1982).

Although tricyclic antidepressants are a mainstay in the psychiatric treatment of depression, they present particular problems in older suicidal patients, both because of the increased incidence of untoward side effects in older patients, and also because an overdose may be lethal. Tricyclic antidepressants can produce orthostatic hypotension, tachyrhythmia, and congestive heart failure. Pulse and blood pressure should be carefully monitored during treatment, and patients should be warned to rise slowly from a sitting or lying position.

Standard tricyclic antidepressants produce the anticholinergic side effects of dry mouth, constipation, urinary hesitancy or retention, tachycardia, delirium, hallucinosis, and blurred vision, and these effects are more pronounced and disturbing to older individuals than younger individuals. Older people who experience dry mouth from these medications may suffer from increased caries, demineralization of teeth, and decreased taste acuity. Constipation is common in sedentary older patients and, if untreated, may lead to symptoms that are interpreted as somatization, such as bloating, belching, flatus, faintness, and anxiety. Thus older persons taking tricyclics should be taken seriously when they express abdominal complaints, and the offending medication discontinued if response to improved diet and mild laxatives is ineffective. Untreated constipation can lead to fecal impaction, stercoral ulcer, and anal fissures. Likewise, urinary retention may lead to overflow incontinence which is often mistaken for incontinence of neurological origin. The delirium and hallucinosis of the tricyclics, especially in otherwise debilitated or demented elderly patients, may be attributed to organic brain syndrome or dementia, and left untreated. Age-related changes in drug metabolism, absorption, and excretion present particular problems. Older adults are likely to be taking several drugs, increasing the risk of negative drug interactions.

Very careful thought should be given to the possibility of overdose with medications. Lethal overdoses have occurred with older adults following ingestion of as little as 5g of imipramine (Tofranil), about thirty days' worth for a patient receiving 150 mg daily. Certain antidepressant medications, such as trazodone (Desyrel) and fluoxetine hydrochloride, are safer if overdose should occur than the tricyclic antidepressants. They may be preferable for first line treatment of depression in suicidal elderly.

In older patients, the general rule for pharmacological treatment is "start low and go slow." Although newer antidepressants appear to have certain advantages in older patients, it is prudent to begin with an established drug such as desipramine (Norpramin) with a low incidence of side effects at a dose of 10–25 mg daily. If the patient is unable to tolerate the anticholinergic side effects of the tricyclic antidepressants, trazodone or fluoxetine would be appropriate treatments. If orthostatic hypotension is problematic for the patient, nortriptyline (Aventyl) is an appropriate alternative initial drug. Most antidepressant medications take from two to four weeks to produce the desired effect.

MAO Inhibitors

MAO inhibitors block monoamine oxidase, an enzyme widely distributed in the central nervous system and also peripherally. Optimal drug response requires at least 80 percent inhibition of this enzyme. MAO inhibitors produce marked clinical improvement in patients of any age who are unresponsive to tricyclics. Phenelzine sulfate (Nardil), tranylcypromine sulfate (Parnate), and isocarboxazid (Marplan) are the major drugs of choice.

MAO inhibitors are not recommended as the first choice of treatment in older adults due to their many serious adverse side effects. These drugs negatively interact with many common medications taken by the elderly. MAO inhibitors also inhibit the degradation of tyramine found in many foods and beverages. If an elderly adult eats or drinks these foods or beverages while taking MAOs, a life-threatening hypertensive crisis may result. Insomnia, altered bladder function, stroke, and myocardial infarction are other dangerous side effects.

In prescribing these medications, a general clinical rule is that older patients require one-third to one-half of the usual adult dose of an antidepressant, but this clinical rule of thumb has many exceptions.

Lithium

Lithium is not recommended for treatment of reactive depressions. Manic episodes in recurrent manic-depressives, however, respond to lithium carbonate. The use of lithium with older adults requires strict supervision. Hypothyroidism, cardiac sinus node dysfunction, anorexia, nausea, edema, excessive thirst, and frequent urination are some of the possible side effects to expect. Required dosages of lithium are smaller in older adults. Doses may begin as low as 50 mg/day with increases every three or four days until a serum level of 0.4–0.7 mEq/L is achieved (Borson & Veith, 1985).

Minor Tranquilizers

Diazepam (Valium) is not the drug of choice to treat depressed elders; however, it may be useful in low doses for older adults who cannot tolerate tricyclics due to cardiac problems. Sedation, blurred vision, diplopia, auditory and visual hallucinations, restlessness and agitation, and other side effects may result from the use of these agents.

Stimulants

Stimulants such as Ritalin may be useful as a temporary measure in elevating depressed mood. These agents may be used in the time period before the desired effect has been achieved with tricyclics. Stimulants should not be used in the presence of glaucoma, arrhythmic cardiovascular disease, and agitated states.

Side effects of amphetamines include hypertension, insomnia, anxiety, and the danger of drug dependence. Blood pressure should be carefully monitored. Stimulants should not be used with MAO inhibitors.

Table 15 presents an overview of psychotropic agents with dosage information and side effects.

ELECTROCONVULSIVE THERAPY

Despite adverse publicity, electroconvulsive therapy remains one of the most effective treatments in the psychiatric armamentarium, provided it is used to treat appropriate disorders under appropriate conditions. When electroconvulsive therapy is used to treat major depression, it results in more rapid improvement and shorter hospital stays than tricyclic antidepressant therapy (Markowitz, Brown, & Sweeney, 1987). In the suicidal elderly patient with melancholia or psychotic depression, electroconvulsive therapy may well be the treatment of choice. For older patients, as for younger patients, unilateral electroconvulsive therapy with brief pulse wave stimulus is the preferred means, since unilateral electroconvulsive therapy tends to produce substantially less cognitive memory impairment than bilateral electroconclusive therapy (Weiner, 1979).

Electroconvulsive therapy is generally regarded as a safe treatment in older patients. Data from younger patients attest to electroconvulsive therapy's safety in comparison to tricyclic antidepressant, although similar studies have not been done in the elderly. Despite its relative safety, complications from electroconvulsive therapy in older patients can be significant, particularly if patients are medically ill or if they continue to take psychotropic medications during this treatment. In one study, complications were particularly frequent in the oldest-old and included such conditions as high blood pressure following stimulation, hypotension, persistent tachycardia, falls, and pneumonia (Burke, Rubin, Zorumski, & Wetzel, 1987). Thus older patients must be carefully assessed for the appropriateness of electroconvulsive therapy to ensure that the possibility of complications are minimized. Appropriate steps to minimize risk would be discontinuing all psychotropic medications prior to treatment, although occasionally in a severely delusional or agitated patient this is not possible; employing pre-electroconvulsive therapy evaluation (EEG or CT scan of head, CBC, SMA 18, urinalysis, and spinal films); and carefully weighing the potential anesthesia risk by using a

Table 15
Psychopharmacotherapy for Depression in Elderly Patients*

Drugs	Dosage	Side Effects
Tricyclics		
Imipramine (Tofranil)	25 mg/ 24 hr, increased to 100 mg/24 hr third week; maximum of 250 mg/24 hr possible, if no side effect	Blurred vision, glaucoma, dry mouth, urinary retention and delayed micturition Constipation, edema Dizziness, tachycardia, palpitations
Desipramine (Pertofran) Amitriptyline (Elavil) Doxepin (Sinequan)		
Nortriptyline (Aventyl)	10 mg/24 hr increased to 50 mg/ 24 hr episodes	Arrhythmias, myocardial infarctions, hypotensive Parkinsonian tremors numbness, ataxia Central anticholinergic syndrome
MAO inhibitors		
Phenetizine (Nardil)	Start at 15 mg/24 hr; increase to maximum of 60 mg/24 hr	Hypertensive crisis can be precipitated by interaction with other drugs Blurred vision, chills, gastrointestinal complaints, weakness, agitation Mania, tachycardia

Table 15 (Continued)

Drugs	Dosage	Side Effects
Lithium		
Lithium Carbonate (Lithonate)	Start at 300 mg/24 hr; increase slowly and monitor blood levels regularly. Levels of 0.6 mEq/L may be adequate. Levels should not exceed 1.5 mEq/L.	Anorexia, nausea, diarrhea, excessive thirst and urination Ataxia, hyperreflexia, muscle spasms, confusion, coma
Minor Tranquilizer		
Diazepam (Valium)	Start at 2 mg/24 hr, increase gradually with careful monitoring	Drowsiness, aggravation of glaucoma, blurred vision, paradoxical excitement Possible habituation following prolonged administration
Stimulants		
d = Amphetamine	2.5–5 mg twice a day; short-term use only	Tachycardia, hypertension, insomnia, jitters Dependence and withdrawal syndrome with regular use

*From B. S. Kopell, Management of depression in the elderly, in R. E. Ebaugh (Ed.), Management of common problems in geriatric medicine, (date), pp. 129–130.

standard risk measurement. In all cases, the attending psychiatrist should seek anesthesiology consultation, monitor the patient's EEG, EKG, and blood pressure during the treatment, and provide post-treatment observation to protect the patient against problems associated with delirium, falls, or aspiration. Careful, systematic assessment of the patient's mental and physical status during the course of electroconvulsive therapy is required so that treatment can be stopped if problems begin to emerge.

PSYCHOTHERAPY

Several forms of psychotherapy may be used with the depressed elderly, including insight-oriented, behavioral, cognitive, supportive, and milieu therapy. "Psychodynamic therapies are based on theories of personality that emphasize the dynamic interplay of the physiological substrate of the individual and the social forces of the environment as mediated by inner psychological states" (Storandt 1983, p. 19). The theories of S. Freud (1955) and C. Jung (1934) form the basis for most psychodynamic psychotherapy. They focus on the importance of symbols, images, and dreams and emphasize the role of unconscious feelings, impulses, and emotions in determining unconscious feelings, moods, and behaviors. The major goal of psychodynamic psychotherapy is to facilitate the patient's development of insight into disturbing behaviors and feelings (Gotestam, 1980). The emphasis in psychotherapy is on experiencing, as opposed to understanding in an intellectual sense. Psychotherapy is "therapeutic communication." The therapist must determine why the patient is thinking, feeling, and acting in a particular manner at a particular time (Verwoerdt, 1976). Psychoanalytic theory assumes pathology is rooted in unconscious past conflict and insight can be developed via review and interpretation of individual history (Keller & Bromley, 1989).

E. Bibring (1954), outlines five major uses of psychotherapy: (1) suggestion, in the form of hypnosis or some form of inducing ideas, impulses, and emotions, to facilitate emotional expression, gain insight, or help the patient face reality and deal with problems; (2) abreaction, or emotional discharge of dammed up tensions through emotionally charged verbalizations; (3) manipulation of the patients's ideas and emotions through mobilizing various emotional systems; (4) clarification of issues and emotions; and (5) insight, or conscious understanding and interpretation of unconscious material, thoughts, and emotions. A. Verwoerdt (1976) describes the following techniques of psychotherapy: nonverbal communication, empathy, optimistic attitude, hope and reassurance, preservation of dignity, and management of maladaptive defenses. The most common psychotherapeutic technique used by psychiatrists is psychodynamic psychotherapy. The same general principles and goals guide both individual and group psychotherapy.

Freud (1955), posited that the elderly would be poor candidates for psy-

chotherapy; however, recent clinical and empirical observations challenge
Freud's position (Zung, 1980; Levy, Derogatis, Gallagher & Gatz, 1980;
Brink, 1979; Gallagher, 1981; Gallagher & Thompson, 1982). The first published report on psychotherapy with the elderly was by J. Martin and D.
De Gruchy in 1930. However, as M. Lawton (1976) points out, there is very
limited literature on the effects of psychotherapy on depressed elderly. S.
Zarit (1980), in response to Freud's assertion that the old are too rigid in
their defenses for psychotherapy to be effective, asks how one can remain
rigid and adapt to the biological and social changes of aging. He further
suggests that the approach to psychotherapy is different when one treats the
elderly. As we age, we have more losses with different implications. The
loss is permanent. Treatment should focus on positive foci such as listening
supportively, learning the meaning of the loss to the individual, helping the
client regain some sense of mastery over his life, learning new behavioral
skills, asserting coping skills that may have been important in the past,
gaining a sense of control through planning and settling any unfinished
business.

Group psychotherapy may also be a very helpful treatment for elderly
patients. Group psychotherapy was first successfully used with the elderly
in 1950 by A. Silver. K. Wolff (1963), A. Stein (1959), and others have
reported favorable changes using group psychotherapy with older depressed
patients.

In this section the focus is on individual psychotherapy. Psychiatric problems occur when the equilibrium between stress and intolerance becomes
unbalanced and reaches or exceeds the ability to cope. The goal is to become
integrated and comfortable in surroundings and recognize that problems are
not due to aging but are caused by physical or situational change (Keller &
Bromley, 1989). For a detailed discussion and review of the literature on
several types of psychotherapy conducted with depressed elderly individuals, the reader is referred to a recent chapter "Behavioral and Dynamic
Psychotherapy with the Elderly" (Gotestam, 1980).

Insight-Oriented

Insight-oriented psychotherapy, influenced by the work of Freud, is based
largely on psychoanalytic principles and involves the therapist heavily in
treatment. The therapist facilitates and interprets feelings and behavior.
Early memories are reactivated to mobilize feelings associated with them.
The expression of fears, anxieties, doubt, guilt, and other emotions is encouraged by the therapist. Unconscious and suppressed emotions are
brought to the level of consciousness so that they may be recognized, faced,
and dealt with in a positive way. Insight is achieved when the patient can
recognize the nature and cause of his or her particular problem or maladaptive defense(s) and can recognize reasonable solutions or alternative re-

sponses that are more adaptive. Insight-oriented psychotherapy aims to strengthen the ego and reduce anxiety and depression. According to Verwoerdt (1976), "through intrapsychic alterations the ego emerges as a more mature and effective mental agency" (p. 136).

The use of insight therapy with individuals over 45 was discouraged by Freud, who indicated that "after 45 the patient's character would be too inflexible to make the necessary personality changes which were brought about by increased insight" (Gotestam 1980, p. 786). Brief psychodynamic therapy in which rigidity and increased dependency of the elderly are used as therapeutic tools was developed by A. Goldfarb (Goldfarb & Turner, 1953). This technique, in which the therapist takes on the role of parent, allows the client to attain gratification for emotional needs and to build high self-esteem. The therapist, seen as a "protective parent," becomes a "significant other" who can provide help and hope to the dependent elder. The older client is allowed to "defeat" the parent which is a way to help him or her gain strength. Other psychotherapists have also reported success with this approach (Godbole & Verinis, 1974; Rechtschatten, 1959). Insight-oriented psychotherapy requires the therapist to take an active role in directing therapy, providing guidance and reassurance, and actively intervening in the patient's life.

Behavioral

Behavioral psychotherapy, guided by the principles of classical conditioning (Pavlov, 1955) and operant conditioning (Skinner, 1936), has also been used effectively to relieve late life depression. Behavioralists view depression and other mental health problems as learned behaviors. According to behavioralists, the focus of therapy should be on the particular overt problem behavior or thought pattern, not on the internal subjective experience for the client. Changing the principles by which behavior is learned can effectively change or eliminate the problem behavior or negative thought pattern (Beck, 1967). Focusing on overt behavior and thought processes, behavioral therapy uses relaxation, systemic desensitization, and reinforcement techniques (Keller & Bromley, 1989).

Classical conditioning is "the learning process by which neutral cues (or stimuli) become associated with emotional reactions" (Edinberg 1985, p. 170). Two classical conditioning techniques, systematic desensitization and relaxation, are frequently used with elderly persons to diminish anxiety. The older adult is taught how to relax. Patients can be taught to associate the feelings of being relaxed with cue words such as "calm." Elderly patients can also be taught "successive relaxation techniques" (Jacobson, 1938), in which various muscle groups in the body are systematically relaxed.

Operant conditioning techniques, also referred to as behavior modification, are based on the premise that "maladaptive behaviors can be altered by manipulating stimulus variables or reinforcements" (Whanger, 1980, p. 457). Use of positive or negative reinforcement, extinction procedures, and token economies have all proven effective with older adults. Reduced depression in elderly subjects treated with behavioral psychotherapy has been reported by D. Gallagher and L. Thompson (1982). Gallagher (1981) reports reduced depression in elderly clients after they received supportive group psychotherapy and behavioral therapy. B. Mishara and R. Kastenbaum (1973) found that living in a token economy, in that positive behaviors are rewarded by tokens which may be exchanged for food, cigarettes, and privileges, and negative behaviors are discouraged through loss of tokens, significantly reduced the incidence of suicidal behavior among hospitalized elderly veterans.

Cognitive

One of the most popular current psychotherapies, cognitive or cognitive-behavioral therapy, is grounded in the theories and concepts proposed by Aaron Beck and his colleagues at the University of Pennsylvania. Beck (1967) proposed cognitive theory to explain the etiology of reactive depression. According to A. Beck, "central to the pathogenesis of depression are the individual's attitudes toward self, the social environment, and the future" (Blazer 1982, p. 80). Individuals who have negative views about themselves and the world around them and who regard themselves as unworthy, undesirable, or useless are especially vulnerable to reactive depression when confronted with stressful events or life crises. Beck also suggests that "the affective response is determined by the way an individual structures his experiences. Thus, if an individual's conceptualization of the situation has an unpleasant context, he will experience a corresponding unpleasant affective response" (Blazer, 1982, p. 81).

Beck uses three concepts to explain depression: negative "cognitive triad," which encompasses negative perceptions of self, present situations, and the future; underlying beliefs or "schemas" developed out of past experiences, which determine how an individual interprets situations and events; and "cognitive errors" in logic and information processing that support negative (depressive) self-concepts. Cognitive theory posits that feelings of hopelessness and worthlessness lead to depression.

Cognitive therapy also emphasizes patients' internal experiences, thoughts, wishes, and attitudes, rather than focusing exclusively on overt behavior. The aim of cognitive therapy for elderly patients is to change negative thoughts or cognitions and distorted perceptions that reinforce negative self-concepts and lead to depressed feelings. Cognitive restructuring of events and situations, in which more positive interpretations are substituted, is a major goal of this therapy.

Cognitive therapy focuses on overt behavior and thought processes (Keller

& Bromley, 1989) and involves uncovering and identifying negative thoughts by: (1) teaching patients how to identify negative thoughts and self-statements that lead to depression, (2) instructing patients how to examine the evidence for or against such thoughts, and (3) changing patients' attitudes and negative world views so they begin to develop more reality-oriented and adaptive interpretations of their worlds. The focus is on present-day problems and the therapist takes an active role in teaching the patient problem solving and coping skills. Feelings of mastery and pleasurable experiences are encouraged. The therapist also helps patients identify underlying negative themes that lead to negative cognitions. In elderly patients several such themes may be present such as "I'm too old to change," "Old people are not good for anything," and "If only some situation would change, I would not be depressed."

The effectiveness of cognitive therapy has been demonstrated in reducing late life depression. In one study of thirty patients age 55 and over, who were diagnosed as suffering from major depressive disorders (Gallagher & Thompson, 1983), subjects were divided into three treatment groups: those in one group received cognitive therapy, patients in the second group received behavioral therapy, and the third group of patients were treated with brief psychotherapy. The greatest improvements in depression, (assessed using four different scales designed to measure depression) were found in those subjects receiving behavioral and cognitive psychotherapy. Other researchers have similarly reported on the effectiveness of cognitive therapy in reducing depression in elderly clients (Haley, 1983; Steuer, 1982). All of these therapies may be effective in reducing suicidal feelings, impulses, and behaviors in older patients.

REMINISCENCE AND LIFE REVIEW THERAPY

Reminiscence may be defined as "the act, process, or fact of recalling or remembering the past" (Butler, 1964, p. 266). When reminiscing, one remembers past life events, experiences, people, and places. The activity can be mental or verbal. One may recall thoughts or feelings, even smells or sounds, connected with the past. Thoughts of the past may emerge as "stray, seemingly insignificant thoughts about self, or may become continuous (Butler, 1971, p. 49). Reminiscence may produce nostalgia, pleasure, an idealized past, or mild regret. On the other hand, it may lead to anxiety, guilt, depression, or despair. "Memory pains us and shames us and entertains us and serves the sense of self and its continuity" (Butler, 1964, p. 266).

Life review encompasses reminiscence, but includes much more. In a life review one does not just remember the past; one analyzes, evaluates, restructures, and reconstructs past life events and experiences and their meanings to arrive at a better understanding of one's life. The process puts the past into coherent order and proper perspective in light of present values, attitudes, and life experiences. The life review, more common in late life but apparent in all life stages, is thus an active process of personality reorganization. J. Birren (1964) describes it as "setting one's house in order." During life review, the elderly "integrate life as it has been lived in relation to how it might have been lived" (p. 275). Older adults who have not completed some of the "unfinished business" from their past may suffer from feelings of guilt, remorse, and turmoil. All of these feelings may contribute to depression in late life.

Therapeutic Values

Freud referred to neurotic illnesses as "diseases of reminiscence" (Butler, 1963, p. 523), suggesting the therapeutic value of remembering and the psychopathology of repressing, forgetting, or removing memories from conscious awareness. In the same vein, R. Butler (1963) noted that "recovering important memories is a basic ingredient of the curative process in psychoanalysis and necessary for change" (p. 525). In this view, reminiscence and life review are a natural form of personal psychotherapy. Life review helps to reduce psychic tension and restore psychic balance and is necessary to personality development (Jung, 1934). To arrive at a sense of integrity over despair, older individuals must review their lives and come to the conclusion that their lives were inevitable, meaningful, and worthy of having been lived (Erikson, 1950). If they accept their lives and feel they have done all they could and they do not wish anything different, then they will arrive at a sense of integrity over despair and gain wisdom.

Empirical findings confirm the therapeutic value of reminiscence and life review for older adults suffering from depression. Based on clinical data collected from a large-scale study of human aging conducted at the National Institute of Mental Health from 1955 to 1961, Butler (1980-1981) reported several examples of positive personal change in subjects after they engaged in reminiscence and life review. The therapeutic benefits ranged from a better ability to cope with aging and death to greatly improved relations with family members. From his clinical observations, Butler concluded that "people get much out of the opportunity to express thoughts and feelings to someone willing to listen" (Butler, 1980-1981, p. 37). In his study of twenty-four white males aged 65 and over, C. Lewis (1971) found a positive relationship between reminiscence and maintaining a positive self-concept, especially in times of pervasive stress. He found reminiscence helps one get through various life crises, particularly the loss of a spouse. In a more recent study of ninety-one subjects between the ages of 58 and 98, M. Romaniuk and J. Romaniuk (1981) concluded that "interpersonal reminiscence appears to be a pleasant activity and is essentially a method of bolstering self-esteem during the course of social interactions. Apparently, self-esteem is maintained through recollections which demonstrate current personal worth and utility or past worth" (p. 68).

Life Review Therapy

Life review therapy is defined by Lewis and Butler (1974) as a psychoanalytically oriented action process in which the therapist does not initiate a process but rather "taps into an already ongoing self-analysis and participates in it with the older person" (p. 166). The technique is an effective way for older adults to do the necessary developmental work of late life, primarily reaching a sense of integrity over despair and coming to terms with death. Life review therapy helps individuals put their pasts into perspective in the light of present events, values, and attitudes. It allows them to experience and acknowledge important emotions and to integrate them into the self, which is essential for healthy functioning. The intervention strategy can be used to help reduce loneliness, enhance self-esteem, increase morale, and extend cognitive functioning (Reedy & Birren, 1980). By helping elderly individuals bring past events back to mind and to re-live, re-experience, and savor them, therapists can aid them in identifying and mitigating real guilt, exorcising problematic childhood identifications, resolving intense earlier conflicts, reconciling family relationships, and transmitting knowledge values to others (Pincus, 1970). In addition, such therapy can help older persons integrate the aging experience into the entire life process and see death as a natural part of life.

By carefully listening as older persons relate and reconstruct the past by telling their life stories, the therapist can begin to see and understand critical issues and unresolved conflicts, feelings of guilt over past mistakes or wrongdoings, concerns over inability as a parent, and other fears, anxieties, and doubts. The degree of emotion with which certain past events or people are recalled provides a clue as to the nature and intensity of feelings about them. Nuances and slips of the tongue can provide clues about self-image, the amount of stress the patient is experiencing, and the types of relationship the person hopes to foster. Listening intently to patients also provides the opportunity to form an interpersonal bond with them and to re-awaken their interests (Butler, 1961). Moreover, a sensitive listener can help elderly patients put past events in proper perspective and turn the life review into "a positive attempt to reconcile life, to confront real guilt, and to find meaning in their lives, especially in the presence of acceptance and support from others" (Lewis & Butler, 1974, p. 169).

There are three steps in life review therapy: recording of a detailed life history, careful observation, and systematic eliciting of memories. To elicit memories, individuals are encouraged to write or tape their autobiographies or detailed personal life histories. They are encouraged to focus on a particular person, life event, or period of significance. Life review therapy techniques include pilgrimages to important places from the past, reunions (church, class, and family), genealogy construction, and the use of memorabilia (scrapbooks, photo albums, and old letters). Life review therapy may be done in a group situation or on an individual level. It is particularly important that the therapist, who chooses life review therapy as an intervention technique to help the troubled older person, be an effective listener and be able to use the skills of exploration, focusing, and probing to help individuals order their pasts as coherent wholes (Pincus, 1970). The objective should be to help the depressed older person to achieve a sense of meaning and to maintain integrity over despair, thereby decreasing the risk of suicide. By reducing feelings of despair, the risk of suicide is greatly reduced also.

CREATIVE ARTS THERAPY

The use of dance, song, and visual arts in religious and magical ways to cure physical or emotional ills dates back to antiquity. Aristotle recognized the value of dramatic play for relaxation "as a medicine" and noted the value of tragedy as catharsis because it allows for the "purgation of emotion" (Courtney, 1968, p. 10), and Greek tragedies encouraged the expression of such emotions as pity and fear as the actors identified with characters.

During the twentieth century there has been dramatic growth in and acceptance of the use of creative arts or expressive therapy with the sick. Creative arts therapies are closely allied with and have been greatly influenced by psychoanalysis, humanistic psychoanalysis, and humanistic psychology. The therapeutic value of the drawing or painting of dreams, which are experienced as visual images and difficult to express in words, was recognized by both Freud (1955) and Jung (1964).

The arts allow for creative expression, development of personal insight, and self-awareness. Similarly, spontaneity, flexibility, and originality resulting from the creative process are encouraged through the use of creative therapies. Art, whether in music, visual media, drama, or dance, is naturally therapeutic. Often, the creative process enables persons to uncover aspects of the self that are blocked from conscious sight. The arts provide a means of expanding the consciousness, of naturally becoming more aware of the self, particularly of the connection between mind and body. It forces persons to become more in personal tune with their senses (sight, hearing, and touch) and bodies. The arts also provide a means to achieve identity. The search for identity, the sense of who one is and where one stands, has always led to music, art, and drama.

Visual Arts

Many therapists have effectively used the visual arts as therapy with the elderly (Dwedney, 1977; Landgarten, 1981; Weiss, 1984). Art therapy has proven to be particularly effective for persons experiencing chronic pain. The expression of pain and the accompanying feelings of anger, rage, guilt, or sorrow through artwork permits catharsis and leads to successful management of the feeling (Landgarten, 1981). Art work is one method of working through feelings of depression for older adults. Art work expressing feelings can be shared and discussed with positive results. Individuals can obtain therapeutic benefits by examining their own feelings and emotions as expressed in concrete form in art works.

Music Therapy

Practitioners have used music therapy effectively with the elderly. Music therapy has been used with older participants as an outlet for creative expression, as a vehicle to invoke powerful emotions, and as an aid in grief work and in dealing with the experience of death and dying. Music encourages group participation. Alleviation of feelings of loneliness, hopelessness, depression, and despair in elderly participants has been reported (Bright, 1985; Kartman, 1980).

Music therapy has been used to treat a number of different problems of elderly clients. It has been used effectively with aging residents in long-term care facilities to help alleviate depression and stress (Kartman, 1980). Exposure to player piano music resulted in improved life satisfaction and feelings of well-being for elderly subjects (Olson, 1984). The role of music in combating the loneliness, isolation, and depression of older people has been emphasized by R. Bright (1985). Music is useful in psychotherapy with the old. Through its strong powers of association and memory-evoking properties, music can help to bring past and present feelings and emotions to the surface so they can be expressed and therapeutically explored.

Psychodrama

As a therapeutic technique, creative dramatics has its roots in dramatic play and is closely related to psychodrama. Psychodrama grew out of Jacob Moreno's (1934) experience with Viennese children at play. Derived from the Greek terms *psyche*, meaning "mind or soul," and *dramein*, meaning "to do or to act," psychodrama refers to the doing or acting of thoughts and emotions through speech, gestures, and movement (Duke, 1974). In psychodrama individuals play roles and create parts; the emphasis is on spontaneity, creativity, action, process, self-disclosure, risk taking, and the here and now. The individual acts out unconscious thoughts, feelings, and impulses to recapitulate unsolved problems and experience catharsis. The group drama encourages empathy as the players identify with one another. Like psychodrama, creative expression of thoughts, feelings and emotions are encouraged through verbal and non-verbal means of communication.

In the last decade, creative dramatics has been used increasingly with older persons. From data she collected on the effects of drama on the elderly, P. Gray (1974) cites the following as major benefits: opportunity to be of service to others, increased self-confidence resulting from successful memorization and good performance, communication and social interaction skills developed through the group experience, and the emotional outlet provided by the experience. One study demonstrated that elderly individuals who participate in the creative drama experience begin to communicate and see themselves as useful again; life takes on new meaning (Burger, 1980). Based on her study, B. Davis (1985) reports that "drama helps older adults integrate their thoughts, words, actions, and emotions through original improvisation in which they draw on their life experience" (p. 315). Based on analysis of quantitive and qualitative data, P. Clark and N. Osgood (1985) concluded that participation in applied theater decreases loneliness and increases life satisfaction. Those who engage in the drama activities see themselves as younger than those who do not.

Dance

Dance as a form of therapeutic intervention has its basis in the development of modern dance and has been used successfully with older adults. S. Zandt and L. Lorenzen (1985), who have used dance with seniors, found that dance helped people relax, reduced stress, and provided tranquility. Older dancers said they felt less lonely, less depressed, and more self-assured as a result of their dancing. E. Garnet (1974) used movement sequences that employ rhythmic use of swings, twists, stretches, pulls, and pushes to meet physical needs and stimulate somatic and psychological feelings of comfort, ease, and humor in elderly subjects. I. Fersh (1981) concludes that dance/movement therapy with elderly clients can be an enlightening experience that can inspire the therapist and clients to face life and death with love and energy.

Therapeutic Values of Creative Arts Therapy

Creative arts offer the older adult choice. In creative art activities the individual chooses the medium (clay, wood, and fibers), chooses the colors and textures, chooses what to make and how to make it. The art object is personalized. Dance and drama activities also offer opportunities for individual expression. The individual decides what to say or do and in what manner. Choice builds pride, confidence, self-esteem, and a sense of control to offset the negative psychological effects of loss. Through participating in creative activities older adults come to view themselves as active, vital, useful human beings.

The arts are inspirational, infusing the older adult with spirit and zest for life and hope for the future. Creative therapy is a valuable means of releasing fear and doubt, guilt and grief, and decreasing hopelessness, emotions that plague many potentially suicidal elderly individuals. Creative therapy provides a positive experience of participation in a social group, with accompanying feelings of acceptance and belonging, self-esteem and self-concept, and personal competence, mastery, and accomplishment. As such, the arts represent a major technique for reducing suicidal risk in older adults.

SUPPORT GROUP THERAPY

Support group therapy is one therapy that can effectively reduce depression and suicidal behavior in older individuals. Social support encompasses interpersonal communication and interaction, protective feedback, love and understanding, caring and concern, affection and companionship, financial assistance, respect, and acceptance. Social support is usually provided by family members and kin, close friends, and neighbors. Such support can also be provided by a support group composed of individuals who are facing the same problems and have the same needs and concerns. Blazer (1980) notes that "decreased social support may be of more importance in the increased prevalence of depression in late life than personality style, and intrapsychic conflicts, or genetic predisposition" (p. 261).

Therapeutic Values of Support Groups

The principle of mutual aid or joint struggle against common problems underlies the development of mutual help or support groups. Support groups are patterned after the family or small community and are expressive in nature. They offer members understanding and acceptance as unique personalities with both good and bad qualities, with both strengths and weaknesses. They offer a place where emotions can be freely expressed and where recognition, status, and security are offered. Most support groups are established by and for individuals who are stigmatized, either for a short time or permanently (Traunstein & Steinman, 1973). For example, widows may feel they are "misfits," "marginals," or "fifth wheels" in a couple-oriented society. The very word *widow* has negative connotations and carries a stigma for many women. In a support group, these individuals can find acceptance among others suffering the same plight. When everyone shares the same stigma, one finds acceptance, and feelings of isolation and marginality are reduced.

In a support group, the members (1) learn by their participation in developing and evaluating a social microcosm, (2) learn by giving and receiving feedback, (3) have the unique opportunity to be both helpers and helpees, and (4) learn by the consensual validation of multiple perspectives (Bednar & Kaul, 1978). As noted by I. Yalom (1970) and I. Burnside (1988), the group offers opportunities for people to confront feelings of alienation by providing for free expression of feelings and experiences with group members who are "in the same boat." Participating in a support group can instill hope in members who see others successfully coping with similar problems or life experiences (Yalom, 1970).

Types of Support Groups

In the last decade the popularity of support groups has greatly increased. Currently, support groups exist for widows and widowers, Alzheimer's victims and their family caregivers, cancer patients, heart patients, persons with arthritis, and depressed elderly dealing with the problems of grief, loss, and aging. Those working with support groups have noted the many positive effects of such groups on the elderly. Burnside (1976; 1988) has described her success with groups of grievers, indicating that such groups help the members by facilitating adjustment to the loss of a spouse and preventing subsequent problems.

B. Petty, T. Moeller, and R. Campbell (1976) organized support groups for elderly persons with arthritis. Most of the individuals were experiencing moderate depression in adjusting to the aging process. Participation in a support group decreased feelings of loneliness, depression, and unhappiness, increased knowledge of physical functioning, and resulted in better communication with family and friends and a desire to be more actively involved in life. The members also came to feel that their frustration and problems were "normal" and a part of aging. They made new friends and learned how to use community resources more effectively through their participation in the group. S. Hiltz (1977), who started a program for widows in 1970, reported positive effects. Weekly discussion groups were successful in alleviating feelings of loneliness and providing assurance that the widow was not unique, that others faced similar challenges. Members of the groups cited emotional support as the major benefit obtained from participation. Someone to listen and give sympathy were the benefits most valued by the widows.

Older adults in the community and in institutions can profit from involvement in support groups of all types. Clinicians working with depressed residents in institutions will find support groups a valuable adjunct to therapy. The recently bereaved, those suffering from a particular physical condition such as arthritis, those dealing with the loss of physical function or mobility, and residents who have recently moved in and are experiencing difficulty adjusting to their new environment could all benefit from participation in a support group.

Characteristics of support groups are a consideration. Based on his experience with groups, Lowy (1967) cited three important factors in effective group work: authority, structure and language, and sharing common symbols and meanings. The group's structure must provide a basis for relating and accomplishing group goals. A format or standard procedure and use of a common language will serve to provide this structure. By including authorative research and sharing of emotions and feelings, the group becomes a support system that provides new ways of thinking about issues.

PSYCHOSOCIAL NURSING INTERVENTIONS

Loneliness is a universal phenomenon. More than 80 percent of the institutionalized elderly are likely to show symptoms of isolation and loneliness (Aguilar, 1978). Depression is also prevalent among older residents of long-term care facilities. Residents of long-term care institutions often express feelings of loneliness and emptiness, loss of self-esteem and diminished morale, and loss of control during depressive episodes. Thus it is of utmost importance that morale, self-esteem, and a sense of control in older adults be preserved.

Interpersonal strategies to alleviate depressive symptomotology are effective interventions with older clients. Openness, acceptance, trust, honesty, and respect characterize role behaviors of participants in therapeutic interactions (Barrell & Wyman, 1989). The key to achieving success or failure is the quality of the relationship between health care providers and older persons. Nurses are instrumental in all types of group work in long-term care facilities. Communicating through one-on-one interaction and touch can combat loneliness, increase self-esteem and control, and reduce depression in older adults. These interventions will be discussed in the following paragraphs.

Group Work

The role of nursing in group work with the elderly has been well documented by Burnside (1973, 1976, 1980), P. Ebersole (1976), and others in the discipline of nursing. Group therapy, as Ebersole (1976) points out, is the treatment of choice in many cases, and "the testing of the efficacy of working with groups of elders is left for the most part to nurses" (p. 184). Success in group work can be measured in part by decreased interpersonal friction, personal isolation, and a noticeable change in affect (Ebersole, 1976, p. 184). Interventions such as counseling, group activities, and physiologic assessment are well within the skill repertoire of the clinician and advanced practitioner in gerontologic nursing.

Nurses in long-term care play a pivotal role in forming and leading support and reminiscence groups. Group work requires well-developed interpersonal skills necessary for supportive listening, encouraging self-expression, facilitating interaction among members, and motivating staff to support group development. Nurses working in long-term care settings can cultivate these skills.

Nursing home staff can support group work by helping elder group members select clothing, providing ample time to prepare for attending the group, demonstrating interest, listening, assuring the elder's attendance at groups, rewarding even small attempts to change behavior or complete tasks (Burnside, 1976), and treating older adults with positive personal regard.

One-to-One Interaction

One effective nursing intervention is the development of one-to-one relationships, interpersonal relationships that promote nurturance, warmth, and feedback and provide meaningful relationships with the elderly. Therapeutic interventions by staff include taking time to talk with residents, expressing interest in their activities, and orientating them to reality. Facilitating self-help, establishing and maintaining scheduled activities, assisting residents to keep a daily schedule, offering choices, providing clear feedback, providing privacy when giving personal care, and listening are all integral to maintaining the relationship. Aguilar's (1978) study of loneliness in a group of nursing home residents found that nursing intervention in the forms mentioned above reduced loneliness significantly.

Touch

Touch can be a powerful nursing intervention with lonely individuals. The need for touch never grows old for persons who are lonely, who reach out for human contact, who experience increased stress and illness, and who seek caring and comfort. Touch is therapeutic because of its healing nature, and, therefore, it is a necessary ingredient in the interpersonal relationships (Burnside, 1980). Touch facilitates non-verbal communication, caring and warmth, and recognizes the wholeness of the individual (Bahr & Gress, 1984; Burnside, 1976). It also provides tactile stimulation necessary to reduce sensory deprivation (Wolanin & Phillips, 1981) and can increase feelings of well-being. Family members and others concerned about older depressed individuals can also use touch in a therapeutic way.

Affective touch, as defined by Burnside (1980, p. 504), expresses caring, concern, affection or control. With the elderly in long-term care facilities, use of touch with each other frequently leads to smiling, laughing, and other positive demonstrations of feelings. This, in turn, increases contact with their surroundings, and their interactions (Davis, 1984, p. 154). As A. Wolanin and L. Phillips (1981) point out, "It is through the senses that one perceives their world, and by using this information, people are able to exist in their environment" (p. 200).

Touching is helpful in communicating a sense of love and concern, substituting for the missing closeness of family and friends no longer available, and reaching for human contact. While it can be an uncomfortable encounter for some health professionals, the experience of sharing touching moments with others has meaning for elder persons. Each nursing intervention with an older adult can be planned to include touch. Nurses, other care providers, and family members should be sensitive to non-verbal requests for touching, e.g., back scratching, assistance with dressing, reaching out, and hand holding. These experiences are mutually satisfying for staff and residents. It is important to the relationship that care providers examine their own attitudes and feelings with regard to the use of touch and closeness with others, both emotionally and physically, in the process of developing a skillful and effective use of touch (Langland & Panicucci, 1982, p. 155). As Bob Hope's famous one-liner expresses it, "People who don't cuddle, curdle."

Depression in the elderly is eminently treatable. Pharmacologic intervention and electroconvulsive therapy are available to medical practitioners treating older depressed adults. In addition to these medical treatments, a wide range of psychosocial therapies are effective in treating depressed elders. Creative arts therapy, reminiscence therapy, support group therapy, psychotherapy, and other psychosocial therapies should all be introduced into the institutional setting.

Nursing staff provide the majority of care to residents of long-term care facilities. It is crucial that they are responsive to the emotional needs of residents. One-to-one nursing, effective touch, and other nursing interventions can help reduce residents' feelings of loneliness, emptiness, and meaninglessness and enhance their daily lives. All of the therapeutic modalities discussed can be employed by staff to reduce depression and prevent suicide among residents.

8

INSTITUTIONAL CHANGES AND PREVENTION OF ELDERLY SUICIDE

Suicides among the aging population are likely to be reduced by accurate diagnosis and treatment of depression; early detection and treatment of physical illness and health problems; increased involvement with family, friends, and others; increased involvement in social activities; and greater attention to the needs and problems occasioned by retirement, bereavement, and other life changes accompanying life patterns and the aging process. In addition to these measures, specific steps may be taken to improve the quality of staff working with institutionalized residents, and to enhance the institutional environment. The treatment of depression was discussed in a previous chapter. This chapter focuses on environmental manipulation and staff issues relevant to suicide prevention in long-term care facilities.

ENVIRONMENTAL MANIPULATION

B. Mishara and R. Kastenbaum (1973) examined the impact of a changed environment on the intentional suicidal behavior of forty residents on a medical unit of a large state hospital to learn whether enriching an environment would alter suicidal behavior. Subjects were divided into three groups: *persons living in a token economy* in which desirable behaviors were rewarded by tokens that could be exchanged for goods, i.e., confections and privileges and permission to leave the unit, whereas undesirable behaviors were not, and, in some cases tokens were recalled; *persons on an enrichment ward* that offered cheerful surroundings, more activities, increased social stimulation, personal food choices, and personal grooming; and *persons living on a traditional custodial care ward*. Trained observers systematically observed residents on each of the three wards over a period of nine months.

Mishara and Kastenbaum's Self-Injurious Behavior Scale was used to record resident behaviors during this time. Analyses of data showed that residents living on the token and enrichment wards engaged in significantly less suicidal behavior than did residents living on the traditional custodial wards. Mishara and Kastenbaum concluded that the nature and quality of the environment significantly influenced the level of suicidal behavior in persons residing on these units. Persons who live in "better environments" engage in less suicidal behavior.

To prevent suicide among elderly persons in institutions, facilities can restructure an environment conducive to meeting resident needs for freedom of choice and personal autonomy, privacy, and personal space. Other supportive and enriching approaches include appropriate and necessary architectural design and safety features; a well-trained and caring staff who recognize the uniqueness and individuality of each older adult as a human being; dignified and respectful treatment of residents not as objects or naughty children; and various recreational, social, and health-related services and resources.

IMPROVING THE PHYSICAL ENVIRONMENT

In the last twenty-five years, more attention has been directed toward the effect of the social environment on health and well-being, while attention to the physical environment has been slow. The physical environment, or the "built" environment as it is termed, encompasses space, objects, architecture, physical design features, and outdoor grounds. The physical environment is known to exert a powerful influence on social relationships, quality of daily life, and physical and mental health of residents. Several elements in the physical environment can be designed to enhance mental and physical functioning, independence, and autonomy. O. Lindsley (1964) and G. Beyer and F. Nierstrasz (1967) describe a "prosthetic environment" in which various physical aids are provided and accessible to increase mobility, and to prevent falls and injuries in the elderly. Other inducements include sensory and cognitive stimulation through the use of large mural calendars, communication (reality orientation) boards and reinforcement through verbal exchange, and a host of other creative and practical innovations. Prosthetic environments then, are designed to compensate for physical, cognitive, and sensory losses experienced by older persons, and to enhance physical and mental competence, individuality, independence, and self-esteem.

To compensate for visual impediments that accompany the aging process, lighting should be indirect and low glare; colors bright, cheerful, and varied from room to room and unit to unit to facilitate orientation; floors clean but without glossiness and glare. To compensate for auditory changes, background noise should be kept to a minimum, so that conversation can be clear, low-toned, and louder if necessary. Music, if pleasant to the ear, can also enhance the physical environment. Soothing music can calm an over-stimulated environment, while sprightly music can aid in stimulation. Physical aids such as signs, calendars, large-faced clocks, painted arrows, and communication boards make the environment more understandable and predictable and less confusing, while compensating for visual, auditory, and cognitive alterations, which characterize many elders in institutions. Comfort needs can be met by carefully controlling air temperature and quality, eliminating drafts, and providing comfortable furniture appropropriate to the physical needs of older persons, i.e., proper height, firmness, contour, and durability. Safety features include wheelchair ramps, pull bars (mandatory in most nursing homes), absence of steps, nonslip flooring, lowered, reachable cabinets, and other innovations. Finally, landscaping, gardening, fountains, lighting, pictures, art work, music and living plants can contribute significantly to the asthetic beauty of the physical environment so necessary to the promotion of normalcy. In designing such environments for the elderly, emphasis must be placed on the enhancement of personal freedom, independence, privacy, and autonomy of residents.

Providing Privacy

Privacy has been identified as a factor influencing behavior and attitudes of older individuals essential to positive self-regard, self-reflection, autonomy, and emotional release (Koncelik, 1976; Lawton, 1977; Windley & Scheidt, 1980; Tate, 1980; Louis, 1983). The following environmental manipulations can enhance privacy: creating physical boundaries to assist the resident in maintaining "private territory" (Johnson, 1979); using curtains between beds in multi-bedrooms, adding a dresser or chest from home, and assisting the resident in rearranging the room to facilitate privacy; arranging small dining areas limited to resident self-selection to reduce crowding and social overload; grouped furniture to encourage small group interaction, rather than large, often overstimulated placement; private bathrooms, or at the very least, privacy to meet basic physiologic needs, well-being, and social functioning; as state and federal regulations reflect—knock before entering a room, a common courtesy, asking permission to enter rather than intruding unwelcomed on the personal territory of the individual; and respecting the need for solitude and intimacy. Privacy can be further facilitated by designing private rooms, doors that lock, and small private areas. In a large facility, it is important to design spaces to create the sense of living in a smaller physical place, to reduce feelings of being overwhelmed, or without control, and to increase the feeling of privacy. Designing smaller facilities or modifying larger ones to accommodate the person's need for personal space, privacy, autonomy, and individuality could potentially reduce suicidal behavior.

The Value of Pets

Pets as companions add joy, fun, and zest to an otherwise lonely life, and a living object to lavish love and care on. Pets may be introduced into the environments of older people as a therapeutic aid in relieving depression, mood changes, and other feeling states. Pets are known to improve physical health, reduce loneliness, enhance socialization, and advance socioemotional well-being (S. Corson et al., 1977; Katchner, 1982; Mugford & M'Comisky, 1975; Cuszak & Smith, 1984; Frank, 1984). Emotionally and physically needy persons have benefited from the warmth, smell, and touch of animals. Persons who are unable to establish social relations with others are often able to give their attention to a pet (Frank, 1984). Many elders have grown up having pets of their own, and many others have sorrowfully left their pet behind when they entered the instuitutional setting. Pets have become "significant others" to some in the absence of human companionship.

Introducing a pet who is responsive and eager for attention may bridge the gap between contact with reality and withdrawal for older persons (Frank, 1984), which can serve as a catalyst to socializing (Davis, 1984) and, in turn, create adaptive and satisfying social interactions. A special rapport of unconditional acceptance exists between animals and the elderly. Both are in need of physical contact, and both are willing to respond to each other's need (Davis, 1984).

A live, domestic puppy visitation study was conducted by G. Francis, J. Turner, and S. Johnson (1985), with twenty-one elderly discharged chronic psychiatric patients in two adult homes. Pet therapy was found to be an inexpensive and simple intervention strategy that significantly improved life quality. The Humane Society, as a supplier of animals for use in pet therapy, can be a vital community resource. In a recent study by G. Francis and B. Munjas (1988), using a similar modality, plush animals were introduced to sixty-two male patients, 57-96 years of age, in a Veterans Administration Medical Center. The purpose of the study was to determine whether plush animals contributed to improved health, self-concept, life satisfaction, psychologic well-being, social functioning, and reduced depressive symptomology. Findings in this study were positively related. In her recent study of the impact of pets on elderly residents of nursing homes, H. Hendy (1987) discovered a positive change in resident alertness and smiling when pets were introduced into the facility.

STAFF DEVELOPMENT AND IMPROVEMENT

Improving the quality of life and care delivery through nursing personnel who work with residents of long-term care institutions is critical to suicide prevention among this aging population. Many older adults living in institutions have limited contact with family, neighbors, and friends; thus staff members provide the resident's major source of daily contact and support. Unfortunately staff in such facilities are often inadequately prepared to meet this important challenge and sufficiently disillusioned in their work situation to leave their jobs. These two factors alone threaten the quality and security of the environment.

In order that quality can be improved, some major changes are necessary in the nursing home industry. Macrolevel changes in staffing patterns, pay scales, working hours and conditions, and recruitment and retention of qualified personnel are needed. In addition, changes at the institutional level can be made, primarily in training and education, which focus specifically on the needs, concerns, and problems of aging and the clues and warning signs of depression and suicide in elders. This section discusses staff turnover and the need for education and staff development. Various strategies to improve the working conditions of personnel in long-term care facilities are suggested, reducing the threat of suicide in elders in long-term care institutions and promoting and increasing greater quality of care and life is the ultimate goal.

The Impact of Staff Turnover

Because of the incredibly poor working conditions in many long-term care facilities in the United States, nursing homes invariably have a very high attrition rate at all levels in the organizational structure. Annual turnover rates among all nursing home employees average well in excess of 100 percent and vary from state to state (Halbur, 1982; 1986). R. Stryker (1981) found rates in excess of 700 percent in her research on staff turnover in nursing homes. Statistical analysis of data obtained from the authors' nursing home study (Osgood & Brant, 1990) revealed that more than 50 percent of the responding facilities had turnover rates in excess of 50 percent.

In R. Wallace and T. Brubaker's (1984) study of turnover rates, nurses averaged 61 percent, while nurses aides averaged 105 percent. Staff turnover rates in nursing homes in excess of 50 percent become problematic for the facility, because regular worker effectiveness begins to disintegrate (Halbur, 1982; 1986; Stryker, 1981). High rates of turnover in institutions are thought to increase depression, disengagement, and disorientation among residents, which, in turn could produce isolation, hopelessness, and disappointment, all elements that place the resident at risk for suicide.

Staffing problems have caused much dissension among workers. Inequitable assignments, inadequate and unsafe coverage, inaccessibility to middle managers, use of temporary pools, and excessive overtime scheduling to provide necessary shift coverage are a few of the causes for disgruntlement. Why do employees terminate employment? Factors cited for staff turnover in nursing homes are many. Included here are resident characteristics, habits, likes and dislikes; physical and verbal abuse of employees and physical or cognitive impairment of the resident (Holder, 1987; Phillips, 1987); exploitation (Halbur, 1982); diminished morale (Erickson, 1987; Stryker, 1982); few, if any, monetary or reward incentives; and unsafe care practices especially toward the Medicaid patient (Halbur, 1982; Halbur & Fears, 1986; Ricker-Smith, 1982; Waxman, Carner, & Berkenstock, 1984). Because turnover affects quality of services and costs the company money (Swindeman, 1987), turnover costs, time loss, employee morale, and resident effects must also be considered in this discussion.

Turnover costs are administrative costs related to how limited resources are to be used to replace staff (Hanson, 1982). Time loss relates to the investment in acquiring, hiring, and orienting new staff, which impacts directly on staff time used to complete assignments, and time spent with residents (Halbur, 1982). Employee morale is an essential factor in providing quality of care. If morale is low, productivity is decreased and turnover of staff is increased (Erickson, 1987; Stryker, 1981). Negative effects on residents from staff turnover are numerous. The following may result from turnover: delivery of superficial and indifferent care by untrained or minimally trained new employees, loss of sustained relationships with staff "friends" (Stryker, 1981; Ricker-Smith, 1982), residing in a facility cited for poor to life-threatening care (Ricker-Smith, 1982, p. 1077), overprescribing and overuse of psychotrophic medication, or other forms of restraint (Waxman, Carner, & Berkenstock, 1984).

Macrolevel Changes in Nursing

Results of a recent survey conducted by the American Health Care Association (1988) highlight the problems of staff shortages and high staff turnover in the industry. According to this study the problems are a result of difficulty in recruiting new staff and problems in retention of existing staff members. Staff members surveyed reported low salaries as the primary reason for not accepting a position in long-term care or for leaving a position in the field. The next most often cited problems were problems with shift scheduling and other working conditions related to patients such as dealing with incontinence. Surveyors also concluded that benefits offered by long-term care facilities were not attractive enough to entice or retain nursing personnel in long-term care facilities. Some of these are concerns in the industry and in the nursing profession, which must be addressed at a broader level.

The Commission on Nursing appointed by the secretary of Health and Human Services (Ousley, 1989) has recently issued its recommendations to aid the long-term care industry in solving the nursing shortage and meeting the problem of high staff turnover (Ousley, 1989). The commission recommended the following: (1) equitable compensation of nurses and adequate funding to support quality nursing services; (2) adoption of innovative staffing patterns at the facility level to appropriately utilize different levels of education, competence, and experience among RNs as well as LPNs and ancillary nursing personnel; (3) encouragement of active involvement of nurses in decision-making bodies at national, state, and local levels, as well as increased decision-making powers at the individual institutional level; and (4) decreasing nonfinancial barriers to education.

The commission recommended that Congress and the Health Care Financing Administration (HCFA) direct the creation of a specific payment methodology to ensure equity between hospital nursing salaries and salaries for nurses working in long-term care facilities. The commission further recommended that Congress and HCFA expand their recognition of nurses' clinical decision making and patient care assessment by providing RNs the authority to certify and recertify Medicare and Medicaid nursing home beneficiaries.

In addition to macrolevel recommendations in the areas of salaries and decision making, the commission made recommendations directed toward the nursing profession and schools of nursing. Specifically, the commission encouraged schools of nursing to more actively pursue nontraditional students, LPNs, nurse assistants, low-income minorities, and others into their programs. They recommended flexible programs with evening and weekend courses and remedial courses. The commission also recognized the need for more specific geriatric and gerontologic components in curriculum of nursing schools and more on-site placements in nursing homes.

Improving Morale in the Work Environment

Recruitment and retention of staff is of major importance to the improvement of morale among employees, because the highest rate of turnover usually occurs in the first three months of employment. While recruitment efforts are the responsibility of the total facility, formal recruiting techniques rest with administrators and department heads. However, serving on a selection committee for screening qualified new applicants may be one way for staff to become team members. Participatory management incorporates the team concept where every employee is a coworker, and the concept is filtered from the top of the organizational structure to staff below. Serving on committees is one aspect of participatory management. Another committee might be the Policy Review Committee for Recruitment and Retention. Providing incentives is essential for meeting self-esteem and morale needs of nursing home personnel.

An approach to designing staffing patterns is to computerize them, rather than to use valuable nursing time in their tedious development. Staffing patterns can be designed to be cyclic, for example, or molded into whatever pattern works best to meet the staffing needs of the facility. Every employee must be committed to making it work and to carrying their own load. It is never fair for team members to purposefully relinquish their work responsibility to another without permission.

Economic benefits translate to pay scales and benefits accorded employees in long-term care institutions as governed by the administration or the corporation ownership. The old saying "You get what you pay for" certainly applies here. A pay rate of $7.65 per hour for a RN with a sound gerontologic background, compares very poorly with a pay rate of $20 to $30 or more per hour in an acute facility in today's economy. It is clear that to raise the morale of staff and discourage staff turnover, reimbursement for services at the prevailing rate in the surrounding area is a necessary first step.

Work hours and conditions should be understood on hiring and outlined in the job description. If participatory management is the model in use, changes are made by mutual agreement. Work schedules should be made with provisions for relief from high-stress work (Holder, 1987). Employees are within their right to ask for agreements in writing. Contracting may be the answer for the professional. Accommodations for break times, lunches free of desk work, and assurance to leave the shift at the appropriate time are not benefits, but expectations of the job. Adequate benefits include paid health insurance, sick leave, incremental vacations, and holidays. A positive incentive is tuition reimbursement for educational courses to upgrade knowledge and skill, because the facility directly benefits. Institutions should also consider offering free or low-priced day care for children of staff members. Lutheran Home had a very successful experience with day care on the premises. Staff benefited greatly and residents loved the contact with children.

As T. Swindeman (1987) suggests, administrators who want strong teams hire beyond the regulatory minimum for staffing and maintain consistent personnel policies, outlined and available for review. Salaries based on the prevailing market would include cash bonuses for those who exceed productivity goals. Encouraging regular employee feedback at departmental meetings and on opinion surveys as well as providing education through orientation, training, staff development, and continuing education produce an informed and effective participatory team.

Staff Education

Nurses throughout the country will assume a pivotal role in meeting the health care needs of a growing population of older adults, particularly the vulnerable old in nursing homes and related facilities. The building of a knowledge base related to physical, psychological, and social functioning, processes of normal aging, adaptations and alterations associated with the functional and spiritual parameters of aging is essential to gerontologic nursing practice. The challenge of gerontologic nursing is that it is both unique and complex. A continuous process of learning to creatively meet the health care needs of a growing population of older adults in the long-term care settings is long overdue and the need is acute (Brant, 1990).

Multiple educational needs, which must be met to enhance staff quality, have been identified in the literature. Among these are improved formal orientation programs of one week or more for non-professional staff (Stryker, 1981); educational programs to improve interpersonal skills, communication, sensitivity awareness, use of therapeutic touch, and dealing with one's own emotions and attitudes (Erickson, 1987; Jeffries, 1987); and values clarification (Values clarification, 1983).

It has been estimated that 50 to 80 percent of the residents in nursing homes have mental problems (Cohn, Smyer, Garfein, Droogas, & MaloneBeach, 1987; Zarit, 1980). H. Waxman, E. Carner, and G. Berkenstock (1984) state that between 43 and 75 percent of nursing home patients have a prescription for a psychotropic drug and large numbers of residents have a diagnosible psychiatric condition. In the nursing home, personnel have little or no training in mental health and aging, and patients are rarely seen by any type of mental health professional (Zarit, 1980). M. Cohn, M. Smyer, A. Garfein, A. Droogas, and E. MaloneBeach (1987) report that few efforts are made to provide for the special needs of mental illness in most nursing homes. Aides, who provide the bulk of the patient care, are usually the first to see a change, but have no special education to help them evaluate its meaning. Their study, conducted in Pennsylvania as a nursing home survey of 704 residents, attempted to identify aide perception versus administrative perception of the need for specialized training to better relate to eleven disruptive mental health behaviors. The behaviors studied were hostility, threats, or abusive behavior; disorientation; hallucinations and delusions; withdrawal and depression; suicidal behavior; agitation, wandering, and screaming; problematic grief reactions; sensory deprivation; inappropriate sexual behavior; drug and alcohol abuse and misuse; and lack of family contact.

Of the 247 aides who responded to the survey, 54 percent had worked in long-term care more than five years (Cohn, Smyer, Garfein, Droogas, & MaloneBeach, 1987). There were repeated requests for specific cost-effective behavioral training. The authors indicated that behavioral approaches for nursing homes have been shown to be effective and provide concrete actions for caregivers. The approach also reinforces resident optimal functioning by promoting independence. One serious critique, however, is the finding that administrators report more training for each problem than do nurses aides. Nurse aides also report that existing training does not assist in effective management of the mental health problems. The research of Cohn and colleagues (1987) suggests the need to provide not only specific training, but methods that are most effective.

Vocational education programs, which are now federally mandated for all states, offer helpful resources for curriculum development and course planning. These programs offer information on teaching techniques and content development, as well as providing relevant audiovisual and other materials. Staff responsible for organizing and conducting in-service and training programs in long-term care facilities could easily access these programs within their state.

A ready reference library and curriculum resource guides, developed by Regional Geriatric Education Centers (Brant, 1990) for program planning and library selection, are useful in staff education. Seminars, lectures, group study for educational programs offered by the facility, and external connections to colleges and universities where continuing education could be obtained by long-term care personnel are useful adjuncts in staff training. Another approach to education is to contract with nursing schools to bring education to the institution by experts.

The Teaching Nursing Home Project, funded by the Robert Wood Johnson Foundation, has become an excellent example of how colleges and universities can work in conjunction with long-term care facilities. Working together, staff from both institutions are able to share information on various problems and discover creative solutions. Through such a cooperative program quality of life and care of residents in long-term care facilities can be greatly improved (McCraken Knight, 1984).

One aim of the teaching nursing home was creating a viable staff development program within long-term care institutions. In-service care programs, based on assessment of learning needs of nursing staff, are developed and made available on a monthly basis to all professional and non-professional personnel.

The teaching nursing home involved various methods of conveying valuable information to staff, including using bulletin boards, placing information in monthly clinical care newsletters, and addressing specific needs of staff on each shift (McCracken Knight, 1984). Generating and disseminating knowledge through these learning methods offers an exciting avenue of learning to nursing homes interested in staff development and improved patient care.

Suicide prevention will be enhanced greatly by effective suicide education specifically designed and detailed to cover all aspects of the prevention process, with emphasis on clues and warning signs of depression and suicide and identification of resources available to help suicidal elders (J. McIntosh, 1987c).

J. McIntosh (1987c) offers a helpful guide to "education and training with emphasis on the elderly as an appropriate starting point for educational efforts" (p. 129). McIntosh emphasizes the need for training in five content categories.

The first area of education involves dispelling the myths about suicide. Many caregivers still believe that suicide happens without warning, that individuals who talk about suicide never really do it, and that counseling individuals about their suicidal feelings and ideations puts the idea of suicide into their heads. These and other myths hamper effective recognition of suicidal intent and intervention.

The second major area of training consists of identifying residents most at risk of committing suicide. Many staff members are not aware of demographic characteristics associated with high suicide risk. Similarly, they are not aware of psychosocial factors that place elderly individuals at increased risk. Identification of suicidal clues and warning signs is the next important content area to be included in such a program. Staff need to be taught the verbal, behavioral, and situational clues to suicide in older adults.

Another important area for education is in the area of assessment of lethality potential. Staff members need to be able to assess the seriousness of suicidal thoughts and recognize the existence of a suicide plan. Educational efforts should be aimed at helping staff members identify overt suicide and intentional life-threatening behaviors. Education directed at increasing staff awareness of specific techniques for interacting with suicidal individuals is also needed. Staff members who have excellent clinical skills may lack experience with such individuals and may have limited knowledge of crisis intervention techniques.

The final area of education consists of providing staff members with knowledge about resources available in the community. Mental health professionals, crisis or suicide prevention centers, and other appropriate services should be identified for staff.

Treatment of depression and adequate provision for services to meet the physical and mental health needs of residents are essential to suicide prevention. Environmental changes to accommodate the need for privacy, freedom, and individual autonomy, are also important in reducing suicidal risk among older residents of long-term care facilities. Macrolevel changes in the nursing profession and the health care industry are essential to reduce the nursing shortage in facilities. At the level of the individual institution, staff development and training and improved benefits are important measures to reduce the problem of staff shortage and staff turnover. Specific suicide prevention education should be a part of each facility's in-service training and staff development program.

9

SUICIDE AND EUTHANASIA:
ETHICAL DILEMMAS
AND LEGAL ISSUES

It is ironic that as human life has been prolonged, more and more elderly individuals are choosing to terminate their lives. Statistical evidence shows an alarming concentration of suicides among older people, particularly among males 85 years and older. Many elderly persons who commit or contemplate suicide reside in long-term care institutions. Because the life expectancy of Americans has increased, an ever-larger proportion of society is made up of elderly people. Increased life expectancy; prolonged periods of chronic illness and disability, partially resulting from advances in medical technology; increased risk of institutionalization; and other such conditions may create conditions that older people may not wish to endure.

Recent societal changes and trends in medicine and the health care industry pose moral and ethical issues that must not only be recognized, but that call for difficult decisions regarding both individual choices and public policies, especially in the modern world where aggressive medical strategies can greatly prolong life. The values on which such medical measures are based can come into open conflict with those that vest the right of self-determination within the individual's free choice. There are strong arguments in favor of the individual's right to self-determination. There are equally strong arguments opposed to suicide and euthanasia. The antecedents of these positions may be found in the religious, legal, social, and attitudinal commitments of Western civilization that are the bases of both stable societal behavior and social change. These arguments and positions will be examined in this chapter. Contemporary legislation regarding suicide and euthanasia among the elderly, grounded in these positions, will also be discussed. In this chapter we will also examine some of the sociomedical changes related to suicide and euthanasia.

SUICIDE AND EUTHANASIA IN PERSPECTIVE

Suicide

Suicide implies the conscious, intentional taking of one's own life. There are three major types of suicide: overt suicide, ILTB, and assisted suicide. *Overt suicide* is a recognizable, intentional act of self-destruction such as wrist-slashing, use of firearms, or hanging. *ILTB* consists of repeated self-destructive behavior(s) by individuals, which result in physical harm or tissue damage or which could bring about a premature end to life. Non-adherence to medical regimens, refusal to eat or drink, and ingestion of foreign substances or objects are examples of ILTB. *Assisted suicide*, sometimes referred to as "mercy killing," is any conduct intended to encourage the suicide of another. Unlike euthanasia, in which consent of the victim is not necessary, assisted suicide implies the consent of and, in many cases, the request of the victim. Mixing a poison cocktail and leaving it by the patient's bedside, placing a lethal dose of drugs within reach of the patient, and increasing the dosage of morphine to a lethal level are all examples of assisted suicide. Assisted suicide is a crime in all states.

The following types of ethical question need to be examined: Do old people living in long-term care facilities ever have the right to die? In the face of limited resources and rising costs for institutional care, is suicide sometimes the best solution?

Euthanasia

The term euthanasia derives from the Greek words *eu*, meaning "good or easy," and *thanatos*, meaning "death". Implicit in the concept of a good or easy death is the idea that a continuation of life for that person would involve intolerable levels of pain and suffering. This apparently benign term has acquired many different meanings, which have created shock, distress, and confusion. It has been used synonymously with genocide, murder, mercy killing, death with dignity, right to die, and painless inducement of death. To some it connotes an action the individual performs equivalent to suicide; to others it signifies an action performed for or on the individual by others. Some would define the same action as euthanasia if an individual's life were terminated by a physician, while they would consider it mercy killing if that same action were performed by a family member.

Non-consenting euthanasia involves killing someone without that person's desire, request, consent, or knowledge. *Voluntary euthanasia* describes a situation where an adult of sound mind requests assistance in dying, to save himself or herself from further suffering. *Active euthanasia* consists of taking measures or instituting procedures that would probably hasten death, with the aim of ending futile suffering on the part of the individual. *Mercy killing,* defined as willful actions to end another's life instituted at that person's request, can be seen as a form of voluntary active euthanasia. *Passive euthanasia* has been described as a negative act, or a lack of action. By withholding medications or procedures that would extend life and sustain an individual in a marginal condition, i.e., by refraining from action, the hopelessly ill patient is permitted to die. Elderly persons in nursing homes are more likely to be suffering from chronic debilitating illnesses. Contemporary arguments and legal decisions surrounding the issue of euthanasia, therefore, are particularly relevant to this group. The following question needs to be considered in light of these issues: Should those individuals who have outlived all family and friends and who suffer from a painful, debilitating illness and no hope for a meaningful and productive future life be forced to live?

SOCIOMEDICAL CHANGES

Attitudes and laws governing suicide and euthanasia exhibit the same cultural lag as do other societal entities. Reverence for the authority of antiquity has encouraged us to rely more on what has been said or done in former times than on the realities of current conditions. Attempts to scrutinize this area objectively, and to apply ethical principles are consonant with changing times, novel conditions, and contemporary imperatives.

Foremost among these changing societal conditions are the unprecedented technological development of medicine, the change in the status of the physician from private practitioner to employee earning a salary in a bureaucracy, the increasing number and percentage of the oldest-old, the increased costs of health care in general, and the disproportionate amount of medical resources consumed by the oldest-old population. Perhaps most important on an individual level, there has been a rejection of medical paternalism and an increased emphasis on self-determination.

Changing Roles of Physicians and Patients

In recent years, patients have increasingly begun to question the authority of physicians to make unilateral decisions concerning their lives. Within more traditional role definitions both patient and doctor accepted the physician's role as a paternalistic one. The physician was the sole repository of the arcane knowledge of medicine, and was seen as the only person capable of making informed decisions. Furthermore, the physician's motives were seen as altruistic and benign: the doctor's goal was to help patients and to keep them healthy and alive. The physician was supposed to have a collective orientation and to be affectively neutral.

Under the traditional medical model of care, it was mutually agreed that illness, disease, and dying overwhelmed patients, rendering them incompetent to make reasonable judgments, or even to know their own interests.

Even if it meant withholding information from the patient, the all-wise physician decided what was best for the patient and proceeded with the planned course of treatment. Moreover, because the physician was presumably acting with a collective orientation, i.e., in the best interests of the patient, it was not necessary to have the patient's consent. Implicit in this scheme was the assumption that there was value consensus—that the value system of the patient coincided with that of the physician.

Current doctor-patient relationships have changed considerably, along with an altered public perception of physicians in general. Many patients today reject the former paternalistic view and desire greater autonomy and self-determination in the decision-making process about medical care. This is especially evident in decisions affecting whether the patient will live or die, and it is here that the change has truly significant implications for the elderly population.

There are now patients who prefer to refuse medical treatment if it will only prolong the length of their lives, without reference to the quality of those lives. There are patients who appear to have a greater fear of what the physician will do *to* them, rather than what the physician will do *for* them. There are patients who believe that medical judgments should not be the sole determinants of whether they should live or die and that mere biological survival may not be a first-order value. In essence, there are now patients who believe that not all critical choices should be made by physicians without regard to the patient's own hierarchy of values. Consonant with a general client revolt in the larger society, a vigorous patients' rights movement has emerged demanding patient input or control over medical decisions.

One of the most debated issues in recent years has been whether under certain conditions, such as terminal illness, people have the *right* to choose death, or whether the decision (to choose life) still remains in the hands of the physician. What if the patient refuses medical treatment that would prolong life? Does the physician have the right to impose medical treatment, or should the physician have the choice of allowing the patient to die? Legislation regarding living wills, as well as intervention of the courts in such cases, appear to be outgrowths of changing attitudes toward the role of physicians.

Physicians themselves are also viewing roles differently. The ethical norm against helping patients die is a central part of the oldest traditions of medicine. It was institutionalized in the Hippocratic Oath, formulated in the fourth century B.C. That oath expressly forbade physicians from taking measures to hasten a patient's death. Specifically, it mandates that "I will not give anyone a lethal dose if asked to do so, nor will I suggest such a course" (A. Flew, 1974, p. 35). Besides forbidding assistance in suicide, the oath also requires a physician to use treatment to help the sick according to the physician's ability and judgment, but never with a view to injury and wrongdoing.

While these proscriptions appeared quite straightforward in a formulation that defined a doctor's duty as saving lives, modern critics such as Flew (1974) have pointed out that the fundamental undertaking of helping the sick may conflict with the promise not to give lethal medicine to anyone, even if asked to do so. Furthermore, such commitments can change. The Hippocratic Oath is no longer the powerful injunction that it once was. For example, abortion, which was also prohibited under the oath, is now permitted almost universally. The proscription against assisted suicide apparently is being re-examined, as well. Thus views are changing, with a greater awareness of rights by patients and greater respect for those rights by physicians. In addition, society itself is changing. Increasingly, the courts have been pressured to define those rights in relation to the terminally ill. Recent court decisions that allow patients the right to refuse life-prolonging measures reflect societal support for the shift in the control of clinical decisions from paternalistic physicians to patients. Moreover, the direction of these changes has been in response to one of increasing support for the right-to-die and death-with-dignity advocates.

Technological Advances in Medicine

For most of its history, medicine was relatively powerless to do much about illness, disease, and death. Due to fairly recent technological developments within medical science, life expectancy has been extended dramatically, both at birth, and in old age. Thus not only are an increasingly large number of people living through serious illnesses to old age, but also it is now possible to sustain the bodily functions of individuals almost indefinitely. As a consequence, lives of the very ill can be extended well beyond the point at which they might otherwise have died in the past. (Pneumonia, for example, was referred to by Dr. William Osler, the noted medical scholar, as "the old man's friend.") Underlying these changes is the fact that, today, most people who die are elderly; in 1985, 70 percent of the 2 million people who died were 65 or older. With longevity the chances of a lingering death are greatly increased. Accordingly, there are those who see this change as not necessarily extending life, but *prolonging the process of dying* (Downing, 1974).

Two important issues emerging from these changes in medicine are whether continuing to lengthen life expectancy will increase the rates of disabling dependency among the aged, or whether the elderly will be able to function independently. J. Fries (1980) argues that there will be a "compression of morbidity," predicting that the amount of time spent in later years relatively free of chronic illness and accompanying disabilities will continue to increase. The decrease in chronic disease would be accompanied by a decrease in the need for medical care and a drop in the average period of decreased vigor prior to death. In other words, morbidity and senescence would be compressed. E. Palmore (1986) in a recent study also found support for this position. According to this view, the onset of disabling impairment would be delayed, so that individuals would live healthy alert lives for a long time; death when it came (at about age 85) would be quick.

E. Schneider and J. Brody (1983), however, refute the compression of morbidity viewpoint that rates of chronic diseases and disabilities have declined in the elderly. In fact, they maintain that these rates may actually have increased. K. Manton and B. Soldo (1985) affirm that although various factors contributing to the severity and ultimately terminal outcome of chronic diseases have been controlled, the diseases themselves have not been eliminated. If the onset of these illnesses and disabilities is not delayed, they predict that the rates of dependency and lingering death will rise. This is a truly significant debate, with important policy implications. At present, convincing support for either side has not been forthcoming.

The Aging of the Population

Because modern medicine and technology have facilitated or supported growing numbers of people to live into old age, the number of those over the age of 65 exceeds the number of teenagers in the United States. It is projected that the number of elderly will double in twenty years to 60 million. However, the oldest-old cohort are the fastest-growing age group in the country and are expected to triple in number during that same time span.

The rate of increase in the oldest-old population has been truly impressive. For example, there are now twenty times as many people over 85 as there were at the turn of this century. In 1960, there were 0.9 million people in that age category or above; this number increased to 2.3 million in 1980, a gain of 156 percent in twenty years. It is estimated that in the year 2000 the number of persons 85 years and older will increase to 5.4 million; it will reach over 7.6 million by 2020, and is expected to reach or exceed 13 million by the year 2040 (Longino, 1988).

These gains are significant for an age group that has been identified as the one most at risk in terms of physical disabilities, institutionalization, isolation, and mental depression. The percentage of older persons suffering from significant depressive symptomatology increases with age, as does the rate of chronic illness and functional disability. Manton and his associates (1987) ask whether the increase in depressive symptomatology in those 85 and over, paralleled by an increase in physical disabilities and chronic diseases occupying a larger proportion of their life spans, will also increase the rate of suicide for the oldest-old. The implications are equally relevant regarding the issue of euthanasia.

THE BURDEN OF RISING COSTS

We spend more of our national wealth on health care for all segments of the population than any other advanced nation. In 1986, the United States spent 11.1 percent of its gross national product (GNP) on health care. By contrast, Britain spent 6.2 percent on health care; Japan, 6.7 percent; West Germany, 8.1 percent; France and Canada, 8.5 percent; and Sweden, 9.0 percent (Lohr, *The New York Times*, 1988, p. A12). In reviewing overall health care costs in the United States, the disproportionate utilization of the system by the elderly often becomes the focus for advocates of budget cutting, reevaluation of priorities, and redistribution of resources.

The increase in the number of the elderly, noted earlier, has been accompanied by a phenomenal increase in their health care costs and in projections that these costs will continue to rise. At present, 40 percent of all visits to physicians involve persons over age 65, suggesting that when faced with increasing numbers of elderly patients, all physicians in the future should have adequate training in geriatrics. Nursing homes are currently populated by elderly patients whose average age is 82 years. Projections from current trends to the year 2000 indicate that the number of elderly people in nursing homes will increase by nearly 70 percent (Kapp and Bigot, 1985). Expenditures among the elderly population itself are disproportionate: 25 to 35 percent of Medicare allocations are spent on the 5 to 6 percent of enrollees who will die within that year (Lubitz and Prihoda, 1984).

In the early 1960s, less than 15 percent of the federal budget was allocated to those 65 and over; by 1985 that percentage had ballooned to 28 percent (Maddox, 1988). In that same year, the elderly cohort that represented 11 percent of the total population consumed 29 percent of all health care expenditures. In the year 2040, when the elderly will comprise 21 percent of the population, it is expected that they will consume 45 percent of all health care expenditures in the United States (Callahan, 1987).

Health Care Cost Containment

The idea of rationing health care, especially for the elderly, is not new. Britain's National Health Service, for example, founded over forty years ago, promised to provide every citizen with equal access to "whatever medical treatment he requires, in whatever form he requires" (quoted by Lohr in *The New York Times*, 1988, p. 12). The system is now faced with long waiting lines for medical care and service cutbacks that impact on all patients, but that can be particularly significant for elderly individuals when treatment decisions are made on a triage basis. For example, there is one-third less dialysis in Britain and the overall treatment of chronic renal failure is less than half what it is in the United States. In decisions regarding who will receive the limited dialysis facilities, chronological age is often factored into the equation (Rationing Hospital Care, 1984). In England, surgeries per capita are performed half as frequently as they are in the United States. For cataract operations, which are usually the domain of the elderly, there is a waiting period of more than a year for a patient seeking an operation at the Newcastle Hospital, with a staff of 3,500 (Lohr, *The New York Times*, 1988, p. 12). Whether this situation is a reflection of implicit policy or merely a response to inadequate resources, it shows an ordering of priorities in which the elderly are far from the top (Rationing Hospital Care, 1984).

In the United States, there is strong evidence that such priorities already operate on an informal level. For example, investigators have recently found that the level of health care for the elderly in general, and nursing home patients in particular, is not up to the same high standards of medical care available to the patients of other age groups and other treatment locations. M. Kapp and A. Bigot (1985) report, for example, that "Physicians often attempt to avoid visiting their patients once they have entered a nursing home and, when a visit is made, frequently rush through their examination and treatment" (p. 115). In a study of 1,680 women with breast cancer who were treated in seventeen community hospitals (Chu, Diehr, Feigl, Glaefke, Begg, Glicksman, & Ford, 1987), it was found that there was a linear trend for older patients to receive fewer services such as biopsies prior to definitive treatment, number of lymph nodes examined, chemotherapy, or radiation therapy.

Discussions of rationing of health care for the elderly as a means of reducing the cost of health care nationally have surfaced in recent years in the form of questions and speculation. Alexander Leaf (1984) hints at it, for example, when he writes, "With costs now in excess of 10 percent of the gross national product, health care has begun to encroach on the support for other social needs such as housing, transportation, education, heating, recreation, and so forth which may be as important to the quality of life as medical care . . . " (p. 718). He believes that priorities must be assigned and that we must face many questions such as "Who gets treated?" He points out that under Medicare, all those who require treatment for end-stage renal disease are entitled to renal dialysis or kidney transplantation; in 1982, 72,800 people availed themselves of those services at a cost of 1.8 billion. T. St. Martin (1980) makes a similar type of prediction. As more individuals come to realize that aging populations compete for scarce resources that are related to well-being, he believes that there will be an increasing tendency to apply some sort of triage concept in health care. Evidently the corollary to "Who gets treated?" will become "Who deserves more to continue living?" The physician will be called on to distinguish between a decision to withdraw life support to pursue the best interests of the patient, and withdrawal of life support based on cost-effective medical rationing.

Age-Based Rationing of Health Care

The discussions regarding health care cost containment were conducted on a level that did not violate or offend the value system of Western society, in which all individuals' lives are presumed to be equally important. In 1986 however, Richard D. Lamm, a former governor of Colorado (who is currently director of the Center for Public Policy and Contemporary Issues at the University of Denver), caused a great deal of furor by stating publicly that the infirm elderly had a duty "to die and get out of the way" ("Health Debate Rages over Rationing by Age" *AARP, News Bulletin* 1988). Even more significant, however, is the explication of this attitude in the form of a public policy statement by a leading, well-respected ethicist, Daniel Callahan. Callahan, who is cofounder and director of the Hastings Center, a nationally recognized institute for studies of medical ethics, has published a proposed answer to the dilemma of rising medical costs, and the disproportionate amount consumed by the elderly.

Callahan (1987) believes that we must change our thinking about health care for the elderly. He points out that the gap between expanding health care needs of the elderly and the limited economic resources is great and will continue to widen. Setting limits on the medical care that can be provided for the elderly is his answer to the increased number and proportion of elderly, whose chronic illnesses require expensive medical treatment.

Ethicist Callahan, who is 57 years old, calls for "A willingness to ask once again how we might creatively and honorably accept aging and death when we become old, and not always struggle to overcome them" (p. 24). In his system of proposed rationing of medical care, sick old people should be prepared to forego long, expensive (and what he considers will eventually be useless) medical care: "the conquest of one disease only guarantees death from some other disease" (p. 59).

Callahan believes that a long life is not necessarily a better life. The primary orientation and aspirations of the elderly should be to the young and the generations to come rather than to the advancement of the welfare of their own group. He calls for greater intergenerational equity and believes that "the future is best left in the hands of the energetic and adaptable young" (p. 27).

Our present system of health care for the elderly, maintains Callahan, neither will nor should work. The high expenses at the end of life have not been found to be the result of overly aggressive, intensive high-technology medical care. This indicates that it is not possible to be optimistic about large-scale savings in caring for the elderly by merely attacking the type of care they receive.

He claims that the government has been expected to bear an unreasonable burden in the past and suggests that it must ration its care to the elderly to meet the needs of all other groups within the society. "Government cannot be expected to bear, without restraint, the growing social and economic costs of health care for the elderly. It must draw lines, because technological advances almost guarantee escalating and unlimited costs which cannot be met, and because in any case it has a responsibility to other age groups and other social needs, not just to the welfare of the elderly" (p. 116).

In his proposed new system, Callahan's primary emphasis in the care of the elderly would be the relief of suffering. The government does have a duty to help people live out a natural life span (about seventy-five years). Beyond this point, the government should be responsible only for providing the means necessary to relieve undue suffering, so that the individual lives out "a fitting span of life followed by a tolerable death" (p. 64). Tolerable death is defined as one that occurs at that point in the life span when "(a) one's life possibilities have on the whole been accomplished; (b) one's moral obligations to those for whom one has had responsibility have been discharged; and (c) one's death will not seem to others an offense to sense or sensibility, or tempt others to despair and rage at the finitude of human existence" (p. 66). Another stipulation about "tolerable death" is that it should not be accompanied by unbearable or degrading pain. Callahan, however, argues against euthanasia because he believes that it would signal a direct contradiction to an effort to give meaning and significance to old age.

All of the societal changes discussed above are reflected in changing attitudes toward the elderly, and particularly toward a more permissive stance regarding terminally ill suicide and voluntary passive euthanasia. Indications of such changes are found in policy statements by the medical profession, the church, and the government, as well as by individuals responding to public opinion polls. The issue is by no means resolved, and both the positive and negative aspects of both suicide and euthanasia are still being debated. In the next section, we will discuss arguments for and against the right to suicide and euthanasia. These arguments are particularly relevant for residents of long-term care facilities, who are the most likely to be older and suffering from chronic illnesses or are in pain or terminally ill.

THE DEBATES IN CONTEMPORARY PERSPECTIVE

Contemporary legal and moral views of suicide are the result of a long process of cultural evolution. That process brought together and melded values that were developed in several earlier civilizations. Specifically, suicide is viewed within a set of moral restraints that had their origins in both the Greek and Roman civilizations, and within the Judeo-Christian traditions as these developed in subsequent centuries.

The Case against Euthanasia and Suicide

A powerful set of influences on contemporary values comes from Greek and Roman heritages. Their views concerning suicide were very clear. Under the Greeks and the Romans, arguments against suicide insisted that human beings were God's property. In the sixth century B.C. Pythagoras rejected suicide on the grounds that "we are the chattels of God . . . and without his command we have no right to make our escape" (quoted in Gillon, 1986, p. 211). Perhaps influenced by the suicide of his mentor, Socrates, Plato claimed that man was a soldier of God and must not leave his post until God called. In addition, whether or not one could commit suicide came under the aegis of the state; Aristotle rejected suicide as contrary to man's civic duty. And indeed, the Greeks considered suicide a heinous crime—self-murder—and punishment was severe. Concurrent with these draconian punishments for "unjustified" suicides, there was a sanctioning of suicide in cases of incurable or terminal illness.

In the Roman Empire, if an individual committed suicide after having been denied the privilege by the magistrate, disgrace was heaped on his body, and it was buried in the most humiliating fashion. However, here as well, there was a distinction made in the case of terminal illness; petitioning to end one's life because of such a condition was considered a valid reason by the courts (Gillon, 1986).

The centuries of dominance of Western society by Christianity both reinforced earlier values and shaped them in new ways. Today among Christians, human life is held to be sacred, and, therefore, the taking of human life, regardless of reason, is wrong. Life is a gift from God to be revered, and this sanctity of life is an absolute value. Only God, who has dominion over life and death, can take life.

The positions of St. Augustine and St. Thomas Aquinas make it clear that any form of suicide was considered contrary to natural law and God's will. Thus in the fifth century St. Augustine (1950), the great leader of the early Christian church, proclaimed that it was an individual's duty to take care of God's property entrusted to him or her. In *The City of God*, he condemned suicide as a "detestable and damnable wickedness." In other words, our bodies and souls belong to God, and the individual who takes his or her own life sins against God. Not only was suicide a direct violation of the Sixth Commandment, "Thou shalt not kill," but it was also an unpardonable sin that deprived a person of the opportunity for repentance and penitence.

Eight centuries later, St. Thomas Aquinas (1964) reinforced this belief in *Summa Theologiae*: "Suicide is the destruction of the temple of God and a violation of the property rights of Jesus Christ." Not only did suicide usurp God's power over creation and death, but it was also contrary to man's natural inclination and the law of nature.

In addition to objections on religious grounds, opponents of euthanasia and the right to suicide stress a number of arguments based on medical and social grounds. They point out that doctors are neither omniscient nor infallible; the prognosis that a patient is terminal is never completely certain, and misdiagnoses are certainly possible. There have been many instances where patients who had been diagnosed as terminal have had unexplainable remissions. Opponents of positive euthanasia fear that even the most skilled physicians do make errors, and an error that results from positive euthanasia can never be reversed.

Linked with the above view is the possibility that if new treatments or cures should become available, they cannot be tried if euthanasia or suicide has occurred. In addition, R. Twycross (1981) believes that with increased education and technology in the art of pain relief, persons dying in painful agony would become a thing of the past. Because much of the supporting evidence for legislation allowing voluntary euthanasia rests on instances in which pain and other symptoms have been inadequately treated or controlled, he believes that it would be unwise to pursue euthanasia legislation prematurely.

Some see suicide of the elderly as a symptom and response to the stresses of old age such as physical disability, dependency, economic status changes, and loneliness. If these conditions of the elderly were addressed and alleviated, they argue, suicides and assisted suicides would decrease (Koppel, 1977). In persons with cancer, A. Weisman (1974) believes, social dissonance, due to loss of functioning and integration, is more important in their decisions to commit suicide than is physical disfigurement and deterioration. He found most significant the fact that these patients felt lonely, isolated, depressed, and without hope.

K. Siegel and P. Tuckel (1985) tested the assumption that persons with cancer commit suicide more frequently than members of the general population. They found that the rate of suicide among cancer patients did not exceed that of the general population. These authors also suggest that it is the patient's intrapsychic organization, and not the disease itself, that is the critical factor in determining whether the individual is suicidal or nonsuicidal.

The concept of rational suicide implies that older adults who choose to take their own lives are making a rational decision. On an individual level, R. Brandt (1980) argues that persons in a state of despair may be wrong when they attempt to make a rational decision. They may overlook other possible courses of action, and they may be unable to see the consequences of their behavior. D. Mayo (1980) believes that, even if we warn individuals of this possibility, the warning provides little safeguard against irrational suicide. In addition, there are reported situations where a patient who wished to die had a change of heart. In such cases, G. Murphy (1973) states that "The 'right' to suicide is a 'right' desired only temporarily" (p. 472).

There is also opposition to the individual's right to suicide from a social point of view. The individual does not exist in a social vacuum, it is argued, but as part of a relational network. Therefore, "a suicide will almost always have harmful consequences to other individuals" (Clements, 1980, p. 113). One of the most frequently raised socially based arguments against positive euthanasia or assisted suicide among the elderly is the concept of the "wedge" or "slippery slope." It is feared that legalizing voluntary euthanasia or assisted suicide could lead to involuntary and even compulsory euthanasia, and the elimination of people judged as inferior or undesirable. The atrocities committed by the Nazis in the 1930s provide an example of the dangers of euthanasia. The Nazis began enforced sterilization of persons who had hereditary illnesses and the systematic elimination of severely disabled and chronically ill individuals. This included the mentally defective, psychotics, epileptics, and those suffering from infantile paralysis. Then the program expanded to Parkinson's disease and multiple sclerosis, as well as those suffering from infirmities of old age. The objective was the destruction of *lebensunverten Leben*,"life unworthy of life"—another descriptive term for this population was *unnutze Esser*, or "useless eater"—figuratively, people devoid of value taking food from the mouths of the worthy (Humphrey & Wickett, 1986, p. 22).

Lessons from the past, opponents maintain, remain as guidelines for future policies. That is, the argument goes, if euthanasia were sanctioned for the elderly incurably ill, the potential for abuse is so great that it could result, even today, in the extension to the unwanted deformed, handicapped, psychotic, senile, and functionally dependent elderly. "If euthanasia is granted to the first class, can it long be denied to the second? . . . Each step is so short; the slope so slippery; our values in this age so uncertain and unstable" (Editoral, 1961). "The fatal error of German medicine was to think it could accept a little killing at its own initiative and under its own authority and not be forced, inexorably, to accept more killing at someone else's initiative and under the state's authority" (Derr, quoted in Wheeler, 1988, pp. A1, A6).

In a debate sponsored by the National Council on the Aging, Nat Hentoff, social commentator and writer for the New York newspaper *The Village Voice*, raised this specter when he referred to Callahan's proposals in *Setting Limits* as "morally depraved." He stated that this type of thinking was the first step down the "slippery slope" that leads to condoning the outright extermination of those considered "undesirable" ("Health Debate Rages Over Rationing by Age," quoted in *AARP News Bulletin*, 1988).

The Case for Euthanasia and Suicide

The Stoic thinkers of antiquity held that quality of life, not quantity, is the ultimate criterion of the "good life." Both the Stoics and the Epicureans considered suicide as a matter of individual conscience and the ultimate expression of human freedom and human dignity.

Many of those who today advocate suicide among the elderly advocate essentially a right to die, a right to self-determination, and death with dignity as the key elements. Many who favor rational suicide in late life, especially when pain and suffering are present, call for love and compassion and a quick and painless end to suffering. Still others emphasize the burdens that older sicker members place on their families and on society as a whole and suggest we might all be better off if such individuals would exit early.

R. Sartorius (1983) and other libertarians argue that the old are free to choose death over life. The liberty of the individual is the supreme value and the right of self-determination the ultimate individual freedom in our society. G. Williams (1973), M. Barrington (1969), and others all support the view that the old have the right to end their own lives when and as they see fit. Some supporters of this position claim there is a Constitutionally guaranteed inalienable right to death just as there is an inalienable right to life. The patients'-rights view similarly regards voluntary death as an option to be welcomed in preference to continued hopeless suffering. Sir Thomas More provided for active euthanasia at the person's request in his *Utopia*. Derek Humphrey, founder of the Hemlock Society, declares that "the right to die when and as we choose is the ultimate human liberty."

The right to die position claims that a man's life belongs to himself, not to God or to the state. Hence, he has a right to take his own life if he so chooses. As John Locke stated, "every man has a property in his own person. This nobody has any right to but himself." To own one's life is to own one's self. We own our own bodies and our own lives, thus suicide is legitimate and we have the moral right to use or misuse our life as we choose. This personal property argument and the closely related argument of the right to privacy have been involved in recent court decisions.

An additional argument often made in support of older adults' right to commit suicide suggests that death is the choice of the old person and it does not affect or infringe upon the rights of others nor does it harm society (Beckwith, 1979). D. Portwood (1978) and K. Lebacqz and H. Englehardt (1980) justify suicide in terminal illness because in such a situation we cannot fulfill our obligations to others and, therefore, are not bound by our obligations to them.

Closely related to the right to die position are the death-with-dignity and quality-of-life arguments in support of suicide and assisted suicide for the old. Many proponents of these positions claim that life in old age is sometimes no longer worth living. The negatives outweigh the positives and the pains outweigh the pleasures to such an extent that suicide is preferable to life. In the words of the famous Scottish skeptic, David Hume (1983), "it is permissible and even laudable to quit life whenever one is tired of life and haunted by pain and misery." In *On Suicide* he advocates suicide as the ultimate preventive against pain and misfortune. Norman Cousins (1975), editor of the *Saturday Review*, commented, "Death is not the greatest loss in life. The greatest loss is what dies inside us while we live. The unbearable tragedy is to live without dignity or sensitivity."

A. Downing (1974) takes the view that what is essentially human in us is the capacity for thought and love and aesthetic experience. A person who has been stripped of his personality and personhood by the ravages of pain and debilitating illness is no longer essentially human, but is reduced to the level of an animal. Downing is of the opinion that most of us, faced with such a possibility, would choose a dignified death if we were legally allowed to. He claims it is our basic human right to choose when death is an enemy or a friend and to act accordingly in our own best interests.

In her book, *Common Sense Suicide: The Final Right*, Portwood (1978), presents arguments that advocate a right to suicide among elderly individuals who know it is time for them to die. Portwood discusses the changes that most often occur with advancing age, particularly the losses and the negative physical, social, and economic changes. One of the concepts she employs is "balance sheet suicide." The concept implies that a competent older person can set off the unacceptable or intolerable aspects of his or her life against the chances for betterment and find the result weighted on the side of death. When the absence of life is more attractive than its presence, the older individual should have the right to commit suicide.

Aged suicide is portrayed by G. Lesnoff-Caravaglia (1980) as being motivated by an interest in "closing life with meaning, rather than despairing at the meaninglessness of life." The person wishes an end to life and a peace. Lesnoff-Caravaglia argues that in modern technological society the old moral/philosophical views and condemnations of suicide are no longer valid because life is different in this era and suicide must be considered in that light.

The situation ethics perspective, expounded on by J. Fletcher (1967), provides that no act is inherently good or bad, right or wrong, moral or immoral. The moral value of any action always depends on the situation. What ought to be done is whatever maximizes human well-being. Fletcher holds that suicide is morally permissible when it is freely chosen, minimizes the suffering of the individual, and does not invade the well-being of others. As Fletcher stated, "Every person's fight with death is lost before it begins. What makes the struggle worthwhile, therefore, cannot lie in the outcome. It lies in the dignity with which the fight is waged and the way it finds an end." The decision to die is extremely personal. Integrity of persons and respect for their freedom is the operative ethical principle in dealing with a suicide decision. Fletcher (1980) states that "last-ditch pro-vitalists still mumble threateningly about 'what the Nazis did,' but in fact the Nazis were never engaged in either euthanasia or mercy killing. What they did was merciless killing, either genocidal or for ruthless experimental purposes" (p. 294).

Proponents of rational suicide see the act as justifiable only in certain specifically defined situations, where "dying well" is an important consideration. B. Beckwith (1979) believes that "dying persons should be allowed to end their lives quickly and painlessly whenever they please, and . . . we should facilitate and applaud such conduct . . . both the dying who prefer a painless, dignified death by suicide and those who do not, should be free to do as they please" (p. 231). He indicates that, unfortunately, under present conditions, the great majority of elderly will die slowly, consciously, painfully. Besides personal suffering, they will also cause much trouble and cost to their families and/or society. P. Paelz (1980) also believes that, particularly in "cases in which the process of dying threatens to destroy a man's humanity before death itself intervenes" (p. 71), suicide may be morally permissible; he suggests that it be considered analogous to killing a person in self-defense, and justified morally on that basis.

LEGAL PERSPECTIVES

Background

In early English as well as Continental legal theory, suicide was treated as both a sin and a felony. This outlook encompassed the historical precedents that defined it as a crime against God, as well as a crime against the state.

Various organized groups have tried to change societal attitudes concerning people's right to determine when and how they will die. In the United States, The Hemlock Society supports suicide and assisted suicide for those who are terminally ill, while the Society for the Right to Die concentrates on educational programs as well as judicial and legislative action to accomplish the individual's right-to-die with dignity. Living wills, right-to-die bills, and death-with-dignity acts are increasingly gaining support and popularity.

A living will is a document executed while a person is still able to make health care decisions, which expresses that person's medical treatment preferences in the event of a hopeless illness or injury, where that person might be unable to make those preferences known. Living will legislation is a generic term used interchangeably with natural death, death-with-dignity, and right-to-die legislation. They affirm that the terminally ill have the right to choose when and how they die and that this right should remain inviolate as long as these individuals do not cause harm to others.

In discussing the role of such groups in fostering the aims of rational suicide, K. Siegel and P. Tuckel (1984) claim that "with the passage of time, there has been a progression in the aims of these groups from decriminalizing suicide, to fostering the right of the individual to refuse extraordinary life-preserving measures, to actively assisting in self-termination" (p. 263). The first two aims have largely been accomplished, and are currently integrated into our legal system. The question of actively assisting in self-termination is still being debated.

Many highly regarded theologians, physicians, and ethicists have expressed the conviction that both active and passive euthanasia are morally justifiable under certain circumstances. Supporters of legalized voluntary euthanasia believe that, in certain situations, people have a basic human right to decide for themselves when death is "more of a friend than an enemy" (Downing, 1974). "Just as the right to live is a fundamental human right, to be protected from all incursions, so the right to die should also be recognized and protected" (Russell, 1975, p. 232). According to this view, love and compassion should impel the public to support efforts to make voluntary euthanasia legal, because it "would permit an adult person of sound mind, whose life is ending with much suffering, to choose between an easy death and a hard one, and to obtain medical aid in implementing that choice" (Mathews, 1974, p. 29).

Many proponents of euthanasia argue that euthanasia should be a legal right without any penalty or stigma. Flew (1974) points out that a legal right is different from a moral right and it is not necessarily a moral duty to exercise whatever legal right one may have. He characterizes the present law, which tries to prevent those who suffer from obtaining a quick and painless death, as cruel and degrading and one that robs people of dignity.

From a legal perspective, there are two primary arguments for the legitimization of suicide and assisted suicide. The first is that the law should not enforce purported duties to oneself, such as the purported duty not to kill oneself, because this violates the fundamental moral right of self-determination. The second claim is that there is no evidence that decriminalizing assisted suicides would have significant antisocial results. The state should respect the individual's freedom to engage in acts that are self-destructive or immoral—as long as this freedom does not directly and significantly injure others (Engelhardt & Malloy, 1982). The state should function only as a protective vehicle of self-determination and individual freedom. According to this view, suicide and aiding and abetting suicide should be statutorily defined as noncriminal.

There are legal arguments against sanctioning suicide, assisted suicide, and euthanasia. In judicial and legislative circles a twofold rationale prevails for intervening in issues of suicide and assisted suicide: The first is the paternalistic view—the state has a right to intervene, because it is the state that is responsible for guarding the best interests of its individual subjects. The second is based on the concept of "public welfare—the state can and should intervene in an individual's life for the sake of the collective well-being. Under these views, the state is protecting both the individual and society when it makes determinations regarding the individual's right to take his own or another's life.

Legislation

California was the first state to introduce a right-to-die bill. In 1976, that state legalized wills that rejected the use of life-support equipment or extraordinary medical techniques to prolong life. Increasingly, other state courts have upheld the patient's right to freedom from unwanted intervention in the process of dying. Currently, thirty-eight states and the District of Columbia now have laws permitting living wills (Shipp, *The New York Times*, Oct. 15, 1988, pp. 1, 36). The legal grounds for justification have been the individual's right of privacy, as well as a common law right of self-determination, both of which have been judged to supersede the interests of the state. This was articulated in a 1914 New York Court of Appeals when Judge Benjamin Cardozo wrote, "every human being of adult years and sound mind has a right to determine what shall be done with his own body" (quoted by Shipp, *The New York Times*, October 15, 1988, p. 16).

Beginning with the landmark case of Karen Ann Quinlan in 1976, which granted her parents' request to remove the comatose Karen from a respirator, there has been an evolutionary trend toward legalizing increased individual choice in determining the fate of extremely ill patients. At first, life support measures other than feeding and hydration were allowed to be terminated, but food and water could not be withheld from patients by their own request (*In re Quinlan*, 70 N.J. 10, 355 A. 2d 647, *Garger v. New Jersey*, 429 U.S. 922 [1976] overruled in part *In re Conroy*, 98 N.J. 321, 486 A. 2d 1209 [1985]).

The question of competency has also undergone transitions in legal determinations of this issue. At first, patients were allowed to refuse life-sustaining treatment if the refusal was not only voluntary but also competent and informed. By 1985, the New Jersey Supreme Court ruled that all forms of life support, including nutrition, may be withheld from incompetent as well as competent terminally ill patients. Incompetent patients were deemed entitled to choose, either themselves or through a surrogate, whether they wished to continue life-sustaining treatment or not. It was also the first case where the court eliminated the distinction between feeding and other forms of life support measures (*In re Conroy*, 98 N.J. 321, 486 A. 2d 1209 [1985]).

Competency has been a very serious issue in determining whether or not one should be allowed to give or refuse informed consent for a proposed course of action that might result in one's death. Ultimately, even though the decisions involve medical questions, it is the *law* rather than the medical profession that decides who is competent and who is not.

There are a number of notable examples where the courts determined that patients were competent to make decisions not to accept medical care, despite physicians' attempts to have them declared incompetent on the basis that they would die without the proposed treatment. This happened in 1978, when a 72-year old male refused to have his gangrenous leg amputated. During the lawsuit subsequently brought by his doctors, psychiatrists were split in their opinions, and the judge actually visited the patient in the hospital before deciding that the man was competent. The court found that the right of privacy permits a patient to decline treatment where extensive bodily invasion is involved (*Matter of Robert Quackenbush, An Alleged Incompetent*, 383 A. 2d 785 [Morris Co. Ct., N.J. 1978]). In another landmark case, a man who was terminally ill with Lou Gehrig's disease posted a sign beside his bed asking the physicians to "pull the cord." When doctors refused, the patient sued, arguing that he had a constitutional right to die naturally and without interference. When the Appellate Court of Florida ruled in his favor, he yanked out his own life-support systems and died forty hours later. Florida courts have also ruled that treatment such as blood transfusions can be rejected on religious grounds.

In cases where the patient was incapable of making his or her wishes known, the Quinlan case has served as a precedent. For example, Eileen Farrell (*In re Farrell*, 108 N.J. 335, 529 A. 2d 404 [1987]) suffered from Lou Gehrig's disease, and her husband requested on her behalf that she be removed from a mechanical respirator. Even though she died before the case came to court, the Supreme Court of New Jersey agreed to judge the case after her death "because of the extreme importance of the issue" (Sullivan, *The New York Times*, June 25, 1987, p. B12). In a seven to zero decision, the court ruled that none of the traditional state interests in the case, i.e., preserving life, preventing suicide, safeguarding the integrity of the medical profession, and protecting innocent third parties, would outweigh Mrs. Farrell's right to decide to withdraw the life-sustaining procedures. The court's opinion further stated that: "As medical technology has been advancing the doctrine of informed consent has been developing . . . the patient's right to give an informed refusal to medical treatment [is] the logical correlative of the right to give informed consent" (Garibaldi, *The New York Times*, June 25, 1987, p. B12).

In the case of withholding food and water, which also represented a watershed legal decision, the families of two nursing home patients who were in irreversible comas, petitioned to have their feeding tubes removed. The nursing home refused to do so on the grounds that it would constitute euthanasia. The Supreme Court of New Jersey rejected the arguments of the nursing home, declaring that death would not be caused by the removal of the forced feeding devices, but by the patients' underlying medical problems (*In re Jobes*, 108 N.J. 394, 529 A.2dd 434 [1987] and *In re Peter*, 365, 529 A.2d 419 [1987]).

In writing the opinions in the cases of Nancy Ellen Jobes and Hilda M.

Peter, the judge made some statements that reflect the emergent legal stance regarding medical choices. In the Jobes case, in 1987, the judge Justice Marie L. Garibaldi, stated that, "Embarking on this task, we are mindful that the patient's right to self-determination is the guiding principle in determining whether to continue or withdraw life-sustaining medical treatment. . . . Family members are best qualified to make substitute judgments for incompetent patients" (Garibaldi, 1987). In commenting on the Peter case, the judge wrote:

All patients, competent or incompetent, with some limited cognitive ability or in a persistent vegetative state, terminally ill or not terminally ill, are entitled to choose whether they want life-sustaining medical treatment.

Medical choices are private, regardless of whether a patient is able to make them personally or must rely on a surrogate. They are not to be decided by societal standards of reasonableness or normalcy. Rather, it is the patient's preferences—formed by his or her unique personal experience—that should control (Garibaldi, 1987).

Thus if persons are incompetent, the right to reject treatment still applies. For the purpose of exercising the patient's right of informed consent, it is necessary to have a guardian appointed to make decisions, and family members are seen as appropriate surrogates.

In California, legislation was recently passed authorizing the use of a document called the "durable power of attorney for health care." This allows adults to sign health care proxies designating another person to make decisions on their behalf, regarding the withholding of any medical treatment if they become incapacitated. A person could thus choose his or her own surrogate in the event of future incompetence. Six other states have laws permitting this practice: Illinois, Maine, Nevada, New York, Rhode Island, and Vermont. Other states accomplish the same thing when a person grants a durable power of attorney to another. This legal device is recognized in varying degrees in all fifty states.

That a written document is sometimes necessary was demonstrated by a recent New York Court of Appeals ruling. When physicians determined that the 77-year-old Mrs. O'Connor required a feeding device known as a nasogastric tube (a tube that goes through the nose to her digestive tract) Mrs. O'Connor's two daughters objected, claiming that their mother would never want her life sustained in such circumstances. The hospital argued that without artificial feeding, Mrs. O'Connor would suffer a painful death of starvation and dehydration within seven to ten days. The court ruled that she be kept alive through artificial feeding (Shipp, *The New York Times*, Oct. 15, 1988, pp. 1, 36).

This ruling ran counter to the trend that decisions should lie with the family, because family members best understand the patient's values and preferences. It served to indicate the need to execute in advance specific declarations of the types of treatment a person would want withheld or withdrawn. "The ideal situation," wrote Chief Jusice Sol Wachtler, "is one in which the patient's wishes were expressed in some form of writing, perhaps a living will, while he or she was still competent. The existence of a written document suggests the author's seriousness of purpose and ensures that the court is not being asked to make a life-or-death decision based on casual remarks" (Wachtler, 1988, p. 13).

The state of New Jersey has acknowledged the individual's right to refuse medical treatment when the issue has been adjudicated through their courts. At the same time, it is interesting to note that it is one of the few states that does not have a statute permitting living wills or other such directives in which people certify in advance their preferences about life-sustaining measures in the event that they become incompetent and unable to speak for themselves. However, the recent rulings by the New Jersey Supreme Court, a bellwether in this field, are likely to have a strong influence on courts and legislatures of other states that are grappling with the right to die issue. The rulings clearly place the rights of patients and their wishes over that of the state, and that of the medical profession.

CONCLUSION

One of the most significant policy changes in recent years has been a movement from the oft-stated goal of universal access to high-quality medical care to issues concerning cost efficiency. Some of the consequences of this move have been shortened hospital stays, increased out-patient treatments, a closing of community hospitals catering to the poor, and questions about cost containment in caring for the elderly.

Of special concern to us are some of the solutions being proposed for cost containment in health care for the elderly population. Many of them involve proposals for care delivery, including actual health care rationing for this population group. Under the concept of health care rationing, we have seen suggestions that some treatments—specifically, those that are in scarce supply or are very expensive—be denied to individuals past a certain age. The arguments for such control are instrumental ones, addressing the requirements of the society rather than those of the individual. The medical technology to prolong life has proliferated, while the government's willingness and ability to pay for this sophisticated technology is being strained by the increased number of elderly.

On a more individualized level, rationing or discontinuing health care delivery to the terminally ill elderly has been approached from the humanitarian viewpoint, as a means of alleviating further suffering for the patient who is in the process of dying. We have seen that the increased rates of suicide on the part of these individuals are viewed with a more understanding attitude. In addition, passive euthanasia has received more and more acceptance on the part of the medical establishment, the law, and the population in general.

One of the major problems in dealing with active euthanasia is the fact that once it has been accepted in certain cases, the limits or boundaries become very fluid, with the "slippery slope" possibly leading to inappropriate decisions.

As with most other elements in society, this issue is a dynamic, ever-changing one; each week brings new cases where the courts are being faced with decisions about whether or not to penalize those who helped patients die. At present, the laws allow physicians to refrain from using artificial life-support systems for those terminally ill patients whose wishes have been made known (in specific ways for different states). Relatively recently, the same has been true for withholding food and water. Ironically, while the basis for allowing terminally ill patients to die without interference is a humanitarian one, in the latter case, "natural" death by starvation and dehydration is particularly painful. Whatever the position one takes, the issues must be faced: by policymakers, by medicine, by young people looking toward the future, and by individual elderly persons confronting terminal illness.

REFERENCES

AARP News Bulletin (1988). Health debate rages over rationing by age. 29(6), 12, 13.

Aguilar, V. B. (1978). *Intervening on loneliness in a group of nursing home residents.* Unpublished Master's thesis, School of Nursing, Virginia Commonwealth University, Richmond.

Alexander, L. (1980). Medical science under dictatorship. In D. J. Horan & D. Mall (Eds.), *Death, dying, and euthanasia* (pp. 571-591). Frederick, MD: University Publications of America.

American Health Care Association (1988, Oct.) Staff. *Provider* (21-23).

American Psychiatric Association (1975). *A psychiatric glossary.* New York: Basic Books.

American Psychiatric Association (1980). *Diagnostic and statistical manual of mental disorders* (3rd ed.). Washington, DC: Author.

American Psychiatric Association (1987). *Diagnostic and statistical manual of mental disorders III-R.* Washington, DC: Author.

Appelbaum, S. A. (1963). The problem-solving aspect of suicide. *Journal of Projective Techniques, 27*(3), 259-268.

Arling, G., Nordquist, R., Brant, BA., & Capitman, J. (1987). Nursing home case mix: Patient classification by nursing resource mix. *Medical Care, 25*(1), 9-19.

Bahr, R. T., & Gress, L. D. (1984). *The aging person: Holistic perspectives.* St. Louis, MO: Mosby.

Barnard, C. (1986). The need for euthanasia. In A. B. Downing & B. Smoker (Eds.), *Voluntary euthanasia* (pp. 173-183). Atlantic Highlands, NJ: Humanities Press International.

Barrell, L. M., & Wyman, J. F. (1989). Psychosocial nursing with older adults. In L. M. Brickhead (Ed.), *Psychiatric mental health nursing: The therapeutic use of self* (pp. 567-593). Philadelphia: Lippincott.

Barrington, M. (1969). Apologia for suicide. In A. B. Downing (Ed.), *Euthanasia and the right to die* (pp. 152–172). London: Peter Owen.

Battin, M. P. (1980). Manipulated suicide. *Bioethics Quarterly, 2*(2), 123-134.

Battin, M. P. (1982). *Ethical issues in suicide.* Englewood Cliffs, NJ: Prentice-Hall.

Beck, A. T. (1967). *Depression.* New York: Harper & Row.

Beck, A. T., Ward, C. H., Mendelson, M., Mock, J. E., & Erbaugh, J. K. (1961). An inventory for measuring depression. *Archives of General Psychiatry, 4,* 561-571.

Beck, A. T., Weissman, A., Lester, D., & Trexler, L. (1974). The measurement of pessimism: The hopelessness scale. *Journal of Consulting and Clinical Psychology, 47*(6), 861-865.

Beck, C. M., Rawlins, R. P., & Williams, S. R. (Eds.). (1984). *Mental health-psychiatric nursing.* St. Louis, Mo: Mosby.

Beckwith, B. P. (1979). On the right to suicide by the dying. *Dissent, 26,* 231-233.

Bednar, R., & Kaul, T. (1978) Experimental group research. In S. Garfield, & A. Bergin (Eds.), *Handbook of psychotherapy and behavior change* (2nd ed., pp. 769-815). New York: Wiley.

Belsky, J. (1984). *The psychology of aging: Theory, research and practice.* Belmont, CA: Wadsworth.

Bengtson, V. L. (1979). The aged and their social needs. In E. Seymour (Ed.), *Psychosocial needs of the aged.* Los Angeles: The University of Southern California Press.

Bennett, C. (1980). *Nursing home life: What it is and what it could be.* New York: Tiresias Press.

Berardo, F. M. (1968). Widowhood status in the U.S.: Perspectives on a neglected aspect of the family life cycle. *Family Coordinator, 17*(3), 191-203.

Berardo, F. M. (1970). Survivorship and social isolation: The case of the aged widower. *Family Coordinator, 19*(1), 11-25.

Beyer, G. H., & Nierstrasz, F. H. J. (1967). *Housing the aged in Western countries.* New York: Elsevier.

Bibring, E. (1953). The mechanism of depression. In P. Greenacre (Ed.), *Affective disorders: Psychoanalytic contribution to their study* (pp. 13-48). New York: International Universities Press.

Bibring, E. (1954). Psychoanalysis and dynamic psychotherapies. *Journal of the American Psychoanalytic Association, 2*(4), 745-770.

Bienenfeld, D. (1987). Alcoholism in the elderly. *American Family Physician, 36,* 163-172.

Birren, J. E. (1964). *The psychology of aging.* Englewood Cliffs, NJ: Prentice-Hall.

Birren, J. E., & Sloane, R. B. (Eds.). (1980). *Handbook of mental health and aging.* Englewood Cliffs, NJ: Prentice-Hall.

Blau, D. (1980, Oct.). *Depression in late life: Psychodynamic aspects.* Paper presented at a conference on depression in late life, Cleveland, OH.

Blazer, D. (1980). *Social supports and morality in a community population.* Ph.D. dissertation, Chapel Hill: University of North Carolina Press.

Blazer, D. (Ed.). (1982). *Depression in late life.* St. Louis, MO: Mosby.

Bock, E. W. (1972). Aging and suicide. *Family Coordinator, 21*(1), 71-79.

Bock, E. W., & Webber, I. (1972). Suicide among the elderly. *Journal of Marriage and the Family, 34*(1), 24-31.

Borson, S., & Veith, R. C. (1985). Pharmacological interventions. In N. J. Osgood. *Suicide in the elderly* (pp. 116-30). Rockville, MD: Aspen.

Bostrom, B. A., & Lagerway, W. (1988). The high court of the Hague Case No. 79065, October 21, 1986. *Issues in Law and Medicine*, 3(4), 445-450.

Bragg, M. (1979). *A comparative study of loneliness and depression.* Unpublished Ph.D. dissertation, Los Angeles. University of California.

Brandt, R. B. (1980). The rationality of suicide. In M. P. Battin & D. J. Mayo (Eds.), *Suicide: The philosophical issues* (pp. 117–132). New York: St. Martin's Press.

Brant, B A. (1990) Gerontological nursing. In J. Teitleman and I. Parham, *Fundamentals of geriatrics for health professionals* (pp. 103–119). Westport, CT: Greenwood Press.

Bright, R. (1985). *Music in geriatric care.* (2nd ed.). New York: Alfred.

Brink, T. L. (1979). *Geriatric psychotherapy.* New York: Human Science Press.

Brody , E. M. (1977). *Long-term care of older people: A practical guide.* New York: Human Sciences Press.

Bromberg, S., & Cassel, C. K. (1983). Suicide in the elderly: The limits of paternalism. *Journal of the American Geriatrics Society*, 31(6), 698-703.

Brown, B. L., Goodwin, F. K., Ballenger, J. C., Goyer, P. F., & Major, L. F. (1979). Aggression in humans correlates with cerebrospinal fluid amine metabolites. *Psychiatry Research*, 1(2), 131-139.

Burger, I. (1980). *Creative drama for senior adults.* Wilton, CT: Morehouse-Barlow.

Burke, W. J., Rubin, E. H., Zorumski, C. F., & Wetzel, R. D. (1987). The safety of ECT in geriatric psychiatry. *Journal of the American Geriatrics Society*, 35(6), 516-521.

Burnside, I. M. (1973). Long term group work with the hospitalized aged. In I. M. Burnside (Ed.), *Psychosocial nursing care of the aged* (pp. 84-90). New York: McGraw-Hill.

Burnside, I. M. (1976). *Nursing and the aged.* New York: McGraw-Hill.

Burnside, I. M. (1980). *Nursing and the aged.* (2nd ed.). New York: McGraw-Hill.

Burnside, I. M. (1988). *Nursing and the aged: A self-care approach* (3rd ed.). New York: McGraw-Hill.

Busse, E. W. (1970). *Psychoneurotic reactions and defense mechanisms in the aged.* In E. Palmore (Ed.), *Normal aging* (pp. 84-90). Durham, NC: Duke University Press.

Butler, R. N. (1961). Re-awakening interest. *Nursing Homes*, 10, 8-19.

Butler, R. N. (1963). Recall in retrospection. *Journal of American Geriatric Society*, 11(6), 523-529.

Butler, R. N. (1964). The life review: An interpretation of reminiscence in the aged. In R. Kastenbaum (Ed.), *New thoughts on old age* (p. 265-280). New York: Springer.

Butler, R. N. (1971). Age: the life review. *Psychology Today*, 5, 49-51, 89, 108.

Butler, R. N. (1980–1981). The life review: An unrecognized bonanza. *International Journal of Aging and Human Development*, 12(1), 35-38.

Butler, R., & Lewis, M. (1982). *Aging and mental health: Positive psychosocial and biomedical approaches* (3rd ed.). St. Louis: Mosby.

Callahan, D. (1987). *Setting limits.* New York: Simon & Schuster.

Cantor, N. (1978). A patient's decision to decline lifesaving medical treatment: Bodily integrity versus the preservation of life. In R. F. Weir (Ed.), *Ethical issues in death and dying* (pp. 203-213). New York: Columbia University Press.

Carp, F. (1976). Housing and living environments of old people. In R. Binstock & E. Shanas (Eds.), *Handbook of aging and the social sciences* (pp. 244-271). New York: Van Nostrand Reinhold.

Cath, S. H. (1965). Discussion notes. In M. A. Berezin & S. H. Cath (Eds.), *Geriatric psychiatry: Grief, loss and emotional disorder in the aging process* (pp. 128-129). New York: International Universities Press.

Cattell, H. R. (1988). Elderly suicide in London: An analysis of coroner's inquests. *International Journal of Geriatric Psychiatry, 3,* 251-261.

Chu, J., Diehr, P., Feigl, P., Glaefke, G., Begg, C., Glicksman, A., & Ford, L. (1987). The effect of age on the care of women with breast cancer in community hospitals. *Journal of Gerontology, 42*(2), 185-190.

Clark, P., & Osgood, N. J. (1985). *Seniors on stage: The impact of applied theater techniques on the elderly.* New York: Praeger.

Clements, C. D. (1980). The ethics of not-being: Individual options for suicide. In M. P. Battin & D. Mayo (Eds.), *Suicide: The philosophical issues* (pp. 104-114). New York: St. Martin's Press.

Coble, P. A., Kupfer, D. J., & Shaw, D. H. (1981). Distribution of REM latency in depression. *Biological Psychology, 16,* 453-456.

Cohen, R. (Ed.) (1986). *A home away from home.* Washington, DC: American Association of Retired Persons.

Cohn, M., Smyer, M., Garfein, A., Droogas, A., & MaloneBeach, E. (1987). Perceptions of mental health training in nursing homes: Congruence among administrator's and nurse's aides. *The Journal of Long-Term Care Administration, 15*(2), 20-25.

Colt, G. H. (1987). The history of the suicide survivor: The mark of Cain. In E. J. Dunne, J. L. McIntosh, & K. Dunne-Maxim (Eds.), *Suicide and its aftermath* (pp. 3-18). New York: Norton.

Corson, S. A., Corson, E., Gwynne, P. H., & Arnold, L. (1977). Pet dogs as nonverbal communication links in hospital psychiatry. *Comprehensive Psychiatry, 18,* 61-72.

Council on Ethical and Judicial Affairs, American Medical Association (1986). *Current Opinions of the Council on Ethical and Judicial Affairs of the American Medical Association—1986* (pp. 2-18). Chicago: American Medical Association.

Cousins, N. (1975). Editorial. *Saturday Review,* June 24, p. 4.

Courtney, B. (1968). *Play, drama, and thought.* New York: Drama.

Curry, T., & Ratliffe, R. P. (1973). The effects of nursing home size on resident isolation and life satisfaction. *The Gerontologist, 13*(1), 295-298.

Curry, T., & Ratliffe, B. W. (1973). The effects of home size on resident isolation and life. *The Gerontologist, 13,* 296–298.

Cuszak, O., & Smith, E. (1984). *Pets and the elderly: The therapeutic bond.* New York: Haworth Press.

Darbonne, A. R. (1969). Suicide and age: A suicide note analysis. *Journal of Consulting and Clinical Psychology, 33*(1), 46-50.

Davies, B., & Knapp, M. (1981). *Old people's homes and the production of welfare.* London: Routledge & Kegan Paul.

Davis, A. J. (1984). *Listening and responding.* St. Louis, MO: Mosby.

Davis, B. W. (1985). The impact of creative drama training on psychological states of older adults: An exploratory study. *Gerontologist, 25*(3), 315-321.

Deane, R. T. (1988, Oct.). ACHA's industry survey. *Provider,* pp. 21-23.

Denham, M. J. (1983). *Care of the long-stay elderly patient.* London: Croom Helm.

Dorpat, T. L., Anderson, W. F., & Ripley, H. S. (1968). The relationship of physical illness to suicide. In H. L. P. Resnik (Ed.), *Suicidal behaviors: Diagnosis and management* (pp. 209-219). Boston: Little, Brown.

Downing, A. B. (1974). Euthanasia: The human context. In A. B. Downing (Ed.), *Euthanasia and the right to death* (pp. 13-24). London: Peter Owen.

Dudley, C. J., & Hillary, G. A. (1977). Freedom and alienation in homes for the aged. *The Gerontologist, 17,* (2), 140-145.

Duke, C. (1974). *Creative dramatics and English teaching.* Urbana, IL: National Council of Teachers of English.

Durkheim, E. (1951). *Suicide.* New York: Free Press. (Original work published 1897.)

Dwedney, I. (1977). An art therapy program for geriatric patients. In E. Ulman, & P. Dachinger (Eds.), *Art therapy in theory and practice.* (2nd ed.). New York: Schocken Books.

Ebersole, P. P. (1976). Group work with the aged: A survey of the literature. In I. M. Burnside (Ed.), *Nursing and the aged* (pp. 182-204). New York: McGraw-Hill.

Edinberg, M. (1985). *Mental health practices with the elderly.* Englewood Cliffs, NJ: Prentice-Hall.

Editorial. (1961, Oct.). *Lancet, 2,* 351-352.

Eisdorfer, C., & Wilkie, F. (1977). Stress, disease, aging and behavior. In J. E. Birren & K. W. Schaie (Eds.), *Handbook of the psychology of aging* (pp. 251-275). New York: Van Nostrand Reinhold.

Eliopoulos, C. (1983, Oct.). Nurse staffing in long-term care facilities. *Journal of Nursing Administration, 13*(10), pp. 29-31.

Elwell, F. (1984). The effects of ownership on institutional services. *The Gerontologist, 24*(1), 77-83.

Endicott, J., & Spitzer, R. L. (1978). A diagnostic interview for affective disorders and schizophrenia. *Archives of General Psychiatry, 35*(7), 837-844.

Engelhardt, H. T., & Malloy, M. (1982). Suicide and assisting suicide: A critique of legal sanctions. *Southwestern Law Journal, 36*(4), 1003-1037.

Erickson, J. (1987). Quality and the nursing assistant. *Provider, 13*(4), 4-6.

Erikson, E. (1950). *Childhood and society.* New York: Norton.

Eser, A. (1981). "Sanctity" and "quality" of life in a historical-comparative view. In S. E. Wallace & A. Eser (Eds.), *Suicide and euthanasia* (pp. 103-115). Knoxville: University of Tennessee Press.

Eustis, N. N., Greenberg, J. N., & Patten, S. K. (1984). *Long term care for older persons: A policy perspective* Monterey, CA: Brooks/Cole.

Farber, M. L. (1968). *Theory of suicide.* New York: Funk & Wagnalls.

Farberow, N. L., & Sheidman, E. S. (1970). Suicide and age. In E. S. Sheidman, N. L. Farberow, & R. E. Litman (Eds.), *The psychology of suicide* (pp. 164-174). New York: Science House. (Original work published in 1957.)

Fersh, I. (1981). Dance/movement therapy: A holistic approach to working with the elderly. *Activities, Adaptation, and Aging 2*(1) 21-30.

Fletcher J. (1967). *Moral responsibility: Situation ethics at work.* Philadelphia: Westminster.

Fletcher, J. (1980). Ethics and euthanasia. In D. J. Horan & D. Mall (Eds.), *Death, dying and euthanasia* (pp. 291-304). Frederick, MD: University Publications of America.

Flew, A. (1974). The principle of euthanasia. In A. B. Downing (Ed.), *Euthanasia and the right to death* (pp. 30-47). London: Peter Owen.

Folstein, M. F., Folstein, S. E., & McHugh, P. R. (1975). "Mini-mental state": A practical method for grading the cognitive state of patients for the clinician. *Journal of Psychiatric Research, 12,* 189-198.

Francis, G., Turner, J. T., & Johnson, S. B. (1985). Domestic animal visitation as therapy with adult home residents. *International Journal of Nursing Studies, 22*(3), 201-206.

Francis, G. M., & Munjas, B. A. (1988). Plush animals and the elderly. *Journal of Applied Gerontology, 7*(2), 161-172.

Frank, S. (1984). The touch of love. *Journal of Gerontological Nursing, 10*(1), 28-31.

Freud, S. (1948). *Mourning and melancholia.* Collected papers IV. repr. Hogarth Press, London. (Original work published in 1917.)

Freud, S. (1955). *Origin and development of psychoanalysis.* Chicago: Regnery-Gateway. (Original work published in 1917.)

Fried, C. (1976). Terminating life support: Out of the closet! *New England Journal of Medicine, 295*(7), 390-391.

Fries, J. F. (1980). Aging, natural death, and compression of morbidity. *New England Journal of Medicine, 303*(3), 130-135.

Gallagher, D. (1981). Behavioral group therapy with elderly depressives: An experimental study. In D. Upper & S. Ross (Eds.), *Behavioral group therapy* (pp. 187-224) Champaign, IL: Research Press.

Gallagher, D., Breckenridge, J. N., Steinmetz, J., & Thompson, L. (1983). The Beck depression inventory and research diagnostic criteria: Congruence in an older population. *Journal of Consulting and Clinical Psychology, 51*(6), 945-946.

Gallagher, D., Nies, G., & Thompson, L. (1982). Reliability of the Beck depression inventory with older adults. *Journal of Consulting and Clinical Psychology, 50*(4), 590-591.

Gallagher, D., & Thompson, L. (1982). The treatment of major depressive disorders in older outpatients with brief psychotherapies. *Psychotherapy, Research and Practice, 19*(4), 482-490.

Gallagher, D., & Thompson, L. (1983) Effectiveness of psychotherapy for both endogenous and nonendogenous depression in older adult outpatients. *Journal of Gerontology, 38,* 707-712.

Gallup Report. (1985, Apr.). *235,* 28-29.

Garibaldi, M. L. (1987). *The New York Times.* June 25, p. B12.

Garnet, E. D. (1974). A movement therapy for older people. *Dance Therapy: Focus on Dance, 7,* 59-61.

Gelfand, D. E. (1988). *The aging network: Programs and Services.* New York: Springer.

George, L. K. (1980). *Role transitions in later life.* Monterey, CA: Brooks/Cole.

Gillon, R. (1986). Suicide and voluntary euthanasia: Historical perspective. In A. B. Downing & B. Smoker (Eds.), *Voluntary euthanasia* (pp. 210-229). London: Humanities Press International.

Glasscote, R. M., & Beigel, A. (1976). *Old folks at home: A field study of nursing and board and care homes.* Washington, DC: American Psychiatric Association.

Godbole, A. & Verinis, J. S. (1974). Brief psychotherapy in the treatment of emotional disorders in physically ill geriatric patients. *Gerontologist, 14*(2), 143.

Goffman, E. (1960). Characteristics of total institutions. In M. R. Stein, A. J. Vidich, and D. M. White (Eds.), *Identity and anxiety survival of the person in mass society.* New York: Free Press.

Goffman, E. (1963). *Stigma: Notes on the management of spoiled identity* (pp. 449-479). Englewood Cliffs, NJ: Prentice-Hall.

Golant, S. (1984). *A place to grow old: The meaning of environment in old age.* New York: Columbia University Press.

Goldfarb, A. I., & Turner, H. (1953). Psychotherapy of aged persons: Utilization and effectiveness of brief therapy. *American Journal of Psychiatry, 109,* 916-921.

Gotestam, K. G. (1980). Behavior and dynamic psychotherapy with the elderly. J. E. Birren & R. B. Sloan (Eds.), *Handbook of mental health and aging.* Englewood Cliffs, NJ: Prentice-Hall.

Gove, W. R., & Hughes, M. (1980). Reexamining the ecological fallacy: A study in which aggregate data are critical in investigating pathological effects of living alone. *Social Forces, 58*(4), 1157-1177.

Graber, G. C. (1981). The rationality of suicide. In S. E. Wallace & A. Eser (Eds.), *Suicide and euthanasia* (pp. 51-65). Knoxville: The University of Tennessee Press.

Gray, P. (1974). *Dramatics for the elderly: A guide for residential care and senior centers.* New York: Teachers College, Columbia University.

Greenwald, S. R., & Linn, M. W. (1971). Intercorrelations of data on nursing homes. *The Gerontologist, 11*(4), 337-340.

Gubrium, J. F. (1975). *Living and dying at Murray Manor.* New York: St. Martin's Press.

Gurland, B. J., & Cross, P. S. (1983). Suicide among the elderly. In M. K. Aronson, R. Bennett, & B. J. Gurland (Eds.), *The acting out elderly* (pp. 456-465). New York: Haworth Press.

Halbur, B. (1982). *Turnover among nursing personnel in nursing homes.* Ann Arbor: University of Michigan Press.

Halbur, B. (1986). Managing nursing personnel turnover rates: Strategies for nursing home professionals. *The Journal of Applied Gerontology, 5*(1), 64-75.

Halbur, B., & Fears, N. (1986). Nursing personnel turnover rates turned over: Potential positive effects on resident outcomes in nursing homes. *The Gerontologist, 26*(1), 70–76.

Haley, W. E. (1983). Behavioral self-management: Application to a case of agitation in an elderly chronic patient. *Clinical Gerontology, 3,* 45-52.

Hanson, R. (1982). Managing human resources. *The Journal of Nursing Administration, 12*(12), 17-23.

Harper, M. S. (1986). Introduction. In M. S. Harper & B. D. Lebowitz (Eds.), *Mental illness in nursing homes: Agenda for research*. Washington, DC: U.S. Government Printing Office, DHHS Publication No. (ADM) 86-1459.

Harper, M. S., & Lebowitz, B. D. (1986). *Mental illness in nursing homes: Agenda for research*. Washington, DC: U.S. Government Printing Office, DHHS Publication No. (ADM) 86-1459.

Harrington, C., Newcomer, R. J., Estes, C. L., & Associates. (1985). *Long term care of the elderly: Public policy issues,*. Vol. 157. Beverly Hills, CA: Sage.

Hauerwas, S. (1981). Rational suicide and reasons for living. In S. Hauerwas (Ed.), *Progress in clinical and biological research* (pp. 185-189). New York: Liss.

Hendy, H. M. (1987). Effects of pet and/or people visits on nursing home residents. *International Journal of Aging and Human Development, 25*(4), 279-291.

Henry, A., & Short, J. F. (1954). *Suicide and homicide*. Glencoe, IL: Free Press.

Hiltz, S. R. (1977). *Creating community services for widows*. Port Washington, NY: Rennikat Press.

Hirst, S. P., & Metcalf, B. J. (1984). Promoting self-esteem. *Journal of Gerontological Nursing, 10*(2), 72-77.

Holder, E. (1987). The nursing assistant: To know quality is to give it. *Provider, 13*(4), 36-37; 52.

Holmes, T. H., & Rahe, R. H. (1967). The Social Readjustment Scale. *Journal of Psychosomatic Research, 11*(1), 213-218.

Hume, D. (Ed.) (1983). On suicide. In *Essays, moral, political and literary*. New York: Oxford.

Humphrey, D., & Wickett, A. (1986). *The right to die*. New York: Harper & Row.

Ittleson, W. H., Proshansky, H. M., & Rivlin, L. G. (1970). The environmental psychology of the psychiatric ward. In H. M. Proshansky, W. H. Ittleson, & L. G. Rivlin (Eds.), *Environmental psychology: Man and his physical setting* (pp. 419-438). New York: Holt, Rinehart & Winston.

Jacobson, E. (1938). *Progressive relaxation*. Chicago: University of Chicago Press.

Jaeger, D., & Simmons, L. W. (1970). *The aged ill: Coping with problems and geriatric care*. New York: Appleton-Century Crofts.

Jarvik, L. E. (1975). Thoughts on the psychobiology of aging. *American Psychologist, 30*, 576-583.

Jarvis, G. K., & Boldt, M. (1980). Suicide in the later years. *Essence, 4*, 144-158.

Jeffries, B. (1987). Good management gets top people. *Provider, 13*(2), 4-7.

Jenike, M. A. (1983). Dexamethasone suppression test as a clinical aid in elderly depressed patients. *Journal of American Geriatrics Society, 31*(1), 45-48.

Johnson, C. L., & Grant, L. A. (1985). *The nursing home in American society*. Baltimore, MD: Johns Hopkins University Press.

Johnson, F. L. P. (1979). Response to territorial intrusion by nursing home residents. *Advances in Nursing Science, 1*(4), 21-34.

Jung, C. G. (1934) *Modern man in search of a soul*. New York: Harcourt Brace.

Jung, C. G. (1964). *Man and his symbols*. Garden City, NY: Doubleday.

Kahana, E. (1982). A congruence model of person-environment interaction. In M. P. Lawton, P. Windley, & T. Byerts (Eds.), *Aging and the environment*. New York: Springer.

Kahne, M. (1968). Suicides in mental hospitals: A study of the effects of personnel and patient turnover. *Journal of Health and Social Behavior, 9*(1), 255-266.

Kane, R. (1986). Mental health in nursing homes: Behavioral and social research. In M. S. Harper & B. D. Lebowitz, *Mental illness in nursing homes: Agenda for research* (pp. 347-363). Washington, DC: U.S. Government Printing Office.

Kane, R., & Kane, R. (1987). *Long-term care: Principles, Programs, and Policies.* New York: Springer.

Kaplan, R. P. (1976). Euthanasia legislation: A survey and a model act. *American Journal of Law and Medicine, 2*(1), 41-91.

Kapp, M. B., & Bigot, A. (1985). *Geriatrics and the law.* New York: Springer.

Kaprio, J., Koskenvuo, M., & Rita, H. (1987). Mortality after bereavement: A prospective study of 95,467 widowed persons. *American Journal of Public Health, 77*(2), 283-287.

Kart, C. S., Metress, E. K., & Metress, S. P. (1988). *Aging, health and society.* Boston: Jones and Bartlett.

Kartman, L. L. (1980). The power of music with patients in a nursing home. *Activities, Adaptations, and Aging, 1*(1), 9-15.

Kastenbaum, R. (1964). The structure and function of time perspective. *Journal of Psychosocial Researchers,* (8), 1-11.

Kastenbaum, R. (1969). Death and bereavement in later life. In A. H. Kutscher (Ed.), *Death and bereavement.* Springfield, IL: Thomas.

Katchner, A. H. (1982, Sept/Oct). Are companion animals good for your health? *Ageing,* 2-8.

Kayser-Jones, J. S. (1981). *Old, alone, and neglected: Care of the aged in Scotland and the United States.* Los Angeles: University of California Press.

Keller, J., & Bromley, M. (1989). Psychotherapy with the elderly: A systemic model. In G. Hughston, V. Christopherson, & M. Bonjean (Eds.), *Aging and family therapy: Practitioners perspectives on golden pond.* New York: Harworth.

Kierkegaard, S. (1941). *The sickness unto death.* Princeton, NJ: Princeton University Press. (Original work published 1849.)

Kiernat, J. M. (1983). Environment: The hidden modality. *Physical and Occupational Therapy in Geriatrics, 2* (1), 3-12.

Klein-Schwartz, W., Odera, G. M., & Booze, L. (1983). Poisoning in the elderly. *Journal of the American Geriatrics Society, 31*(4), 195-199.

Knapp, M., & Harrissis, K. (1981). Staff vacancies and turnover in British people's homes. *The Gerontologist, 21*(1), 76-84.

Kobler, A. L., & Stotland, E. (1964). *The end of hope.* New York: Free Press.

Kohn, C., & Bianche, A. (1982). Developing a career ladder for nursing personnel. *The Journal of Long-Term Care Administration, 10,* 4, 25-27.

Koncelik, J. A. (1976). *Designing the open nursing home.* Stroudsburg, PA: Dowden, Hutchinson, & Ross.

Konner, M. (1987). *Becoming a doctor.* New York: Viking.

Koppel, B. S. (1977). Treating the suicidal patient. *Geriatrics, 32*(9), 65-67.

Kovacs, M., Beck, A. T., & Weissman, M. A. (1975). Hopelessness: An indicator of suicidal risk. *Suicide, 51*(2), 98-103.

Kramer, M. (1986). Trends in institutionalization and prevalence of mental disorders in nursing homes. In M. S. Harper & B. D. Lebowitz (Eds.), *Mental illness in nursing homes: Agenda for research*. Washington, DC: U.S. Government Printing Office, DHHS Publication No. (ADM) 86-1459.

Krause, N. (1986). Stress and sex differences in depressive symptoms among older adults. *Journal of Gerontology, 41*(16), 727-731.

Kübler-Ross, E. (1974). *On death and dying*. New York: Macmillan.

Landgarten, H. D. (1981). *Clinical art therapy: A comprehensive guide*. New York: Bruner/Mazel.

Landsberger, B. (1985). *Long-term care for the elderly: A comparative view of layers of care*. London: Croom Helm.

Langland, R. M., & Panicucci, C. L. (1982). Effects of touch on communication with elderly confused clients. *Journal of Gerontological Nursing, 8*(3), 152-154.

LaRue, A., Dessonville, C., & Jarvik, L. (1985). Aging and mental disorders. In J. Birren & K. W. Shaie (Eds.), *Handbook of the psychology of aging* (pp. 664-702). New York: Van Nostrand Reinhold.

Lawton, M. P. (1976). Geropsychological knowledge as a background for psychotherapy with older people. *Journal of Geriatric Psychiatry, 9*(2), 221.

Lawton, M. P. (1977). The impact of the environment on aging and behavior. In J. E. Birren & K. W. Schaie (Eds.), *Handbook of the psychology of aging* (pp. 290-298). New York: Van Nostrand Reinhold.

Lawton, M. P. (1980). Environmental change: The older person as initiator and responder. In N. Datan & N. Lohmann (Eds.), *Transitions of aging* (pp. 171-193) New York: Van Nostrand Reinhold.

Lawton, M. P., & Nahemow, L. (1973). Ecology and the aging process. In C. Eisdorfer and M. P. Lawton (Eds.), *The psychology of adult development and aging* (pp. 316-674). Washington, DC: American Psychological Association.

Lawton, M. P., & Simon, B. (1968). The ecology of social relationships in housing for the elderly. *The Gerontologist, 8*(2), 108-115.

Leaf, A. (1984). Sounding board. *New England Journal of Medicine, 310*(11), 718-721.

Lebacqz, K., & Engelhardt, H. T. (1980). Suicide and convenant. In M. P. Battin & D. J. Mayo (Eds.), *Suicide: The philosophical issues* (pp. 84-89). New York: St. Martin's Press.

Lesnoff-Caravaglia, G. (1980). *Suicide in old age: An ethical dilemma*. Paper presented at the 3rd annual meeting of the Gerontological Society of America, San Diego, CA.

Levy, S., Derogatis, L., Gallagher, D., Gatz, M. (1980). Intervention with older adults and the evaluation of outcome. In L. Poon, (Ed.), *Intervention with older adults: Aging in the 1980s* (pp. 41-61). Washington, DC: American Psychological Association.

Lewis, C. (1971). Reminiscing and self-concept in old age. *Journal of Gerontology, 26*(2), 240-243.

Lewis, M. L., & Butler, R. N. (1974) Life-review therapy: Putting memories to work in individual and group psychotherapy. *Geriatrics, 29*(11), 165-173.

Lindsley, O. R. (1964). Geriatric behavioral prosthetics. In R. Kastenbaum (Ed.), *New thoughts on old age* (pp. 265-280). New York: Springer.

Litman, R. E. (1970). Medical-legal aspects of suicide. In E. S. Shneidman & N. L. Farberow (Eds.), *The psychology of suicide* (pp. 511-530). New York: Science House.

Lohr, S. (1988). *The New York Times.* Aug. 7, pp. A1, A12.

Longino, C. F. (1988). Who are the oldest Americans. *The Gerontologist, 28*(4), 515-523.

Louis, M. (1983). Personal space boundary needs of elderly persons: An empirical study. *Journal of Gerontological Nursing, 7*(7), 395-400.

Louisell, D. W. (1980). Bithanasia: Dying and killing. In D. J. Horan & D. Mall (Eds.), *Death, dying, and euthanasia* (pp. 383-405). Frederick, MD: University Publications of America.

Lowy, L. (1967). Roadblocks in group work practice with older people: A framework for analysis. *Gerontologist, 1*(2), 109-113.

Lowy, L. (1979). *Social work with the aging: The challenge and promise of the later years.* New York: Harper Row.

Lubitz, J., & Prihoda, R. (1984). Uses and costs of medicare services in the last two years of life. *Health Care Financing Review, 5*(3), 117-131.

McCracken, A. (1987). Emotional impact of possession loss. *Journal of Gerontological Nursing, 13,* 2, 14-19.

McCracken Knight, A. M. (1984). Teaching nursing homes: A project update. *Journal of Gerontological Nursing, 10*(6), 14-17.

McIntosh, J. L. (1984). Components of the decline in elderly suicide: Suicide among the young-old and old-old by race and sex. *Death Education, 8*(Supp.), 113-124.

McIntosh, J. L (1985a). Suicide among the elderly: Levels and trends. *American Journal of Orthopsychiatry, 55*(2), 288-293.

McIntosh, J. L. (1985b, Nov 24). *Suicide among minority elderly.* Paper presented at annual meeting of the Gerontological Society of America, New Orleans, LA.

McIntosh, J. L. (1986, Apr. 5). *Cross-ethnic suicide: U. S. trends and levels.* Paper presented at the annual meeting of the American Association of Suicidology, Atlanta, GA.

McIntosh, J. L. (1987a, May 29). *Hispanic suicide in ten U. S. states.* Paper presented at the joint meeting of the American Association of Suicidology and the International Association for Suicide Prevention, San Francisco, CA.

McIntosh, J. L. (1987b, May 28). *Marital status and suicide: Recent U.S. data.* Paper presented at the joint meeting of the American Association for Suicidology and the International Association for Suicide Prevention, San Francisco, CA.

McIntosh, J. (1987c). Suicide: Training and education needs with an emphasis on the elderly. *Gerontology and Geriatrics Education, 7*(314), 125-139.

McIntosh, J. L. (in press). Trends in racial differences in United States suicide statistics. *Death Studies.*

McIntosh, J. L., & Santos, J. F. (1981). Suicide among minority elderly: A preliminary investigation. *Suicide and Life Threatening Behavior, 11*(3), 151-166.

McIntosh, J. L., & Santos, J. F. (1982). Changing patterns in methods of suicide by race and sex. *Suicide and Life-Threatening Behavior, 12*(4), 221-233.

McIntosh, J. L., & Santos, J. F. (1985-1986). Methods of suicide by age: Sex and race differences among the young and old. *International Journal of Aging and Human Development, 22*(2), 123-139.

MacMahon, B., & Pugh, T. (1965). Suicide in the widowed. *American Journal of Epidemiology, 81*(1), 23-31.

Maddox, G. L. (1988). 1987 Boettner Lecture. In *Aging and well-being* (pp. 1-21). PA: Boettner Research Institute.

Manton, K. G., Blazer, D. G., & Woodbury, M. A. (1987). Suicide in middle age and later life: Sex and race specific life table and cohort analyses. *Journal of Gerontology, 42*(2), 219-227.

Manton, K. G., & Soldo, B. J. (1985). Dynamics of health changes in the oldest-old: New perspectives and evidence. *Milbank Memorial Fund Quarterly, 63*(2), 206-285.

Markowitz, J., Brown, R., & Sweeney, J. (1987). Reduced length and cost of hospital stay for major depression in patients treated with ECT. *American Journal of Psychiatry, 144*, 1025-1029.

Maris, R. W. (1969). *Social forces in urban suicide.* Homewood, IL: Dorsey.

Maris, R. W. (1981). *Pathways to suicide: A survey of self-destructive behaviors.* Baltimore, MD: Johns Hopkins University Press.

Martin, J. L. & DeGruchy, D. (1930). *Salvaging old age.* New York: Macmillan.

Mathews, W. R. (1974). Voluntary euthanasia: The ethical aspect. In A. B. Downing (Ed.), *Euthanasia and the right to death* (pp.(25-29). London: Peter Owen.

Mayo, D. J. (1980). Irrational suicide. In M. P. Battin & D. J. Mayo (Eds.), *Suicide: The philosophical issues* (pp. 133-137). New York: St. Martin's Press.

Meerloo, J. (1968). Hidden suicide. In H. L. P. Resnick (Ed.), *Suicidal behaviors: Diagnosis and management* (pp. 13-21). Boston: Little, Brown.

Melville, M. L., & Blazer, D. G. (1985). Depression in the elderly: Etiology and assessment. In N. J. Osgood. *Suicide in the elderly: A practitioner's guide to diagnosis and mental heath intervention* (pp. 14-38). Rockville, MD: Aspen.

Menninger, K. (1938). *Man against himself.* New York: Harcourt Brace Janovich.

Miami Herald (1988). June 3, p. 21A.

Miller, M. (1976). *Suicide among older men.* Ph.D. dissertation, Ann Arbor: University of Michigan.

Miller, M. (1979). *Suicide after sixty: The final alternative.* New York: Springer.

Mishara, B. L., & Kastenbaum, R. (1973). Self-injurious behavior and environmental change in the institutionalized elderly. *International Journal of Aging and Human Development, 4*(2), 133-145.

Moos, R. (1974). *Evaluating treatment environments: A social ecological approach.* New York: Wiley.

Moos, R. (1976). *The human context: Environmental determinants of behavior.* New York: Wiley.

More, Thomas (1964). *Utopia.* New Haven, CT: Yale University Press.

Moreno, J. (1934). *We shall survive: A new approach to human interaction.* Washington, DC: Nervous and Mental Disease.

Mugford, R. A., & M'Comisky, J. G. (1975). Some recent work on the psychotherapeutic value of cage birds with old people. In R. S. Anderson (Ed.), *Pet animals and society.* London, England: Bailliere Tindall.

Murphy, G. E. (1973). Suicide and the right to die. *American Journal of Psychiatry, 130*(4), 472.

National Center for Health Statistics. (annual vol., 1937-1985). *Vital statistics of the United States, Volume II—Mortality.* Washington, DC: U.S. Government Printing Office.

National Center for Health Statistics. (1985a). *The national nursing home survey:*

1985 summary for the United States. Vital and Health Statistics, ser. 13, no. 97. Hyattsville, MD: NCHS.

National Center for Health Statistics. (1985b). *Vital statistics of the United States, 1980. Vol. II—Mortality, part B.* Hyattsville, MD: USDHHS, PHS.

National Center for Health Statistics. (1986). *Inventory of long-term care places.* Vital and Health Statistics, ser. 14, no. 98. Hyattsville, Md: NCHS.

National Center for Health Statistics. (1988). Advanced report of final mortality statistics, 1986. *NCHS Monthly Vital Statistics Report,* 37 (6, Suppl.).

National Conference of Catholic Bishops. (1976). To live in Christ Jesus: A pastoral reflection on the moral life. A pastoral letter on moral values adopted by the National Conference on Catholic Bishops. *The New World,* 84(47), 17.

Nelson, F. L. (1977). Religiosity and self-destructive crises in the institutionalized elderly. *Suicide and Life-Threatening* Behavior, 7(2), 67-74.

Nelson, F. L., & Farberow, N. L. (1980). Indirect self-destructive behavior in the elderly nursing home patient. *Journal of Gerontology,* 35(6), 949-957.

The New Physician. (1987). May-June, 17.

OBRA (Omnibus Budget Reconciliation Act of 1987). (1988). P. L. 100-203. Explanation of the Conference Committee Affecting Medicare-Medicaid Programs. In *Medicare and Medicaid* (Extra edition), Number 545; Part II. Chicago, IL: Commerce Clearing House.

Olson, B. K. (1984). Player piano music as therapy for the elderly. *Journal of Music Therapy,* 21(1), 35-44.

Osgood, N. (1985). *Suicide in the elderly.* Rockville, MD: Aspen.

Osgood, N. J. (1987). The alcohol-suicide connection in late life. *Postgraduate Medicine,* 81(4), 379-384.

Osgood, N. J., & Brant, BA. (1990). Suicide behavior in long-term care facilities. *Suicide and Life-Threatening Behavior,* 20(2), 113-122.

Ousley, M. K. (1989, Feb.). Nursing commission cites problem areas. *Provider,* 15(2), 8-11.

Paelz, P. R. (1980). Suicide: Some theological reflections. In M. P. Battin & D. J. Mayo (Eds.), *Suicide: The philosophical issues* (pp. 71-83). New York: St. Martin's Press.

Palmore, E. B. (1986). Trends in the health of the aged. *Gerontologist,* 26(3), 298-302.

Palola, E., Dorpat, T., & Larson, W. (1982). Alcoholism and suicidal behavior. In D. J. Pittman, & C. R. Snyder (Eds.), *Society, culture and drinking patterns.* New York: Wiley.

Pasquali, L., & Bucher, R. E. (1981). Suicidal attempts according to sex and age. *Acta Psychiatrica y Psicologica de America Latina,* 27(18), 39-43.

Pastalan, L. A., & Carson, D. H. (Eds.). (1970). *Spatial behavior of older people.* Ann Arbor: University of Michigan.

Pavkov, J. (1982). Suicide in the elderly. *Ohio's Health,* 34, 21-28.

Pavlov, I. P. (1955). *Selected works.* (J. Gibbons, Ed., S. Belsky trans.). Moscow: Foreign Languages.

Paykel, E. S., Prusoff, B. A., & Myers, J. K. (1975). Suicide attempts and recent life events. *Archives of General Psychiatry,* 32, 327-333.

Petty, B. J., Moeller, T. R., & Campbell, R. Z. (1976). Support groups for elderly persons in the community. *Gerontologist,* 15(6), 522-528.

Phillips, C. (1987). Staff turnover in nursing homes for the aged: A review and research proposal. *International Journal of Nursing Studies, 24*(1), 45-57

Pincus, A. (1970). Reminiscence in aging and its implications for social work practice. *Social Work, 15*(3), 47-53.

Portwood, D. (1978). *Common sense suicide: The final right.* New York: Dodd, Mead.

Rabin, D. L., & Stockton, P. (1987). *Long-term care for the elderly: A fact book.* New York: Oxford Press.

Rationing hospital care: Lessons from Britain. (1984). *New England Journal of Medicine, 310*(1), 52-56.

Rechtschatten, A. (1959). Psychotherapy with geriatric patients: A review of the literature. *Journal of Gerontology, 14*(1), 73.

Reedy, M. N., & Birren, J. E. (1980, Sept.). *Life review through guided autobiography.* Paper presented at the Annual Meeting of the American Psychological Association, Montreal, Canada.

Richmond Redevelopment and Housing Authority representative. Personal communication, Sept. 6, 1989.

Ricker-Smith, K. (1982). A challenge for public policy: The chronically ill elderly in nursing homes. *Medical Care, XX*(11), 1071-1079.

Rivlin, A. M., & Weiner, J. M. (1988). *Caring for the disabled elderly. Who will pay?* Washington, DC: Brookings Institute.

Romaniuk, M., & Romaniuk, J. (1981). Looking back: An analysis of reminiscence functions and triggers. *Experimental Aging Research, 7*(4), 477-489.

Rosner, F. (1972). Euthanasia. In B. Schoenberg, A. C. Carr, D. Peretz, & A. H. Kutscher (Eds.), *Psychosocial aspects of terminal care* (pp. 309-322). New York: Columbia University Press.

Roy, A., & Linnoila, M. (1986). Alcoholism and suicide. *Suicide and Life-Threatening Behavior, 16*(2), 244-273.

Russell, D., Peplau, L. A., & Cutrona, C. E. (1980). The revised UCLA loneliness scale: Concurrent and discriminant validity evidence. *Journal of Personality and Social Psychology, 39*(3), 472-480.

Russell, R. O. (1975). *Freedom to die: Moral and legal aspects of euthanasia.* New York: Human Sciences Press.

Sadler, W., & Johnson, T. (1980). From loneliness to anomie. In J. Hartog, J. R. Audy, & Y. Cohen (Eds.), *The anatomy of loneliness* (pp. 36-64). New York: International Universities Press.

Sainsbury, P. (1962). Suicide in the middle and later years. In H. T. Blumenthal (Ed.), *Aging around the world: Medical and clinical aspects of aging* (pp. 97-105). New York: Columbia University Press.

St. Augustine. (1950). *The city of God.* New York: Modern Library.

St. Martin, T. (1980). Euthanasia: The three-in-one issue. In D. J. Horan & D. Mall (Eds.), *Death, dying, and euthanasia* (pp. 596-601). Frederick, MD: University Publications of America.

St. Thomas Aquinas. (1964). *Summa theologiae.* Cambridge: Blackfriars.

Sartorius, R. (1973). Coercive suicide prevention: A libertarian perspective. In M. P. Battin & R. W. Maris (Eds.), *Suicide and ethics* (pp. 293-303). New York: Human Sciences Press.

Schildkraut, J. (1965). The catecholamine hypothesis of affective disorders: A review of supporting evidence. *American Journal of Psychiatry, 122*, 509-522.

Schneider, E. L., & Brody, J. A. (1983). Sounding board—Aging, natural death, and the compression of morbidity: Another view. *New England Journal of Medicine, 309*(13), 854-856.

Schultz, N. R., & Moore, D. (1982, Nov.). *Loneliness, correlates, attributions, and coping among older adults.* Paper presented at the annual meeting of the Gerontological Society of America, Boston.

Schulz, R. (1976). Effects of control and predictability on the physical and psychological well-being of the institutionalized aged. *Journal of Personality and Social Psychology, 33*(5), 563-573.

Seiden, R. H. (1981). Mellowing with age: Factors influencing the nonwhite suicide rate. *International Journal of Aging and Human Development, 13*(4), 265-284.

Seligman, M. E. P. (1975). *Helplessness.* San Francisco: Freeman.

Seligman, M. E. P. (1976). Learned helplessness and depression in animals and men. In J. T. Spence, R. C. Carsen, & J. W. Thibaut (Eds.), *Behavioral approaches to therapy* (pp. 111-126). Morristown, NJ: General Learning Press.

Shipp, E. R. (1988). New York's highest court rejects family's plea in right-to-die case. *The New York Times.* Oct. 15, pp. A1, A36.

Shipp, E. R. (1988). Many courts have upheld right to die. *The New York Times.* Oct. 15, p. A36.

Shneidman, E. S. (1985). *Definition of suicide.* New York: Wiley.

Shomaker, D. McD. (1979). Dialectics of nursing homes and aging. *Journal of Gerontological Nursing, 5,* 5, 45-48.

Shuttlesworth, G. E., Rubin, A, & Duffy, M. (1982). Families versus institutions: Incongruent role expectations in the nursing home. *The Gerontologist, 22,* 2, 200-208.

Siegel, K., & Tuckel, P. (1985). Rational suicide and the terminally ill cancer patient. *Omega, 14*(3), 263-269.

Silver, A. (1950). Group psychotherapy with senile psychotic patients. *Geriatrics, 5*(1), 147-150.

Skinner, B. F. (1936). *Behavior of Organisms.* New York: Appleton-Century-Crofts.

Smith, J. C., Mercy, J. A., & Conn, J. M. (1988). Marital status and the risk of suicide. *American Journal of Public Health, 78*(1), 78-80.

Sommer, R., & Osmond, H. (1960). Symptoms of institutional care. *Social Problems, 8*(3), 254-263.

Sounding board. (1984). *New England Journal of Medicine, 310*(11), 718-721.

Spasoff, R., Kraus, A., Beattie, W., Holden, D., Lawson, J., Rodenburg, M., & Woodcock, G. (1978). A longitudinal study of residents of long stay institutions. *The Gerontologist, 18*(3), 281-292.

Spitz, R. (1946). Anaclitic depression. *Psychoanalytic Study of the Child, 2,* 313-342.

Stein, A. (1959, Jan.). *Group psychotherapy in a general hospital: Principles and practice.* Paper presented at the Annual Meeting of the American Group Psychotherapy Association, New York.

Stenger, E. (1964). *Suicide and attempted suicide.* New York Penguin.

Steuer, J. (1982). Psychotherapy for depressed elders. In D. G. Blazer (Ed.), *Depression in late life* (ch.13, pp. 195-221). St. Louis, MO: Mosby.

Steuer, J., Bank, L., Olson, E. J., & Jarvik, L. (1980). Depression, physical health and somatic complaints in the elderly: A study of the Zung self-rating depression scale. *Journal of Gerontology, 35*(5), 683-688.

Storandt, M. (1983). *Counseling and therapy with older adults.* Toronto: Little, Brown.

Stotsky, B. A., & Dominick, J. R. (1969). Mental patients in nursing homes, Part 1: Isolation, depression and regression. *Journal of the American Geriatrics Society, 17*(1), 33-34.

Stryker, R. (1981). *How to reduce employee turnover in nursing homes.* Springfield, IL: Thomas.

Stryker, R. (1982, Summer). The effect of managerial interventions on high personnel turnover in nursing homes. *The Journal of Long-Term Care Administration, 10*(2), 21-33.

Suchman, M. & Wilkes, M. S. (1988). *The New York Times Magazine.* Aug. 21, pp. 44-46.

Sullivan, A. (1980). A Constitutional right to suicide. In M. P. Battin and D. J. Mayo (Eds.), *Suicide: The Philosophical issues* (pp. 229-253). New York: St. Martin's Press.

Sullivan, J. S. (1987). *The New York Times.* June 25, pp. B1, B2.

Swindeman, T. (1987). Anticipate turnover and work against it. *Provider, 13*(2), 14-16.

Tate, J. W. (1980). The need for personal space in institutions for the elderly. *Journal of Gerontological Nursing, 6*(8), 439-449.

Tobin, S. (1974). How nursing homes vary. *The Gerontologist, 14*(5), 516-519.

Tobin, S. S., & Lieberman, M. (1976). *Last home for the aged.* San Francisco: Jossey-Bass.

Traunstein, D. M., & Steinman, R. (1973). Voluntary self-help organizations: An exploratory study. *Journal of Voluntary Action Research, 2*(4), 230-239.

Trout, D. L. (1980). The role of social isolation to suicide. *Suicide and Life-Threatening Behavior, 10*(1), 10-23.

Twycross, R. G. (1981). Voluntary euthanasia. In S. W. Wallace & A. Eser (Eds.), *Suicide and euthanasia* (pp. 88-89). Knoxville: University of Tennessee Press.

Ullman, S. (1984). Ownership costs and facility characteristics in the national long-term health care industry. *Journal of Applied Gerontology, 3*(1), 34-39.

U.S. Bureau of the Census. (1986). Estimates of the population of the United States, by age, sex, and race: 1980 to 1985. *Current Population Reports,* Series P-25, No. 985.

Values clarification for long-term care. (1983). *Creating a career choice for nurses: Long-term care.* NLN Publication #20-1917, 1–4.

Van Praag, H. (1982). Biochemical psychopathological predictors of suicidality. *Bibliotheca Psychiatrica, 162,* 42-60.

Verwoerdt, A. (1976). *Clinical geropsychiatry.* Baltimore, MD: Williams and Wilkins.

Virginia Department for the Aging (1988). *A Consumer's guide to long-term care.* Richmond, VA: Commonwealth of Virgina, funded by the Older Americans Act and the Commonwealth of Virginia.

Vladeck, B. (1980). *Unloving care: The nursing home tragedy.* New York: Basic Books.

Wachtler, S. (1988). Excerpts from the court of appeals. *The New York Times*. Oct. 15, p. A36.

Wallace, R., & Brubaker, T. (1984). Long-term care with short-term workers: An examination of nursing home aide turnover. *Journal of Applied Gerontology*, 3(1), 50-58.

Wang, H. S. (1980). Diagnostic procedures. In Busse, E. W. & Blazer, D. G. (Eds.), *Handbook of geriatric psychiatry* (pp. 285-304). New York: Van Nostrand Reinhold.

Wanzer, S. H., Adelstein, S. J., Cranford, R. E., Federman, D. D., Hook, E. D., Moertel, C. G., Safar, P., Stone, A., Taussig, H. B., & Van Eys, J. (1984). The physician's responsibility toward hopelessly ill patients. *New England Journal of Medicine*, 310(14), 955-959.

Ward, R. A., La Gory, M., & Sherman, S. R. (1988). *The environment for aging: Interpersonal, social, and spatial contexts*. Tuscaloosa: The University of Alabama Press.

Waskow, I. G., & Parloff, M. B. (1975). *Psychotherapy change measures, report on the clinical research branch (NIMH outcomes project)*. Rockville, MD: National Institute of Mental Health.

Waxman, H. M., Carner, E. A., & Berkenstock, G. (1984). Job turnover and job satisfaction among nursing home aides. *The Gerontologist*, 24(5), 503-509.

Weber, H. I. (1980). *Nursing care of the elderly*. Reston, VA: The Reston Publishing Co.

Weber, M. (1958). *The protestant ethic and the spirit of capitalism*. New York: Charles Scribner's Sons.

Weeks, D. G., Michela, J. C., Peplau, L. A., & Bragg, M. E. (1980). The relation between loneliness and depression: A structural equation analysis. *Journal of Personality and Social Psychology*, 39(16), 1238-1244.

Weiner, R. D. (1979). The psychiatric use of electrically induced seizure. *American Journal of Psychiatry* 136(12), 1507-1517.

Weisman, A. D. (1974). *The realization of death*. New York: Aronson.

Weiss, J. C. (1984). *Expressive therapy with elders and the disabled: Touching the heart of life*. New York: Haworth Press.

Welford, A. T. (1962). On changes of performance with age. *Lancet*, 1, 335-339.

Wells, C. E., & Duncan, G. W. (1980). *Neurology for psychiatrists*. Philadelphia: Davis.

Whanger, A. D. (1980). Treatment within the institution. In E. W. Busse, & D. G. Blazer (Eds.), *Handbook of geriatric psychiatry* (pp. 427-452). New York: Van Nostrand Reinhold.

Wheeler, D. J. (1988). Euthanasia: an increasingly pressing issue for ethicists and physicians. *Chronicle of Higher Education*, 35(11), A1, A6.

Wickett, A. (1986). Most mercy killings in living will states. *Hemlock Quarterly*, 23, 3-4.

Williams, G. L. (1973). *The sanctity of life and the criminal law*. New York: Alfred Knopf.

Wilson, M. (1981). Suicidal behavior: Toward an explanation of differences in female and male rates. *Suicide and Life-Threatening Behavior*, 11(3), 131-140.

Windley, P. G., & Scheidt, R. J. (1980). Person-environment dialectics; Implications for competent functioning in old age. In L. W. Poon (ed.), *Aging in the 1980's* (pp. 407-432). Washington, DC: American Psychological Association.

Winokur, G. (1974, Nov.). Lecture given at the Clark Institute of Psychiatry, Toronto, Canada.

Wolanin, M. O., & Phillips, L. R. F. (1981). *Confusion: Prevention and care.* St. Louis, MO: Mosby.

Wolff, K. (1963). Individual psychotherapy with geriatric patients. *Diseases of the Nervous System, 24*(11), 688-691.

Wolff, R. (1970). Observations of depression and suicide in the geriatric patient. In K. Wolff (Ed.), *Patterns of self-destruction: Depression and suicide* (pp. 86-95). Springfield, IL: Thomas.

Yalom, I. D. (1970). *The theory and practice of group psychotherapy.* New York: Basic Books.

Yesavage, J., & Brink, T. L. (1983). Development and validation of a geriatric depression screening scale: A preliminary report. *Journal of Psychiatric Research, 17*, 37-49.

Young, J. E. (1982). Loneliness, depression and cognitive therapy: Theory and application. In L. A. Peplau & D. Perlman (Eds.), *Loneliness: A sourcebook of current theory, research, and therapy* (pp. 379-406). New York: Wiley.

Zandt, S. V. & Lorenzen, L. (1985). You're not too old to dance: Creative movement and older adults. *Activities, Adaptation, and Aging, 6*(4), 121-130.

Zarit, S. (1980). *Aging and mental disorders: Psychological approaches to treatment.* New York: Free Press.

Zung, W. (1980). Affective disorders. In E. Busse & D. G. Blazer (Eds.), *Handbook of geriatric psychiatry* (pp. 338-367). New York: Van Nostrand Reinhold.

INDEX

About the Authors

NANCY J. OSGOOD is Associate Professor in the Department of Gerontology and Sociology at the Medical College of Virginia, Virginia Commonwealth University. She is also co-author of *The Science and Practice of Gerontology: A Multidisciplinary Guide* (Greenwood Press, 1989) and *Suicide and the Elderly* (Greenwood, 1986).

BARBARA A. BRANT is an Instructor in Undergraduate and Graduate Gerontologic Nursing at Virginia Commonwealth University. She is an authority on elderly suicide and has presented many papers at major conferences on the subject. She has also written articles that have appeared in *New Age for Seniors*, the *Journal of Suicide and Life-Threatening Behavior*, and *The GNP Newsletter*.

AARON LIPMAN is a Professor at the University of Miami in Coral Gables, Florida. His previous works include *Suicide and Depression in Nursing Homes*, co-authored with Nancy J. Osgood and Barbara A. Brant.